# Preserving Privacy in Data Outsourcing

# Advances in Information Security

## Sushil Jajodia

*Consulting Editor*
*Center for Secure Information Systems*
*George Mason University*
*Fairfax, VA 22030-4444*
*email: jajodia@gmu.edu*

The goals of the Springer International Series on ADVANCES IN INFORMATION SECURITY are, one, to establish the state of the art of, and set the course for future research in information security and, two, to serve as a central reference source for advanced and timely topics in information security research and development. The scope of this series includes all aspects of computer and network security and related areas such as fault tolerance and software assurance.

ADVANCES IN INFORMATION SECURITY aims to publish thorough and cohesive overviews of specific topics in information security, as well as works that are larger in scope or that contain more detailed background information than can be accommodated in shorter survey articles. The series also serves as a forum for topics that may not have reached a level of maturity to warrant a comprehensive textbook treatment.

Researchers, as well as developers, are encouraged to contact Professor Sushil Jajodia with ideas for books under this series.

For a complete list of titles published in this series, go to www.springer.com/series/5576

Sara Foresti

# Preserving Privacy
# in Data Outsourcing

Foreword by Pierangela Samarati

 Springer

Sara Foresti
Università degli Studi di Milano
Dipartimento di Tecnologie dell'informazione
Via Bramante 65
26013 Crema
Italy

ISSN 1568-2633
ISBN 978-1-4614-2699-8          ISBN 978-1-4419-7659-8 (eBook)
DOI 10.1007/978-1-4419-7659-8
Springer New York Dordrecht Heidelberg London

Printed on acid-free paper

Springer is part of Springer Science+Business Media (www.springer.com)

# Foreword

Data outsourcing is emerging today as a successful paradigm allowing organizations as well as users to exploit external services for the distribution of resources. As a matter of fact, organizations often find it more secure and economically viable to resort to external servers for IT services and data management, maintaining instead their in-house focus on their main core business. Similarly, users are increasingly resorting to external services for storing and distributing user-generated content, as witnessed by the success and large adoption of services like YouTube, MySpace, and Flickr.

In such novel outsourcing and storage/distribution scenarios, it is of primary importance to guarantee proper security and privacy to the data as well as to users. The problem is particularly complex due to the fact that the servers responsible for data storage and access services may not be completely trusted. Outsourced data often contain sensitive information whose release should be strictly controlled and whose access may not even be allowed to the external server. To respond to this problem, existing data outsourcing proposals typically assume data to be outsourced in encrypted form and associate with the data additional indexing information to allow the execution of queries on the encrypted data themselves, thus not requiring the external servers to decrypt data for query computation. While providing a fundamental layer of protection, data encryption does not provide a complete response to the problem of efficiently, effectively, and flexibly providing privacy on outsourced data and many challenges still need to be addressed.

First, in many scenarios access to outsourced data may be selective. How can we guarantee users different views over the outsourced data? Can we outsource to the external server, besides the data, also the management and enforcement of authorizations? If encryption depends on authorizations how can we avoid the need of re-uploading new versions of the resources when authorizations change?

Second, while encryption and decryption are computationally viable, query execution of encrypted data is inevitably more expensive and possibly only for limited kinds of queries. Also, encryption might represent an over protection when what is sensitive are not the data themselves but the associations among data. Can we then depart from encryption, for example, fragmenting data so to break sensitive associations? How can data be fragmented and what assumptions do we need to make on the physical fragments and on the servers storing them? How can query execution work on fragmented data?

Third, in some scenarios there may be the need to perform distributed queries involving data stored at different servers and therefore entailing collaboration and information sharing among the servers for the query computation. How can we establish authorizations regulating information sharing among servers? How can we measure the information carried by derived relations in query computation? How can we define and enforce a query plan that allows collaborative query execution and complies with the different authorizations to be enforced?

This book addresses the three aspects above illustrating state of the art for them and analyzing the problems to be tackled. It investigates different directions and proposes possible approaches to their solution, also providing a response to some of the issues and insights for open problems. It represents a precious source for scholars and researchers interested in security and privacy, in particular with reference to the data outsourcing context, offering them a nice overview and analysis of different issues to be considered and problems addressed together with approaches to their resolutions. Providing a fine investigation of the issues and highlighting open problems, the book can also represent a source of inspiration for future research.

*Pierangela Samarati*

# Preface

The increasing availability of large collections of personal information as well as of data storage facilities for supporting data-intensive services, support the view that service providers will be more and more requested to be responsible for the storage and the efficient and reliable dissemination of information, thus realizing a "data outsourcing" architecture. Within a data outsourcing architecture data are stored together with application front-ends at the sites of an external server who takes full charges of their management. While publishing data on external servers may increase service availability, reducing data owners' burden of managing data, data outsourcing introduces new privacy and security concerns since the server storing the data may be *honest-but-curious*. A honest-but-curious server honestly manages the data but may not be trusted by the data owner to read their content. To ensure adequate privacy protection, a traditional solution consists in encrypting the outsourced data, thus preventing outside attacks as well as infiltration from the server itself. Such traditional solutions have however the disadvantage of reducing query execution efficiency and of preventing selective information release. This introduces then the need to develop new models and methods for the definition and enforcement of access control and privacy restrictions on outsourced data while ensuring an efficient query execution.

In this book, we present a comprehensive approach for protecting sensitive information when it is stored on systems that are not under the data owner's control. There are mainly three security requirements that need to be considered when designing a system for ensuring confidentiality of data stored and managed by a honest-but-curious server. The first requirement is *access control enforcement* to limit the ability of authorized users to access system's resources. In traditional contexts, a trusted module of the data management system is in charge of enforcing the access control policy. In the considered scenario, the service provider is not trusted for enforcing the access control policy and the data owner is not willing to mediate access requests to filter query results. We therefore propose a new access control system, based on selective encryption, that does not require the presence of a trusted module in the system for the enforcement of the policy. The second requirement is *privacy protection* to limit the visibility of stored/published data to non authorized users while minimizing the adoption of encryption. Data collections often contain personally identifiable information that needs to be protected both at storage and when disseminated to other parties. As an example, medical data cannot be stored or published along with the identity of the patients they refer to. To guarantee privacy protection and to limit the use of encryption, in this book we first propose a solution for modeling in a simple while powerful way privacy requirements through confidentiality constraints, which are defined as sets of data whose joint visibility must be prevented. We then propose a mechanism for the enforcement of confidentiality constraints based on the combined use of fragmentation and encryption techniques: associations broken by fragmentation will be visible only to those users who are authorized to know the associations themselves. The third requirement is *safe data integration* to limit the ability of authorized users to exchange data for distributed query evaluation. As a matter of fact, often different sources storing the personal information of users need to collaborate to achieve a common goal. However, such data integration and sharing may be subject to confidentiality constraints, since different parties may be allowed to access different portions of the data. We therefore propose both a model for conveniently representing data exchange constraints and a mechanism for their enforcement during the distributed query evaluation process.

In this book, we address all these three security requirements by defining a model and a mechanism for enforcing access control on outsourced data; by introducing a fragmentation and encryption approach for enforcing privacy constraints; and by designing a technique for regulating data flows among different parties. The main contributions can be summarized as follows.

- With respect to the access control enforcement on outsourced data, the original results are: the combined use of selective encryption and key derivation strategies for access control enforcement; the introduction of a notion of minimality of an encryption policy to correctly enforce an access control policy without reducing the efficiency in key derivation; the development of a heuristic approach for computing a minimal encryption policy in polynomial time; the introduction of a two-layer encryption model for the management of policy updates.
- With respect to the definition of a model for enforcing privacy protection, the original results are: the definition of confidentiality constraints as a simple while complete method for modeling privacy requirements; the introduction of the notion of minimal fragmentation that captures the property of a fragmentation to satisfy the confidentiality constraints while minimizing the number of fragments; the development of an efficient approach for computing a minimal fragmentation, which is a NP-hard problem; the introduction of three notions of local optimality, based on the structure of the fragments composing the solution, on the affinity of the attributes in the fragments, and on a query evaluation cost model, respectively; the proposal of three different approaches for computing fragmentations satisfying the three definitions of optimality.
- With respect to the design of a safe data integration mechanism, the original results are: the definition of permissions as a simple while complete method for modeling data exchange limitations; the modeling of both permissions and queries as relation profiles and their representation through a graph-based model;

the introduction of an approach for the composition of permissions working in polynomial time; the definition of a method that takes data exchange restrictions into account while designing a query execution plan.

*Sara Foresti*

# Acknowledgements

This book is the result of the publication of my Ph.D. thesis. I would like to take this occasion to express my sincere gratitude to all the people who have made both my Ph.D. thesis and this work possible. I would like apologize, before going on, for not being able to express in words all the gratitude all these people deserve.

First of all, I would like to thank my advisor, Pierangela Samarati, for all the time she dedicated to me. During the last five years, she introduced me to scientific research and the joy and enthusiasm she has for this work was contagious and motivating for me. I am grateful to her for the many opportunities she gave me, for her constant presence, support, guidance, and advice. All I know about security and privacy, I learned from her and no page in this book would have been written without her. It has been a honor for me to be one of her Ph.D. students and it is more than an honor and a pleasure for me that she is giving me the possibility to work with her.

A special thank is for my co-advisor, Sabrina De Capitani di Vimercati, for always being there when I needed an advice, both technical and not, for all the time she spent listening and answering to all my (stupid) questions, for her patient, and for helping me to look at things from a different viewpoint. She has been (and is) an important reference point for me.

I am particularly grateful to Sushil Jajodia, who first envisioned the possibility of my Ph.D. thesis to be published as a book and who made it possible. I would also like to thank him for giving me the opportunity to visit the Center for Secure Information Systems (CSIS), George Mason University, VA, USA. I am very grateful to him for his support and for providing a stimulating an enjoyable working atmosphere.

Most of the results illustrated in this book has been obtained thanks to the many profitable discussions to the collaboration with Valentina Ciriani, Sabrina De Capitani di Vimercati, Sushil Jajodia, Stefano Paraboschi, and Pierangela Samarati, who all deserve my gratitude. I would like to thank them, not only for their support and help in the study of different parts of this book (that resulted in different publications acknowledged in the different chapters), but for giving me the opportunity to learn from them and from their outstanding experience.

I would like to especially thank Prof. Vijay Atluri, Prof. Carlo Blundo, Prof. Sushil Jajodia, and Prof. Javier Lopez for their valuable comments, which helped improving the presentation of this work.

I am also extremely grateful to Susan Lagerstrom-Fife, for her support during all the phases preceding the publication of this book, and to Jennifer Maurer. Their support during the preparation of the manuscript has been fundamental.

Last, but not least, I would like to thank my family. All the pages of this book would not be sufficient to express my gratitude to them: their teaching, their support, and their love have been, and will always be, a fundamental reference point for me. A very special thanks is for Eros, for always being there when I needed it, for his support, and for his patience.

# Contents

# Chapter 1
# Introduction

The amount of data stored, processed, and exchanged by private companies and public organizations is rapidly increasing. As a consequence, users are today, with increasing frequency, resorting to service providers for disseminating and sharing resources they want to make available to others. The protection against privacy violations is becoming therefore one of the most important issues that must be addressed in such an open and collaborative context. In this book, we define a comprehensive approach for protecting sensitive information when it is stored on systems that are not under the data owner's direct control. In the remainder of this chapter, we give the motivation and the outline of this book.

## 1.1 Motivation

The rapid evolution of storage, processing, and communication technologies is changing the traditional information system architecture adopted by both private companies and public organizations. This change is necessary for mainly two reasons. First, the amount of information held by organizations is increasing very quickly thanks to the growing storage capacity and computational power of modern devices. Second, the data collected by organizations contain sensitive information (e.g., identifying information, financial data, health diagnosis) whose confidentiality must be preserved.

Systems storing and managing these data collections should be *secure* both from external users breaking the system and from malicious insiders. However, the design, realization, and management of a secure system able to grant the confidentiality of sensitive data might be very expensive. Due to the growing costs of in-house storage and management of large collections of sensitive data, since it demands for both storage capacity and skilled administrative personnel, *data outsourcing and dissemination* services have recently seen considerable growth and promise to become a common component of the future Web, as testifies by the growing success of Web companies offering storage and distribution services (e.g., MySpace, Flickr,

S. Foresti, *Preserving Privacy in Data Outsourcing*, Advances in Information Security 51,
DOI 10.1007/978-1-4419-7659-8_1, © Springer Science+Business Media, LLC 2011

and YouTube). The main consequence of this trend is that companies often store their data on external *honest-but-curious* servers, which are relied upon for ensuring availability of data and for enforcing the basic security control on the data they store. While trustworthy with respect to their services in making published information available, these external systems are however trusted neither to access the content nor to fully enforce access control policy and privacy protection requirements.

It is then clear that users as well as the companies would find an interesting opportunity in the use of a dissemination service offering strong guarantees about the protection of user privacy against both malicious users breaking into the system and the service provider itself. Indeed, besides well-known risks of confidentiality and privacy breaks, threats to outsourced data include improper use of information: the service provider could use substantial parts of a collection of data gathered and organized by the data owner, potentially harming the data owner's market for any product or service that incorporates that collection of information.

There are mainly three security aspects that need to be considered when designing a system for ensuring confidentiality of data stored and managed by a honest-but-curious server, as briefly outlined in the following.

- *Access control enforcement.* Traditional architectures assign a crucial role to the *reference monitor* [7] for access control enforcement. The reference monitor is the system component responsible of the validation of access requests. The scenario considered in this book however challenges one of the basic tenets of traditional architectures, where a trusted server is in charge of defining and enforcing access control policies. This assumption no longer holds here, because the server does not even have to know the access defined (and possibly modified) by the data owner. We therefore need to rethink the notion of access control in open environments, where honest-but-curious servers are in charge of managing the data collection and are not trusted with respect to the data confidentiality.
- *Privacy protection.* The vast amounts of data collected and maintained by organizations often include sensitive personally identifiable information. This trend has raised the attention of both individuals and legislators, which are forcing organizations to provide privacy guarantees over sensitive information when storing, processing or sharing it with others. Indeed, recent regulations [22, 78] explicitly require specific categories of sensitive information to be either *encrypted* or *kept separate* from other personally identifiable information to grant confidentiality. Since encryption makes access to stored data inefficient, because it is not possible to directly evaluate queries on encrypted data, it is necessary to define new solutions that grant data confidentiality and efficient query evaluation.
- *Safe data integration.* More and more emerging scenarios require different parties, each withholding large amounts of independently managed information, to cooperate for sharing their information. Since the data collection detained by each subject contains sensitive information, classical distributed query evaluation mechanisms cannot be adopted [23, 64]. We therefore need an approach for regulating data flows among parties and for redefining query evaluation mechanisms to the aim of fulfilling access control restrictions imposed by each party. Indeed, data flows among the cooperating parties may be prohibited by privacy

constraints, thus making the design of query execution depending on both efficiency principles and privacy constraints.

There are many real-life examples of applications need a mechanism to exchange and disclose data in a selective and secure way. We outline here three possible scenarios.

**Multimedia sharing systems.** The amount of multimedia data people collect every day is quickly increasing. As a consequence, systems offering storage and distribution services for photographs and videos are becoming more and more popular. However, these data may be sensitive (e.g., photographs retracting people) and their wide diffusion on the Internet should be prevented if not explicitly authorized by the data owner. Since the distribution service may not be trusted with respect to data confidentiality, it cannot enforce the access control policy defined by the data owner. Therefore, it is necessary to think to an alternative solution to prevent sensitive data publication.

**Healthcare system.** More and more healthcare systems collect sensitive information about historical and present hospitalizations, diagnosis, and more in general health conditions of patients. Since these data, associated with the identity of patients, are sensitive, their storage, management, and distribution is subject to both state-level and international regulations. As a consequence, any healthcare system should adopt an adequate privacy protection system, which guarantees, for example, that sensitive information is never stored together with patients' identity.

Recently, the functionalities of healthcare systems have been extended, thanks also to the evolution and wide diffusion of network communication technologies, to allow data exchange among cooperating parties, such as medical personnel, pharmacies, insurance companies, and the patients themselves. Even if this solution improves the quality of the service offered to patients, it however needs to be carefully designed to avoid non authorized data disclosure. It is therefore necessary to define a data integration protocol that guarantees data confidentiality.

**Financial system.** Financial systems store sensitive information that needs to be adequately protected. As an example, the data collected by companies for credit card payments are sensitive and need protection both when stored and managed (e.g., credit card numbers and the corresponding security codes cannot be stored together), as demanded by law. Furthermore, thanks also to the wide diffusion of online transactions, the amount of financial data that systems need to manage and protect is increasing very quickly. Financial systems, as well as healthcare systems, need also to cooperate with other parties, managing independent data collections, such as governmental offices, credit card companies, and clients.

From the above description, it is straightforward to see that the security problems envisioned for healthcare systems apply also to the financial scenario, which demands for the same solutions and technologies for guaranteeing data confidentiality in data storage and exchange.

## 1.2 Contribution of the Book

The book provides an analysis of the main problems arising when the data owner does not directly control her data, since they are manager and/or stored by a honest-but-curious server. The contributions of this book focus on the three security aspects above-mentioned, that is, access control enforcement, privacy protection, and safe data integration. In the remainder of this section, we present the contributions in more details.

### 1.2.1 Access Control Enforcement

The first important contribution of this book is the proposal of a model for access control enforcement on encrypted, possibly outsourced, data [15, 41, 44]. The original contribution of our work can be summarized as follows.

**Selective encryption.** An access control system protecting data stored by a honest-but-curious system cannot rely on a trusted component (i.e., the reference monitor) that evaluates clients' requests. Since the data owner cannot act as an intermediary for data accesses, the access control policy should be embedded in the stored data themselves. Preliminary solutions try to overcome this issue proposing a novel access control model and architecture that eliminates the need for a reference monitor and relies on cryptography to ensure confidentiality of the data stored on the server. New solutions instead propose to combine authorization policy and encryption, thus allowing access control enforcement to be delegated together with the data. The great advantage is that the data owner, while specifying the policy, does not need to be involved in its enforcement. The access control system illustrated in this book exploits this same idea: different portions of the data are encrypted using different encryption keys, which are then distributed to users according to their access privileges. The model proposed in this book differs from previous ones since it exploits key derivation methods [8, 31] to limit the number of secret keys that users and the data owner herself need to securely manage. Key derivation methods allow the derivation of a secret key from another key by exploiting a piece of publicly available information. This solution allows us to reduce the amount of sensitive information that users and owners have to protect against third parties.

**Efficient access to data.** Since key derivation requires a search process in the catalog of publicly available information and the evaluation of a function, the key derivation process may become expensive from the client's point of view. In fact, the public catalog is stored at the provider's site and therefore any search operation implies a communication between the client and the server. To limit the burden due to the key derivation process, in this book we propose a solution that tries to minimize the size of the public catalog. Since such a minimization problem is *NP-hard*, we present a heuristic solution that experimentally obtains good results.

**Policy updates.** Since access control enforcement bases on selective encryption, any time the policy changes, it is necessary for the data owner to re-encrypt the data to reflect the new policy. However, the re-encryption process is expensive from the data owner's point of view, since it requires interaction with the remote server. To reduce the burden due to this data exchange process, we propose a two-layer encryption model where a inner layer is imposed by the owner for providing initial protection and an outer layer is imposed by the server to reflect policy modifications. The combination of the two layers provides an efficient and robust solution, which avoids data re-encryption while correctly managing policy updates.

**Collusion model.** An important aspect that should always be taken into account when designing a security system is its protection degree. To this purpose, we analyzed the security of the two-layer model with respect to the risk of collusion among the parties interacting in the considered scenario. In particular, we consider the case when the server, knowing the encryption keys adopted at the outer layer, and a user, knowing a subset of the keys adopted at the inner layer, collude to gain information that none of them is authorized to access. From this analysis, it is clear that the proposed model introduces a low collusion risk, which can be further reduced at the cost of a less efficient query evaluation process.

## 1.2.2 Privacy Protection

The second contribution we present in this book is a system that nicely combines fragmentation and encryption for privacy purposes [29, 27, 28]. The original contribution of our work can be summarized as follows.

**Confidentiality constraints.** The release, storage, and management of data is nowadays subject to a number of rules, imposed by either legislators or data owners, aimed at preserving the privacy of sensitive information. Since not all the data in a collection are sensitive per se, but their association with other information may need to be protected, solutions encrypting the whole data may be an overdo. Therefore, recently solutions combining fragmentation and encryption have been proposed [2]. In this book, we propose a simple while expressive model for representing privacy requirements, called *confidentiality constraints* that exploits fragmentation and encryption for enforcing such constraints. A confidentiality constraint is a set of attributes whose joint visibility should be prevented; a singleton constraint indicates that the values of the single attribute need to be kept private. This model, while simple, nicely captures different privacy requirements that need to be enforced on a data collection (e.g., sensitive data and sensitive associations).

**Minimality.** The main goal of the approach proposed in this book is to minimize the use of encryption for privacy protection. A trivial solution for solving confidentiality constraints consists in creating a fragment for each attribute that does not appear in a singleton constraint. Obviously such a solution is not desiderated, unless demanded by constraints, since it makes query evaluation inefficient. Indeed, since fragments cannot be joined by non authorized users, the client posing the query would be in charge of combining the data extracted from the different fragments. To avoid such a situation, we propose three different models for designing a fragmentation that, while granting privacy protection, maximizes query evaluation efficiency. The three solutions differ in the efficiency measure proposed (i.e., number of fragments, affinity among attributes, query workload).

**Query evaluation.** Data fragmentation is usually transparent to the final user, meaning that queries are formulated on the original schema and then they are reformulated to operate on fragments. Since, as already noted, encryption and fragmentation reduce the efficiency in data retrieval, we propose to add indexes to fragments. Indexes are defined on attributes that do not appear in clear form in the fragment. Also, since indexes may open the door to inference and linking attacks, we carefully analyze the exposure risk due to different indexing methods, considering the external knowledge of a possible malicious user.

### 1.2.3 Safe Data Integration

The third and last contribution we present in this book is a solution for the integration of data from different data sources, which must be subject to confidentiality constraints [42, 43]. The original contribution coming from our work can be summarized as follows.

**Access control model.** We present a simple, yet powerful, approach for the specification and enforcement of permissions regulating data release among data holders collaborating in a distributed computation, to ensure that query processing discloses only data whose release has been explicitly authorized. The model is based on the concept of *profile*, which nicely models both the information carried by the result of a query, and the information whose release is authorized by permissions. To easily evaluate when a data release is allowed by the permissions of the requesting subject, we propose a graph based model. Profiles are then represented by adequately coloring the graph. The process of controlling if a query must be denied or allowed is then based on the comparison of the colors of vertices and edges in the graphs representing the query and the permissions in the system.

**Permission composition.** The amount of data that need to be integrated is potentially large and therefore it is not possible to check queries against single permissions, since the number of permissions to be explicitly defined would increase quickly. We then introduce the principle that a query must be allowed if the information release it (directly or indirectly) entails is allowed by the permissions. In other words, if the subject formulating the query is able to compute its result by combining information she is allowed to access, then the query should be allowed. To enforce this basic principle, we propose a permission composition method, which is based on reachability properties on the graphs representing the profiles of the permissions. The composition method proposed has the great advantage of working in polynomial time, even if the number of possible composed permissions is exponential in the number of base permissions. This is due to a nice dominance property, which we prove in this book, between composed permissions and their components.

**Safe query planning.** Besides defining and composing permissions, it is necessary to evaluate if a query operating in the distributed scenario can be executed (i.e., the query is safe) or if the query must be denied. To this purpose, we characterize the flows of information among the interacting subjects for the evaluation of the given query, considering also different methods for executing join operations between distinct data sources. A query is therefore safe if all the data flows it requires for its evaluation are allowed by the set of (composed) permissions characterizing the system. We present an algorithm that given a query checks if the query can be evaluated without violating the set of permissions regulating the distributed system. If the query can be safely executed, the algorithm we propose also determines which server is in charge for executing which operation.

## 1.3 Organization of the Book

In this chapter, we discussed the motivation and the main objectives of our work and described the major contributions of this book. The remaining chapters are structured as follows.

**Chapter 2** discusses the state of the art of the security aspects related to the objectives of the book. It presents the main results obtained in the data outsourcing scenario, focusing on mechanisms for query evaluation, inference exposure measurement, and data integrity. Also, it introduces preliminary works on access control enforcement, privacy protection, and data integration in the considered scenario.

**Chapter 3** illustrates our access control system for securing data stored at a honest-but-curious server and proposes an efficient mechanism for managing access control policy updates. The risk of collusion among parties is also analyzed to prove the security of the presented solution.

**Chapter 4** addresses the problem of modeling and enforcing privacy requirements to protect sensitive data and/or their associations. It also presents three cost models for computing an optimal fragmentation, that is, a fragmentation that allows efficient query evaluation.

**Chapter 5** focuses on the problem of integrating data made available from different parties and that must satisfy security constraints. It proposes a model for expressing restrictions on data flows among parties and a mechanism for querying distributed data collections under these constraints.

**Chapter 6** summarizes the contributions of this book and outlines future work.

# Chapter 2
# Overview of the State of the Art

This chapter discusses the state of the art in the area of data outsourcing, which is mainly focused on efficient methods for querying encrypted data. We also present some approaches for evaluating the inference exposure due to data publication, and solutions for granting data integrity. A few research efforts have instead addressed the problem of developing access control systems for outsourced data and for securely querying distributed databases.

## 2.1 Introduction

The amount of information held by organizations' databases is increasing very quickly. To respond to this demand, organizations can:

- add data storage and skilled administrative personnel (at a high rate);
- delegate database management to an external service provider (*database outsourcing*), a solution becoming increasingly popular.

In the database outsourcing scenario, usually referred to as *Database As a Service* (DAS), the external service provider provides mechanisms for clients to access the outsourced databases. A major advantage of database outsourcing is related to the high costs of in-house versus outsourced hosting. Outsourcing provides significant cost savings and promises higher availability and more effective disaster protection than in-house operations. On the other hand, database outsourcing poses a major security problem, due to the fact that the external service provider, which is relied upon for ensuring high availability of the outsourced database (i.e., it is trustworthy), cannot always be trusted with respect to the confidentiality of the database content.

Besides well-known risks of confidentiality and privacy breaks, threats to outsourced data include improper use of database information: the server could extract, resell, or commercially use parts of a collection of data gathered and organized by the data owner, potentially harming the data owner's market for any product or service that incorporates that collection of information. Traditional database access

S. Foresti, *Preserving Privacy in Data Outsourcing*, Advances in Information Security 51, DOI 10.1007/978-1-4419-7659-8_2, © Springer Science+Business Media, LLC 2011

control techniques cannot prevent the server itself from making unauthorized access to the data stored in the database. Alternatively, to protect against "honest-but-curious" servers, a protective layer of encryption can be wrapped around sensitive data, preventing outside attacks as well as infiltration from the server itself [38]. This scenario raises many interesting research challenges. First, data encryption introduces the problem of efficiently querying outsourced encrypted data. Since confidentiality demands that data decryption must be possible only at the client-side, techniques have then been proposed, enabling external servers to directly execute queries on encrypted data. Typically, these solutions consist mainly in adding a piece of information, called *index*, to the encrypted data. Indexes are computed based on the plaintext data and preserve some of the original characteristics of the data to allow (partial) query evaluation. However, since indexes carry some information about the original data, they may be exploited as inference channels by malicious users or by the service provider itself. Second, since data are not under the owner's direct control, unauthorized modifications must be prevented to the aim of granting data integrity. For this purpose, different solutions based on different signature mechanisms have been proposed, with the main goal of improving verification efficiency. Third, although index-based solutions represent an effective approach for querying encrypted data, they introduce an overhead in query execution, due to both query formulation through indexes and data decryption and filtering of query results. However, since often what is sensitive in a data collection is the association among attributes more than the values assumed by each attribute per se, new solutions based on the combination of fragmentation and encryption have been proposed to reduce the usage of encryption and to therefore increase query execution efficiency. Fourth, an interesting issue that has not been deeply studied in the data outsourcing scenario is represented by the access control enforcement, which cannot be delegated to the service provider. Finally, when the outsourced data are stored at different servers, new safe data integration mechanisms are needed that should take into consideration the different data protection needs of the cooperating servers.

### 2.1.1 Chapter Outline

In this chapter, we survey the main proposals addressing the data access and security issues arising in the data outsourcing scenario. The remainder of the chapter is organized as follows. Section 2.2 gives an overview of the entities involved in the data outsourcing scenario and of their typical interactions. Section 2.3 describes the main indexing methods proposed in the literature for supporting queries over encrypted data. Section 2.4 addresses inference exposure due to different indexing techniques. Section 2.5 focuses on techniques granting data integrity. Section 2.6 describes solutions efficiently combining fragmentation and encryption for granting privacy protection. Section 2.7 presents the main proposals for access control enforcement on outsourced encrypted data. Section 2.8 illustrates problems and so-

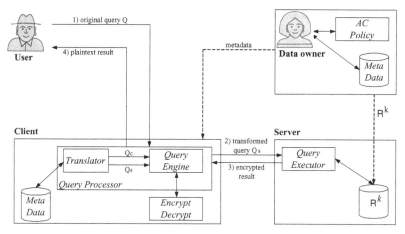

**Fig. 2.1** DAS scenario

lutions for safe data integration in a distributed system. Finally, Sect. 2.9 concludes the chapter.

## 2.2 Basic Scenario and Data Organization

In this section, we describe the entities involved in the DAS scenario, how data are organized in the outsourced database context, and the interactions among the entities in the system for query evaluation.

### 2.2.1 Parties Involved

There are four distinct entities interacting in the DAS scenario (Fig. 2.1):

- a *data owner* (person or organization) produces and outsources resources to make them available for controlled external release;
- a *user* (human entity) presents requests (queries) to the system;
- a *client* front-end transforms the queries posed by users into equivalent queries operating on the encrypted data stored on the server;
- a *server* receives the encrypted data from one or more data owners and makes them available for distribution to clients.

Clients and data owners, when outsourcing data, are assumed to trust the server to faithfully maintain outsourced data. The server is then relied upon for the availability of outsourced data, so the data owner and clients can access data whenever requested. However, the server (which can be "honest-but-curious") is not trusted with the confidentiality of the actual database content, as outsourced data may contain sensitive information that the data owner wants to release only to authorized users. Consequently, it is necessary to prevent the server from making unauthorized accesses to the database. To this purpose, the data owner encrypts her data with a key known only to trusted clients, and sends the encrypted database to the server for storage.

## 2.2.2 Data Organization

A database can be encrypted according to different strategies. In principle, both symmetric and asymmetric encryption can be used at different granularity levels. Symmetric encryption, being cheaper than asymmetric encryption, is usually adopted. The granularity level at which database encryption is performed can depend on the data that need to be accessed. Encryption can then be at the finer grain of [55, 63]:

- *relation*: each relation in the plaintext database is represented through a single encrypted value in the encrypted database; consequently, tuples and attributes are indistinguishable in the released data, and cannot be specified in a query on the encrypted database;
- *attribute*: each column (attribute) in the plaintext relation is represented by a single encrypted value in the encrypted relation;
- *tuple*: each tuple in the plaintext relation is represented by a single encrypted value in the encrypted relation;
- *element*: each cell in the plaintext relation is represented by a single encrypted value in the encrypted relation.

Both relation level and attribute level encryption imply the communication to the requesting client of the whole relation involved in a query, as it is not possible to extract any subset of the tuples in the encrypted representation of the relation. On the other hand, encrypting at element level would require an excessive workload for data owners and clients in encrypting/decrypting data. For balancing client workload and query execution efficiency, most proposals assume that the database is encrypted at tuple level.

While database encryption provides an adequate level of protection for data, it makes impossible for the server to directly execute the users' queries on the encrypted database. Upon receiving a query, the server can only send to the requestor the encrypted relations involved in the query; the client needs then to decrypt such relations and execute the query on them. To allow the server to select a set of tuples to be returned in response to a query, a set of indexes can be associated with the encrypted relation. In this case, the server stores an encrypted relation with an index for each attribute on which conditions may need to be evaluated. For simplicity, we assume the existence of an index for each attribute in each relation of the database. Different kinds of indexes can be defined for the attributes in a relation, depending on the clauses and conditions that need to be remotely evaluated. Given a plaintext

EMPLOYEE

| Emp-Id | Name | YoB | Dept | Salary |
|--------|------|-----|------|--------|
| P01 | Ann | 1980 | Production | 10 |
| R01 | Bob | 1975 | R&D | 15 |
| F01 | Bob | 1985 | Financial | 10 |
| P02 | Carol | 1980 | Production | 20 |
| F02 | Ann | 1980 | Financial | 15 |
| R02 | David | 1978 | R&D | 15 |

(a)

EMPLOYEE$^k$

| Counter | Etuple | $I_1$ | $I_2$ | $I_3$ | $I_4$ | $I_5$ |
|---------|--------|-------|-------|-------|-------|-------|
| 1 | ite6Az*+8wc | $\pi$ | $\alpha$ | $\gamma$ | $\varepsilon$ | $\lambda$ |
| 2 | 8(Xznfeua4!= | $\phi$ | $\beta$ | $\delta$ | $\theta$ | $\lambda$ |
| 3 | Q73gnew321*/ | $\phi$ | $\beta$ | $\gamma$ | $\mu$ | $\lambda$ |
| 4 | -1vs9e892s | $\pi$ | $\alpha$ | $\gamma$ | $\varepsilon$ | $\rho$ |
| 5 | e32rfs4aS+@ | $\pi$ | $\alpha$ | $\gamma$ | $\mu$ | $\lambda$ |
| 6 | r43arg*5[) | $\phi$ | $\beta$ | $\delta$ | $\theta$ | $\lambda$ |

(b)

**Fig. 2.2** An example of plaintext (a) and encrypted (b) relation

database $\mathscr{R}$, each relation $r_i$ over schema $R_i(a_{i1},a_{i2},\ldots,a_{in})$ in $\mathscr{R}$ is mapped onto a relation $r_i^k$ over schema $R_i^k(\underline{Counter}, Etuple, I_{i1}, I_{i2},\ldots,I_{in})$ in the corresponding encrypted database $\mathscr{R}^k$. Here, *Counter* is a numerical attribute added as primary key of the encrypted relation; *Etuple* is the attribute containing the encrypted tuple, whose value is obtained applying an encryption function $E_k$ to the plaintext tuple, where $k$ is the secret key; and $I_{ij}$ is the index associated with the $j$-th attribute $a_{ij}$ in $R_i$. While we assume encrypted tuples and indexes to be in the same relation, we note that indexes can be stored in a separate relation [35].

To illustrate, consider relation `Employee` in Fig. 2.2(a). The corresponding encrypted relation is shown in Fig. 2.2(b), where index values are conventionally represented with Greek letters. The encrypted relation has exactly the same number of tuples as the original relation. For the sake of readability, the tuples in the encrypted relation are listed in the same order with which they appear in the corresponding plaintext relation. The same happens for the order of indexes, which are listed in the same order as the corresponding attributes are listed in the plaintext relation schema. For security reasons, real-world systems do not preserve the order of attributes and tuples and the correspondence between attributes and indexes is maintained by metadata relations that only authorized parties can access [32].

### 2.2.3 Interactions

The introduction of indexes allows the partial evaluation of any query $Q$ at the server-side, provided it is previously translated in an equivalent query operating on the encrypted database. Figure 2.1 summarizes the most important steps necessary for the evaluation of a query submitted by a user.

1. The user submits her query $Q$ referring to the schema of the plaintext database $\mathscr{R}$, and passes it to the client front-end. The user needs not to be aware that data have been outsourced to a third party.
2. The client maps the user's query onto: *i)* an equivalent query $Q_s$, working on the encrypted relations through indexes, and *ii)* an additional query $Q_c$ working on

the results of $Q_s$. Query $Q_s$ is then passed on to the remote server. Note that the client is the unique entity in the system that knows the structure of both $\mathcal{R}$ and $\mathcal{R}^k$ and that can translate the queries the user may submit.

3. The remote server executes the received query $Q_s$ on the encrypted database and returns the result (i.e., a set of encrypted tuples) to the client.
4. The client decrypts the tuples received and eventually discards spurious tuples (i.e., tuples that do not satisfy the query submitted by the user). These spurious tuples are removed by executing query $Q_c$. The final plaintext result is then returned to the user.

Since a client may have limited storage and reduced computation capacity, one of the primary goals of the query execution process is to minimize the workload at the client side, while maximizing the operations that can be computed at the server side [36, 55, 57, 63].

Iyer et al. [55, 63] present a solution for minimizing the client workload that is based on a graphical representation of queries as trees. Since the authors limit their analysis to *select-from-where* queries, each query $Q$="SELECT $A$ FROM $R_1,\ldots,R_n$ WHERE $C$" can be reformulated as an algebra expression of the form $\pi_A(\sigma_C(R_1 \bowtie \ldots \bowtie R_n))$. Each query can then be represented as a binary tree, where leaves correspond to relations $R_1,\ldots,R_n$ and internal nodes represent relational operations, receiving as input the result produced by their children. The tree representing a query is split in two parts: the lower part includes all operations that can be executed by the server, while the upper part contains all operations that cannot be delegated to the server and that therefore need to be executed by the client. In particular, since a query can be represented with different, but equivalent, trees by simply pushing down selections and postponing projections, the basic idea of the proposed solution is to determine a tree representation of the query, where the operations that only the client can execute are in the highest levels of the tree. For instance, if there are two ANDed conditions in the query and only one can be evaluated at the server-side, the selection operation is split in such a way that one condition is evaluated server-side and the other client-side.

Hacigümüs et al. [57] show a method for splitting the query $Q_s$ to be executed on the encrypted data into two sub-queries, $Q_{s1}$ and $Q_{s2}$, where $Q_{s1}$ returns only tuples that belongs to the final result, and query $Q_{s2}$ may contain also spurious tuples. This distinction allows the execution of $Q_c$ over the result of $Q_{s2}$ only, while tuples returned by $Q_{s1}$ can be immediately decrypted. To further reduce the client's workload, Damiani et al. [36] propose an architecture that minimizes storage at the client and introduce the idea of selective decryption of $Q_s$. With selective decryption, the client decrypts the portion of the tuples needed for evaluating $Q_c$, while complete decryption is executed only for tuples that belong to the final result and that will be returned to the final user. The approach is based on a block-cipher encryption algorithm, operating at tuple level, that allows the detection of the blocks containing the attributes necessary to evaluate the conditions in $Q_c$, which are the only ones that need decryption.

It is important to note that the process of transforming $Q$ in $Q_s$ and $Q_c$ greatly depends both on the indexing method adopted and on the clauses and conditions composing query $Q$. There are operations that need to be executed by the client, since the indexing method adopted does not support the specific operations (e.g., range queries are not supported by all types of indexes) and the server is not allowed to decrypt data. Also, there are operations that the server could execute over the index, but that require a pre-computation that only the client can perform and therefore must be postponed in $Q_c$ (e.g., the evaluation of a condition in the HAVING clause, which needs a grouping over an attribute, whose corresponding index has been created by using a method that does not support the GROUP BY clause).

## 2.3  Querying Encrypted Data

When designing a solution for querying encrypted data, one of the most important goals is to minimize the computation at the client-side and to reduce communication overhead. The server therefore should be responsible for the majority of the work. Different indexing approaches allow the execution of different types of queries at the server side.

We now describe in more detail the methods initially proposed to efficiently execute simple queries at the server side, and we give an overview of more recent methods that improve the server's ability to query encrypted data.

### 2.3.1  Bucket-Based Approach

Hacigümüs et al. [58] propose the first method to query encrypted data, which is based on the definition of a number of *buckets* on the attribute domain. Let $r_i$ be a plaintext relation over schema $R_i(a_{i1}, a_{i2}, \ldots, a_{in})$ and $r_i^k$ be the corresponding encrypted relation over schema $R_i^k(\underline{Counter}, Etuple, I_{i1}, \ldots, I_{in})$. Considering an arbitrary plaintext attribute $a_{ij}$ in $R_i$, with domain $D_{ij}$, bucket-based indexing methods partition $D_{ij}$ in a number of non-overlapping subsets of values, called *buckets*, containing contiguous values. This process, called *bucketization*, usually generates buckets that are all of the same size.

Each bucket is then associated with a unique value and the set of these values is the domain for index $I_{ij}$ associated with $a_{ij}$. Given a plaintext tuple $t$ in $r_i$, the value of attribute $a_{ij}$ for $t$ (i.e., $t[a_{ij}]$) belongs to only one bucket defined on $D_{ij}$. The corresponding index value is then the unique value associated with the bucket to which the plaintext value $t[a_{ij}]$ belongs. It is important to note that, for better preserving data secrecy, the domain of index $I_{ij}$ may not follow the same order as the one of the plaintext attribute $a_{ij}$. Attributes $I_3$ and $I_5$ in Fig. 2.2(b) are the indexes obtained by applying the bucketization method defined in Fig. 2.3 for attributes YoB and Salary in Fig. 2.2(a). Note that $I_3$ values do not reflect the order of the domain values it represents, since $1975 < 1985$, while $\delta$ follows $\gamma$ in lexicographic order.

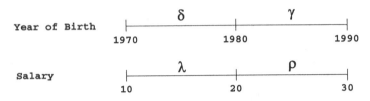

**Fig. 2.3** An example of bucketization

Bucket-based indexing methods allow the server-side evaluation of equality conditions appearing in the WHERE clause, since these conditions can be mapped into equivalent conditions operating on indexes. Given a plaintext condition of the form $a_{ij}=v$, where $v$ is a constant value, the corresponding condition operating on index $I_{ij}$ is $I_{ij}=\beta$, where $\beta$ is the value associated with the bucket containing $v$. As an example, with reference to Fig. 2.3, condition YoB=1985 is transformed into $I_3=\gamma$. Also, equality conditions involving attributes defined on the same domain can be evaluated by the server, provided that attributes characterized by the same domain are indexed using the same bucketization. In this case, a plaintext condition of the form $a_{ij}=a_{ik}$ is translated into condition $I_{ij}=I_{ik}$ operating on indexes.

Bucket-based methods do not easily support range queries. Since the index domain does not necessarily preserve the plaintext domain ordering, a range condition of the form $a_{ij}\geq v$, where $v$ is a constant value, must be mapped into a series of equality conditions operating on index $I_{ij}$ of the form $I_{ij}=\beta_1$ OR $I_{ij}=\beta_2$ OR ... OR $I_{ij}=\beta_k$, where $\beta_1,\ldots,\beta_k$ are the values associated with buckets that correspond to plaintext values greater than or equal to $v$. For instance, with reference to Fig. 2.3, condition YoB>1977 must be translated into $I_3=\gamma$ OR $I_3=\delta$, since both values represent years greater than 1977.

Note that, since the same index value is associated with more than one plaintext value, queries exploiting bucket-based indexes usually produce spurious tuples that need to be filtered out by the client front-end. Spurious tuples are tuples that satisfy the condition over the indexes, but that do not satisfy the original plaintext condition. For instance, with reference to the relations in Fig. 2.2, query "SELECT * FROM Employee WHERE YoB=1985" is translated into "SELECT Etuple FROM Employee[k] WHERE $I_3=\gamma$". The result of the query executed by the server contains tuples 1, 3, 4, and 5; however, only tuple 3 satisfies the original condition as written by the user. Tuples 1, 4, and 5 are spurious and must be discarded by the client during the postprocessing of the $Q_s$ result.

Hore et al. [61] propose an improvement to bucket-based indexing methods by introducing an efficient way for partitioning the domain of attributes. Given an attribute and a query profile on it, the authors present a method for building an efficient index, which tries to minimize the number of spurious tuples in the result of both range and equality queries.

As we will see in Sect. 2.4, one of the main disadvantages of bucket-based indexing methods is that they expose data to inference attacks.

## 2.3.2 Hash-Based Approach

Hash-based index methods are similar to bucket-based methods and are based on the concept of *one-way hash function* [35].

Let $r_i$ be a plaintext relation over schema $R_i(a_{i1}, a_{i2}, \ldots, a_{in})$ and $r_i^k$ be the corresponding encrypted relation over schema $R_i^k(\underline{Counter}, Etuple, I_{i1}, \ldots, I_{in})$. For each attribute $a_{ij}$ in $R_i$ to be indexed, a one-way hash function $h : D_{ij} \rightarrow B_{ij}$ is defined, where $D_{ij}$ is the domain of $a_{ij}$ and $B_{ij}$ is the domain of index $I_{ij}$ associated with $a_{ij}$. Given a plaintext tuple $t$ in $r_i$, the index value corresponding to attribute $a_{ij}$ for $t$ is computed by applying function $h$ to the plaintext value $t[a_{ij}]$.

An important property of any hash function $h$ is its *determinism*; formally, $\forall x, y \in D_{ij} : x = y \Rightarrow h(x) = h(y)$. Another interesting property of hash functions is that the codomain of $h$ is smaller than its domain, so there is the possibility of *collisions*; a collision happens when given two values $x, y \in D_{ij}$ with $x \neq y$, we have that $h(x) = h(y)$. A further property is that $h$ must produce a strong mixing, that is, given two distinct but near values $x, y$ ($|x - y| < \varepsilon$) chosen randomly in $D_{ij}$, the discrete probability distribution of the difference $h(x) - h(y)$ is uniform (the results of the hash function can be arbitrarily different, even for very similar input values). A consequence of strong mixing is that the hash function does not preserve the domain order of the attribute on which it is applied. As an example, consider the relations in Fig. 2.2. Here, the indexes corresponding to attributes Emp-Id, Name, and Dept in relation Employee are computed by applying a hash-based method. The values of attribute Name have been mapped onto two distinct values, namely $\alpha$ and $\beta$; the values of attribute Emp-Id have been mapped onto two distinct values, namely $\pi$ and $\phi$; and the values of attribute Dept have been mapped onto three distinct values, namely $\varepsilon$, $\theta$, and $\mu$. Like for bucket-based methods, hash-based methods allow an efficient evaluation of equality conditions of the form $a_{ij}=v$, where $v$ is a constant value. Each condition $a_{ij}=v$ is transformed into a condition $I_{ij}=h(v)$, where $I_{ij}$ is the index corresponding to $a_{ij}$ in the encrypted relation. For instance, condition Name="Alice" is transformed into $I_2=\alpha$. Also, equality conditions involving attributes defined on the same domain can be evaluated by the server, provided that these attributes are indexed using the same hash function. The main drawback of hash-based methods is that they do not support range queries, for which a solution similar to the one adopted for bucket-based methods is not viable: colliding values are in general not contiguous in the plaintext domain.

If the hash function used for index definition is not collision free, then queries exploiting the index produce spurious tuples that need to be filtered out by the client front-end. A collision-free hash function guarantees absence of spurious tuples, but may expose data to inference (see Sect. 2.4). For instance, assuming that the hash function adopted for attribute Dept in Fig. 2.2(a) is collision-free, condition Dept="Financial" is translated into $I_4=\mu$, that will return only the tuples (in our example, tuples with Counter equal to 3 and 5) that belong to the result of the query that contains the corresponding plaintext condition.

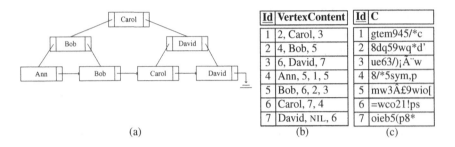

| Id | VertexContent |
|----|---------------|
| 1  | 2, Carol, 3   |
| 2  | 4, Bob, 5     |
| 3  | 6, David, 7   |
| 4  | Ann, 5, 1, 5  |
| 5  | Bob, 6, 2, 3  |
| 6  | Carol, 7, 4   |
| 7  | David, NIL, 6 |

| Id | C            |
|----|--------------|
| 1  | gtem945/*c   |
| 2  | 8dq59wq*d'   |
| 3  | ue63/)¡Ä¨w   |
| 4  | 8/*5sym,p    |
| 5  | mw3Å£9wio[   |
| 6  | =wco21!ps    |
| 7  | oieb5(p8*    |

        (a)                           (b)          (c)

**Fig. 2.4**  An example of B+ tree indexing structure

### 2.3.3 B+ Tree Approach

Both bucket-based and hash-based indexing methods do not easily support range queries, since both these solutions are not order preserving. Damiani et al. [35] propose an indexing method that, while granting data privacy, preserves the order relationship characterizing the domain of attribute $a_{ij}$. This indexing method exploits the traditional B+ tree data structure used by relational DBMSs for physically indexing data. A B+ tree with fan out $n$ is a tree where every vertex can store up to $n-1$ search key values and $n$ pointers and, except for the root and leaf vertices, has at least $\lceil n/2 \rceil$ children. Given an internal vertex storing $f$ key values $k_1, \ldots, k_f$ with $f \leq n-1$, each key value $k_i$ is followed by a pointer $p_i$ and $k_1$ is preceded by a pointer $p_0$. Pointer $p_0$ points to the subtree that contains keys with values lower than $k_1$, $p_f$ points to the subtree that contains keys with values greater than or equal to $k_f$, and each $p_i$ points to the subtree that contains keys with values included in the interval $[k_i, k_{i+1})$. Internal vertices do not directly refer to tuples in the database, but just point to other vertices in the structure; on the contrary, leaf vertices do not contain pointers, but directly refer to the tuples in the database having a specific value for the indexed attribute. Leaf vertices are linked in a chain that allows the efficient execution of range queries. As an example, Fig. 2.4(a) represents the B+ tree index built for attribute Name of relation Employee in Fig. 2.2(a). To access a tuple with key value $k$, value $k$ is first searched in the root vertex of the B+ tree. The tree is then traversed by using the following scheme: if $k < k_1$, pointer $p_0$ is chosen; if $k \geq k_f$, pointer $p_f$ is chosen, otherwise if $k_i \leq k < k_{i+1}$, pointer $p_i$ is chosen. The process continues until a leaf vertex has been examined. If $k$ is not found in any leaf vertex, the relation does not contain any tuple having, for the indexed attribute, value $k$.

A B+ tree index can be usefully adopted for each attribute $a_{ij}$ in the schema of relation $R_i$, provided $a_{ij}$ is defined over a partially ordered domain. The index is built by the data owner over the plaintext values of the attribute, and then stored on the remote server, together with the encrypted database. To this purpose, the B+ tree structure is translated into a specific relation with the two attributes: *Id*, represents the vertex identifier; and *VertexContent*, represents the actual vertex content. The relation has a row for each vertex in the tree and pointers are represented through cross references from the vertex content to other vertex identifiers in the relation. For instance, the B+ tree structure depicted in Fig. 2.4(a) is represented in the encrypted database by the relation in Fig. 2.4(b). Since the relation representing the B+ tree contains sensitive information (i.e., the plaintext values of the attribute on which the B+ tree is built) this relation has to be protected by encrypting its content. To this purpose, encryption is applied at the level of vertex (i.e., of tuple in the relation), to protect the order relationship among plaintext and index values and the mapping between the two domains. The corresponding encrypted relation has therefore two attributes: *Id* that represents, as before, the identifier of the vertex; and *C* that contains the encrypted vertex. Figure 2.4(c) illustrates the encrypted B+ tree relation that corresponds to the plaintext B+ tree relation in Fig. 2.4(b).

The B+ tree based indexing method allows the evaluation of both equality and range conditions appearing in the WHERE clause. Moreover, being order preserving, it also allows the evaluation of ORDER BY and GROUP BY clauses of SQL queries, and of most of the aggregate operators, directly on the encrypted database. Given the plaintext condition $a_{ij} \geq v$, where $v$ is a constant value, it is necessary to traverse the B+ tree stored on the server to find out the leaf vertex representing $v$ for correctly evaluating the considered condition. To this purpose, the client queries the B+ tree relation to retrieve the root, which conventionally is the tuple $t$ with $t[Id]=1$. It then decrypts $t[C]$, evaluates its content and, according to the search process above-mentioned, queries again the remote server to retrieve the next vertex along the path to $v$. The search process continues until a leaf vertex containing $v$ is found (if any). The client then follows the chain of leaf vertices starting from the retrieved leaf to extract all the tuples satisfying condition $a_{ij} \geq v$. For instance, consider the B+ tree in Fig. 2.4(a) defined for attribute Name in relation Employee in Fig. 2.2(a). A query asking for tuples where the value of attribute Name follows "Bob" in the lexicographic order is evaluated as follows. First, the root is retrieved and evaluated: since "Bob" precedes "Carol", the first pointer is chosen and vertex 2 is evaluated. Since "Bob" is equal to the value in the vertex, the second pointer is chosen and vertex 5 is evaluated. Vertex 5 is a leaf, and all tuples in vertices 5, 6, and 7 are returned to the final user.

It is important to note that B+ tree indexes do not produce spurious tuples when executing a query, but the evaluation of conditions is much more expensive for the client with respect to bucket and hash-based methods. For this reason, it may be advisable to combine the B+ tree method with either hash-based or bucket-based indexing, and use the B+ tree index only for evaluating conditions based on intervals. Compared with traditional B+ tree structures used in DBMSs, the vertices in the indexing structure presented here do not have to be of the same size as a disk block; a cost model can then be used to optimize the number of children of a vertex, potentially producing vertices with a large number of children and trees with limited depth. Finally, we note that since the B+ tree content is encrypted, the method is secure against inference attacks (see Sect. 2.4).

### 2.3.4 Order Preserving Encryption Approaches

To support equality and range queries over encrypted data without adopting B+ tree data structures, Agrawal et al. [4] present an *Order Preserving Encryption Schema* (OPES). An OPES function has the advantage of flattening the frequency spectrum of index values, thanks to the introduction of new buckets when needed. It is important to note here that queries executed over this kind of indexes do not return spurious tuples. Also, OPES provides data secrecy only if the intruder does not know the plaintext database or the domain of original attributes.

Order Preserving Encryption with Splitting and Scaling (OPESS) [96] is an evolution of OPES that both supports range queries and does not suffer from inference problems. This indexing method exploits the traditional B-tree data structure used by relational DBMSs for physically indexing data. B-tree data structure is similar to B+ tree data structure, but internal vertices directly refer to tuples in the database and leaves of the tree are not linked in a unique list.

An OPESS index can be usefully adopted for each attribute $a_{ij}$ in the relation schema $R_i$, provided $a_{ij}$ is defined over a partially ordered domain. The index is built by the data owner over the plaintext values of the attribute, and then stored on the remote server, together with the encrypted database. Differently from B+ tree indexing structure, the B-tree data structure exploited by OPESS is built on index values, and not on plaintext values. Therefore, before building the B-tree structure to be remotely stored on the server, OPESS applies two techniques on the original values of $a_{ij}$, called *splitting* and *scaling*, aimed at obtaining a flat frequency distribution of index values.

Consider attribute $a_{ij}$ defined on domain $D_{ij}$ and assume that the values $\{v_1, \ldots, v_n\}$ in the considered relation $r_i$ have occurrences, in the order, equal to $\{f_1, \ldots, f_n\}$. First, a splitting process is performed on $a_{ij}$, producing a number of index values having almost a flat frequency distribution. The splitting process applies to each value $v_h$ assumed by $a_{ij}$ in $r_i$. It determines three consecutive positive integers, $m-1$, $m$, and $m+1$, such that the frequency $f_h$ of value $v_h$ can be expressed as a linear combination of the computed values: $f_h = c_1(m-1) + c_2(m) + c_3(m+1)$, where $c_1$, $c_2$, and $c_3$ are non negative integer values. The plaintext value $v_h$ can therefore be mapped into $c_1$ index values each with $m+1$ occurrences, $c_2$ index values each with $m$ occurrences, and $c_3$ index values each with $m-1$ occurrences. To preserve the order of index values with respect to the original domain of attribute $a_{ij}$, for any two values $v_h < v_l$ and for any index values $i_h$ and $i_l$ associated with $v_h$ and $v_l$ respectively, we need to guarantee that $i_h < i_l$. To this purpose, the authors in [96] propose to exploit an order preserving encryption function. Specifically, for each plaintext value $v_h$, its index values are obtained by adding a randomly chosen string of low order bits to a common string of high order bits computed as follows: $v_h^e = E_k(v_h)$, where $E$ is an order preserving encryption function with key $k$.

Since splitting technique grants the sum of frequencies of indexes representing value $v$ to be exactly the same as the original frequency of $v$, an attacker who knows the frequency distribution of plaintext domain values could exploit this property to break the indexing method adopted. Indeed, the index values mapping a given plaintext value are, by definition, contiguous values. Therefore, the authors in [96] propose to adopt a *scaling* technique together with splitting. Each plaintext value $v_h$ is associated with a scaling factor $s_h$. When $v_h$ is split into $n$ index values, namely $i_1, \ldots, i_n$, each index entry in the B-tree corresponding to $i_h$ is replicated $s_h$ times. Note that all $s_h$ replicas of the index point to the same block of tuples in the encrypted database. After scaling has been applied, the index frequency distribution is not uniform any more. Without knowing the scaling factor used, it is not possible for the attacker to reconstruct the correspondence between plaintext and index values.

The OPESS indexing method allows the evaluation of both equality and range conditions appearing in the WHERE clause. Moreover, being order preserving, it also allows the evaluation of ORDER BY and GROUP BY clauses of SQL queries, and of most of the aggregate operators, directly on the encrypted database. It is important to note that query execution becomes expensive, even if it does not produce spurious tuples, due to the fact that the same plaintext value is mapped into different index values and both splitting and scaling methods need to be inverted for query evaluation.

## 2.3.5 Other Approaches

In addition to the three main indexing methods previously presented, many other solutions have been proposed to support queries on encrypted data. These methods try to better support SQL clauses or to reduce the amount of spurious tuples in the result produced by the remote server.

Wang et al. [97, 98] propose a new indexing method, specific for attributes whose domain is the set of all possible strings over a well defined set of characters, which adapts the hash-based indexing methods to permit direct evaluation of LIKE conditions. The index value associated with any string $s$, composed of $n$ characters $c_1 c_2 \ldots c_n$, is obtained by applying a secure hash function to each pair of subsequent characters in $s$. Given a string $s = c_1 c_2 \ldots c_n = s_1 s_2 \ldots s_{n/2}$, where $s_i = c_{2i} c_{2i+1}$, the corresponding index is computed as $i = h(s_1) h(s_2) \ldots h(s_{n/2})$.

Hacigümüs et al. [57] study a method to remotely support aggregation operators, such as COUNT, SUM, AVG, MIN, and MAX. The method is based on the concept of *privacy homomorphism* [19], which exploits properties of modular algebra to allow the execution over index values of sum, subtraction, and product operations, while not preserving the order relationship characterizing the original domain. Evdokimov et al. [47] formally analyze the security of the method based on privacy homomorphism, with respect to the degree of confidentiality assigned to the remote server. The authors formally introduce a definition of *intrinsic security* for encrypted databases, and it is proved that almost all indexing methods are not intrinsically secure. In particular, methods that do not cause spurious tuples to belong to the result of a query inevitably are exposed to attacks coming from a malicious third party or from the service provider itself.

| Index | Query | | |
|-------|:-----:|:-----:|:-----:|
| | **Equality** | **Range** | **Aggregation** |
| Bucket-based [58] | ● | ○ | – |
| Hash-based [35] | ● | – | ○ |
| B+ Tree [35] | ● | ● | ● |
| OPES [4] | ● | ● | ○ |
| OPESS [96] | ● | ● | ● |
| Character oriented [97, 98] | ● | ○ | – |
| Privacy homomorphism [57] | ● | – | ● |
| PPC [63] | ● | ● | ● |
| Secure index data structures [16, 20, 51, 93, 99] | ● | ○ | – |

● fully supported; ○ partially supported; – not supported

**Fig. 2.5** Indexing methods supporting queries

The *Partition Plaintext and Ciphertext* (PPC) is a new model for storing server-side outsourced data [63]. This model proposes to outsource both plaintext and encrypted information that need to be stored on the remote server. In this model, only sensitive attributes are encrypted and indexed, while the other attributes are released in plaintext form. The authors propose an efficient architecture for the DBMS to store together, and specifically in the same page of memory, both plaintext and encrypted data.

Different working groups [16, 20, 51, 93, 99] introduce other approaches for searching keywords in encrypted documents. These methods are based on the definition of a *secure index data structure*. The secure index data structure allows the server to retrieve all documents containing a particular keyword without the need to know any other information. This is possible because a trapdoor is introduced when encrypting data, and such a trapdoor is then exploited by the client when querying data. Other similar proposals are based on *Identity Based Encryption* techniques for the definition of secure indexing methods. Boneh and Franklin [17] present an encryption method allowing searches over ciphertext data, while not revealing anything about the original data. This method is shown to be secure through rigorous proofs. Although these methods for searching keywords over encrypted data have been originally proposed for searching over audit logs or email repositories, they are also well suited for indexing data in the outsourced database scenario.

Figure 2.5 summarizes the discussion by showing, for each indexing method discussed, what type of query it (partially) supports. Here, an hyphen means that the query is not supported, a black circle means that the query is fully supported, and a white circle means that the query is partially supported.

## 2.4  Evaluation of Inference Exposure

Given a plaintext relation $r$ over schema $R(a_1, a_2, \ldots, a_n)$, it is necessary to decide which attributes need to be indexed, and how the corresponding indexes can be defined. In particular, when defining the indexing method for an attribute, it is important to consider two conflicting requirements: on one side, the indexing information should be related to the data well enough to provide for an effective query execution mechanism; on the other side, the relationship between indexes and data should not open the door to *inference and linking attacks* that can compromise the protection granted by encryption. Different indexing methods can provide different trade-offs between query execution efficiency and data protection from inference. It is therefore necessary to define a measure for the risk of exposure due to the publication of indexes on the remote server.

Although many techniques supporting different kinds of queries in the DAS scenario have been developed, a deep analysis of the level of protection provided by all these methods against inference and linking attacks is missing. In particular, exposure has been evaluated for a few indexing methods only [24, 35, 37, 61].

Hore et al. [61] analyze the security issues related to the use of bucket-based indexing methods. The authors consider data exposure problems in two situations: *i)* the release of a single attribute, and *ii)* the publication of all the indexes associated with a relation. To measure the protection degree granted to the original data by the specific indexing method, the authors propose to exploit two different measures. The first measure is the *variance* of the distribution of values within a bucket $b$. The second measure is the *entropy* of the distribution of values within a bucket $b$. The higher is the variance, the higher is the protection level granted to the data. Therefore, the data owner should maximize, for each bucket in the relation, the corresponding variance. Analogously, the higher is the entropy of a bucket, the higher is the protection level granted to the data. The optimization problem that the data owner has to solve, while planning the bucketization process on a relation, is the *maximization of minimum variance and minimum entropy*, while maximizing query efficiency. Since such an optimization problem is *NP-hard*, Hore et al. [61] propose an approximation method, which fixes a maximum allowed performance degradation. The objective of the algorithm is then to maximize both minimum variance and entropy, while guaranteeing performances not to fall under an imposed threshold.

To the aim of taking into consideration also the risk of exposure due to associations, Hore et al. [61] propose to adopt, as a measure of the privacy granted by indexes when posing a multi-attribute range query, the well known *k-anonymity* concept [83]. Indeed, the result of a range query operating on multiple attributes is exposed to data linkage with publicly available datasets. *k*-Anonymity is widely recognized as a measure of the privacy level granted by a collection of released data, where respondents can be re-identified (or the uncertainty about their identity lower under a predefined threshold $k$) by linking private data with public data collections.

Damiani et al. [24, 35, 37] evaluate the exposure to inference due to the adoption of hash-based indexing methods. Inference exposure is measured by taking into account the prior knowledge of the attacker, thus introducing two different scenarios. In the first scenario, called $Freq+DB^k$, the attacker is supposed to know, in addition to the encrypted database ($DB^k$), the domains of the plaintext attributes and the distribution of plaintext values (*Freq*) in the original database. In the second scenario, called $DB+DB^k$, the attacker is supposed to know both the encrypted ($DB^k$) and the plaintext database (*DB*). In both scenarios, the exposure measure is computed as the probability for the attacker to correctly map index values onto plaintext attribute values. The authors show that, to guarantee a higher degree of protection against inference, it is convenient to use a hash-based method that generates collisions. In case of a hash-based method where the collision factor is equal to 1, meaning that there is no collision, inference exposure measure depends only on the number of attributes used for indexing. In the $DB+DB^k$ scenario, the exposure grows as the number of attributes used for indexing grows. In the $Freq+DB^k$ scenario, the attacker can discover the correspondences between plaintext and indexing values by comparing their occurrence profiles. Intuitively, the exposure grows as the number of attributes with a different occurrence profile grows. For instance, considering relation Employee in Fig. 2.2(a), we can notice that both Salary and the corresponding index $I_5$ have a unique value with one occurrence only, that is, 20 and $\rho$, respectively. We can therefore conclude that the index value corresponding to 20 is $\rho$, and that no other salary value is mapped into $\rho$ as well.

Damiani et al. [37] extend the inference exposure measures presented in [24, 35] to produce an inference measure that can be associated with the whole relation instead of with single attributes. The authors propose two methods for aggregating the exposure risk measures computed at attribute level. The first method exploits the weighted mean operator and weights each attribute $a_i$ proportionally with the risk connected with the disclosure of the values of $a_i$. The second one exploits the *OWA* (Ordered Weighted Averaging) operator, which allows the assignment of different importance values to different sets of attributes, depending on the degree of protection guaranteed by the indexing method adopted for the specific subset of attributes.

Agrawal et al. [4] evaluate the exposure to inference due to the adoption of OPESS as an indexing method, under the $Freq+DB^k$ scenario. They prove that the solution they propose is intrinsically secure, due to the flat frequency distribution of index values and to the additional guarantee given by scaling method, which avoids the combination of the attackers frequency knowledge with the knowledge of the indexing method adopted.

## 2.5 Integrity of Outsourced Data

The database outsourcing scenario usually assumes the server to be "honest-but-curious", and that clients and data owners trust it to faithfully maintain outsourced data. However, this assumption is not always applicable and it is also important to protect the database content from improper modifications (*data integrity*). The approaches proposed in the literature have the main goal of detecting unauthorized updates of remotely stored data [56, 73, 74, 92]. Hacigümüs et al. [56] propose to add a signature to each tuple in the database. The signature is computed by digitally signing, with the private key of the owner, a hash value obtained through the application of a hash function to the tuple content. The signature is then added to the tuple before encryption. When a client receives a tuple, as a result of its query, it can verify if the tuple has been modified by an entity different from the data owner. The verification process consists in recomputing the hash over the tuple content and checking whether there is a match with the value stored in the tuple itself. In addition to tuple level integrity, also relation level integrity (i.e., absence of non authorized insertions and deletions of tuples) needs to be preserved. Therefore, for each relation, a signature computed on the basis of the tuples in the relation is added. An advantage of the proposed method is that relation level signature does not need to be recomputed any time a tuple is inserted or deleted because the old signature can be adapted to the new content, thus saving computation time at the data owner side.

Since an integrity check performed on each tuple in the result set of a query can be quite expensive, Mykletun et al. [73] propose methods for checking the signature of a set of tuples in a single operation. The first method, called *condensed RSA*, works only if the tuples in the set have been signed by the same user; the second method, which is based on bilinear mappings and is less efficient than condensed RSA, is called *BGLS* (from the name of the authors who first proposed this signature method [18]) and works even if the tuples in the set have been signed by different users. A major drawback of these solutions is that they do not guarantee the *immutability property*. Immutability means that it is difficult to obtain a valid aggregated signature from a set of other aggregated signatures. To solve this problem, Mykletun et al. [72] propose alternative solutions based on zero knowledge protocols.

Narasimha and Tsudik [74] present another method, called *Digital Signature Aggregation and Chaining* (DSAC), that is again based on hash functions and signature. Here, the main goal is to evaluate whether the result of a query is *complete* and *correct* with respect to the database content. This solution builds over each relation chains of tuples, one for each attribute that may appear in a query, that are ordered according to the attribute value. The signed hash associated with a tuple is then computed by composing the hash value associated with the immediate predecessors of the considered tuple in all the chains. This solution is quite expensive when there are different chains associated with a relation.

Sion [92] proposes a method to ensure result accuracy and guarantee that the server correctly executes the query on the remote data. The method works for batch queries and is based on the pre-computation of *tokens*. Basically, before outsourcing the database, the data owner pre-computes a set of queries on plaintext data and associates, with each query, a token computed by using a one-way cryptographic hash function on the query results, concatenated with a nonce. Any set of batch queries submitted to the server contains then a subset of pre-computed queries, along with the corresponding tokens, and fake tokens. The server, when answering, has to indicate which are the queries in the batch set that correspond to the given tokens. If the server correctly individuates which tokens are fake, the client is guaranteed that the server has executed all the queries in the set.

## 2.6 Privacy Protection of Databases

Often encryption of the whole database containing sensitive data is an overdo, since not all the data are sensitive per se but only their association needs protection. To reduce the usage of encryption in data outsourcing, thus improving query execution efficiency, it is convenient to combine fragmentation and encryption techniques [2]. In [2] the authors propose an approach where privacy requirements are modeled simply through confidentiality constraints (i.e., sets of attributes whose joint visibility must be prevented) and are enforced by splitting information over two independent database servers (so to break associations of sensitive information) and by encrypting information only when strictly necessary. By assuming that only trusted clients know the two service providers (each of which is not aware of the existence of the other server), sensitive associations among data can be broken by fragmenting the original data. When fragmentation is not sufficient for solving all confidentiality constraints characterizing the data collection, data encryption can be exploited. In this case, the key used for encrypting the data is stored on one server and the encrypted result on the other one. Alternatively, other data obfuscation methods can be exploited; the parameter value is stored on one server and the obfuscated data on the other one. Since the original data collection is divided on two non-communicating servers, the evaluation of queries formulated by trusted users requires the presence of a trusted client for possibly combining the results coming from the two servers. The original query is split in two subqueries operating at each server, which results are then joined and refined by the client. The process of query evaluation becomes therefore expensive, especially if fragmentation does not take into account the query workload characterizing the system (i.e., when attributes frequently appearing in the same query are not stored on the same server). After proving that identifying a fragmentation that minimizes query execution costs at the client side is NP-hard (this problem can be reduced to the hypergraph coloring problem), the authors propose a heuristic algorithm producing good results.

While presenting an interesting idea, the approach in [2] suffers from several limitations. The main limitation is that privacy relies on the complete absence of communication between the two servers, which have to be completely unaware of each other. This assumption is clearly too strong and difficult to enforce in real environments. A collusion among the servers (or the users accessing them) easily breaches privacy. Also, the assumption of two servers limits the number of associations that can be solved by fragmenting data, often forcing the use of encryption. The solution presented in Chap. 4 overcomes the above limitations: it allows storing data even on a single server and minimizes the amount of data represented in encrypted format, therefore allowing for efficient query execution.

A related line of work is represented by [13, 14], where the authors exploit functional dependencies to the aim of correctly enforcing access control policies. In [14] the authors propose a policy based classification of databases that, combined with restriction of the query language, preserves the confidentiality of sensitive information. The classification of a database is based on the concept of classification instance, which is a set of tuples representing the combinations of values that need to be protected. On the basis of the classification instance, it is always possible to identify the set of allowed queries, that is, the queries whose evaluation return tuples that do not correspond to the combinations represented in the classification instance. In [13] the authors define a mechanism for defining constraints that reduce the problem of protecting the data from inferences to the enforcement of access control in relational databases.

## 2.7 Access Control Enforcement in the Outsourcing Scenario

Traditional works on data outsourcing assume all users to have complete access to the whole database by simply knowing the (unique) encryption key adopted for data protection. However, this simplifying assumption does not fit current scenarios where different users may need to see different portions of the data, that is, where *selective access* needs to be enforced, also because the server cannot be delegated such a task. Adding a traditional authorization layer to the current outsourcing scenarios requires that when a client poses a query, both the query and its result have to be filtered by the data owner (who is in charge of enforcing the access control policy), a solution that however is not applicable in a real life scenario. More recent researches [15, 33, 70, 102] have addressed the problem of enforcing selective access on outsourced encrypted data by combining cryptography with authorizations, thus enforcing access control via *selective encryption*. Basically, the idea is to use different keys for encrypting different portions of the database. These keys are then distributed to users according to their access rights.

The naive solution for enforcing access control through selective encryption consists in using a different key for each resource in the system, and in communicating to each user the set of keys associated with the resources she can access. This solution correctly enforces the policy, but it is very expensive since each user needs to keep a number of keys that depends on her privileges. That is, users having many privileges and, probably, often accessing the system, will have a greater number of keys than users having a few privileges and, probably, accessing only rarely the system. To reduce the number of keys a user has to manage, access control mechanisms based on selective encryption exploit *key derivation methods*. A key derivation method is basically a function that, given a key and a piece of publicly available information, allows the computation of another key. The basic idea is that each user is given a small number of keys from which she can derive all the keys needed to access the resources she is authorized to access.

To the aim of using a key derivation method, it is necessary to define which keys can be derived from another key and how. Key derivation methods proposed in the literature are based on the definition of a *key derivation hierarchy*. Given a set of keys $\mathcal{K}$ in the system and a partial order relation $\preceq$ defined on it, the corresponding key derivation hierarchy is usually represented as a pair $(\mathcal{K}, \preceq)$, where $\forall k_i, k_j \in \mathcal{K}$, $k_j \preceq k_i$ iff $k_j$ is derivable from $k_i$. Any key derivation hierarchy can be graphically represented through a directed acyclic graph, having a vertex for each key in $\mathcal{K}$, and a path from $k_i$ to $k_j$ only if $k_j$ can be derived from $k_i$. Depending on the partial order relationship defined on $\mathcal{K}$, the key derivation hierarchy can be: a *chain* (i.e., $\preceq$ defines a total order relation); a *tree*; or a *directed acyclic graph* (DAG). The different key derivation methods can be classified on the basis of the kind of hierarchy they are able to support, as follows.

- The hierarchy is a *chain of vertices* [85]. Key $k_j$ of a vertex is computed on the basis of key $k_i$ of its (unique) direct ancestor (i.e., $k_j = f(k_i)$) and no public information is needed.
- The hierarchy is a *tree* [54, 85, 86]. Key $k_j$ of a vertex is computed on the basis of key $k_i$ of its (unique) parent and on the publicly available label $l_j$ associated with $k_j$ (i.e., $k_j = f(k_i, l_j)$).
- The hierarchy is a *DAG* [6, 8, 31, 59, 62, 67, 69, 87, 91]. Since each vertex in a DAG can have more than one direct ancestor, key derivation methods are in general more complex than the methods used for chains or trees. There are many proposals that work on DAGs; typically they exploit a piece of public information associated with each vertex of the key derivation hierarchy. In [8], Atallah et al. introduce a new class of methods that maintain a piece of public information, called *token*, associated with each edge in the hierarchy. Given two keys, $k_i$ and $k_j$ arbitrarily assigned to two vertices, and a public label $l_j$ associated with $k_j$, a token from $k_i$ to $k_j$ is defined as $t_{i,j} = k_j \oplus h(k_i, l_j)$, where $\oplus$ is the $n$-ary xor operator and $h$ is a secure hash function. Given $t_{i,j}$, any user knowing $k_i$ and with access to public label $l_j$, can compute (derive) $k_j$. All tokens $t_{i,j}$ in the system are stored in a *public catalog*.

It is important to note that key derivation methods operating on trees can be used for chains of vertices, even if the contrary is not true. Analogously, key derivation methods operating on DAGs can be used for trees and chains, while the converse is not true.

Key derivation hierarchies have also been adopted for access control enforcement in contexts different from data outsourcing. For instance, pay-tv systems usually adopt selective encryption for selective access enforcement and key hierarchies to easily distribute encryption keys [12, 79, 94, 95, 100]. Although these applications have some similarities with the DAS scenario, there are important differences that do not make them applicable for data outsourcing. First, in the DAS scenario we need to protect stored data, while in the pay-tv scenario streams of data are the resources that need to be protected. Second, in the DAS scenario key derivation hierarchies are used to reduce the number of keys each user has to keep secret, while in the pay-tv scenario a key derivation hierarchy is exploited for session key distribution.

The main problem any solution adopting selective encryption suffers from is that they require data re-encryption for policy updates, thus causing the data owner's intervention any time the policy is modified. The selective encryption solution proposed in Chap. 3 is organized to both reduce the client burden in data access and the data owner intervention in policy updates.

## 2.8 Safe Data Integration

Data outsourcing scenarios typically assume data to be managed by a unique external server, managing sensitive information. As already noted for solutions combining fragmentation and encryption for privacy purposes, data may also be stored at different servers. Furthermore, emerging scenarios often require different parties to cooperate with other parties to the aim of sharing information and perform distributed computations. Cooperation for query execution implies data to flow among parties. Therefore, it is necessary to provide the system with solutions able to enforce access control restrictions in data exchange for distributed query evaluation. Indeed, classical works on the management of queries in centralized and distributed systems [11, 23, 26, 64, 68, 90, 101] cannot be exploited in such a scenario. These approaches in fact describe how efficient query plans can be obtained, but do not take into consideration constraints on attribute visibility for servers. However, in light of the crucial role that security has in the construction of future large-scale distributed applications, a significant amount of research has recently focused on the problem of processing distributed queries under protection requirements. Most of these works [21, 46, 48, 52, 66, 75] are based on the concept of *access pattern*, a profile associated with each relation/view where each attribute has a value that may either be *i* or *o* (i.e., input or output). When accessing a relation, the values for all *i* attributes must be supplied, to obtain the corresponding values of *o* attributes. Also, queries are represented in terms of Datalog, a query language based on the logic programming paradigm. The main goal of all these works is that of identifying the classes of queries that a given set of access patterns can support; a secondary goal is the definition of query plans that match the profiles of the involved relations, while minimizing some cost parameter (e.g., the number of accesses to data sources [21]). In Chap. 5, we propose a complementary approach to access patterns that can be considered a natural extension of the approach normally used to describe database privileges in a relational schema; our approach introduces a mechanism to define access privileges on join paths; while access patterns describe authorizations as special formulas in a logic programming language for data access. Also, the model presented in Chap. 5 explicitly manages a scenario with different independent subjects who may cooperate in the execution of a query, whereas the work done on access patterns only considers two actors, the owner of the data and a single user accessing the data.

In [80], the authors propose a model based on the definition of authorization views that implicitly define the set of queries that a user can view. A query is allowed if it can be answered using only the information in the authorization views regulating the system. An interesting advantage of this model is the exploitation of referential integrity constraints for the automatic identification of security compliance of queries with respect to views. It is interesting to note that the approach in [80] operates at a low level since it analyzes the integration with a relational DBMS optimizer and focuses on the consideration of "instantiated" queries (i.e., queries that present predicates that force attributes to assume specific values) aiming at evaluate compatibility of the instantiated queries with the authorized views.

The approach proposed in Chap. 5 operates at a higher level, proposing an overall data-model characterizing views and focusing on the data integration scenario at a more abstract level.

Sovereign joins [3] represent an interesting alternative solution for secure information sharing. This method is based on a secure coprocessor, which is involved in query execution, and exploits cryptography to grant privacy. The advantage of sovereign joins is that they extend the plans that allow an execution in the scenario we present; the main obstacle is represented by their high computational cost, due to the use of specific asymmetric cryptography primitives, that make them currently not applicable when large collections of sensitive information must be combined.

## 2.9 Chapter Summary

Database outsourcing is becoming an emerging data management paradigm that introduces many research challenges. In this chapter, we focused on the solutions known in the literature for solving problems related to query execution and access control enforcement. For query execution, different indexing methods have been discussed. These methods mainly focus on supporting specific kind of queries and on minimizing the client burden in query execution. Fragmentation has also been proposed as a method for reducing encryption and improving query execution performance. Access control enforcement is instead a relative new issue for the DAS scenario and has not been deeply studied. The most important proposal for enforcing access control on outsourced encrypted data is based on selective encryption and key derivation strategies. Finally, the evaluation of queries when outsourced data are distributed at different servers requires a deeper collaboration among servers as well as mechanisms regulating the exchange of data among the collaborating parties. This problem has been addressed in some proposals that are based on the access pattern concept.

In the following of this book, we will analyze more in depth the access control, proposing a new mechanism based on selective encryption, and we will study a solution to the well known problem of dynamically manage access control updates. We will also focus on the usage of fragmentation for reducing encryption, trying to overcome the limitations of the proposal in [2]. Furthermore, we will address the problem related to the execution of queries on distributed data, modeling authorized data flows among involved parties in a simple while powerful manner.

# Chapter 3
# Selective Encryption to Enforce Access Control[1]

Data outsourcing is emerging today as a successful paradigm allowing users and organizations to exploit external services for the distribution of resources. A crucial problem to be addressed in this context concerns the enforcement of selective authorization policies and the support of policy updates in dynamic scenarios.

In this chapter, we present a novel solution for the enforcement of access control and the management of its evolution. Encryption is the traditional way in which a third party can be prevented from accessing information it would have otherwise access to, either because it controls a channel transmitting it or because it reads its stored representation. Our proposal is based on the application of selective encryption as a means to enforce authorizations. Also, the model here proposed represents a first solution for efficiently managing policy updates, limiting the adoption of expensive re-encryption techniques.

## 3.1 Introduction

Contrary to the vision of a few years ago, where many predicted that Internet users would have in a short time exploited the availability of pervasive high-bandwidth network connections to activate their own servers, users are today, with increasing frequency, resorting to service providers for disseminating and sharing objects they want to make available to others.

The continuous growth of the amount of digital information to be stored and widely distributed, together with the always increasing storage, support the view that service providers will be more and more requested to be responsible for the storage and the efficient and reliable distribution of content produced by others, realizing a "data outsourcing" architecture on a wide scale. This important trend

---

[1] Part of this chapter appeared under S. De Capitani di Vimercati, S. Foresti, S. Jajodia, S. Paraboschi, and P. Samarati, "Encryption Policies for Regulating Access to Outsourced Data," in ACM Transactions on Database Systems (TODS), Vol. 35:2, April, 2010 [44] ©2010 ACM, Inc. Reprinted by permission http://doi.acm.org/10.1145/1735886.1735891

is particularly clear when we look at the success of services like YouTube, Flickr, Blogger, MySpace, and many others in the "social networking" environment.

When storage and distribution do not involve publicly releasable objects, selective access techniques must be enforced. In this context, it is legitimate for the data owner to demand the data not to be disclosed to the service provider itself, which, while trustworthy to properly carry out the object distribution functions, should not be allowed access to the object content.

The problem of outsourcing object management to a "honest-but-curious" service has recently received considerable attention by the research community and several advancements have been proposed. The different proposals require the owner to encrypt the data before outsourcing them to the remote server. Most proposals assume that the data are encrypted with a single key only [24, 55, 58]. In such a context, either authorized users are assumed to have the complete view on the data or, if different views need to be provided to different users, the data owner needs to participate in the query execution to possibly filter the result computed by the service provider.

A relatively limited research effort has been dedicated to the integration of access control and encryption. A traditional observation of the community working on access control is indeed that the two concepts have to be carefully kept distinct, following the classical principle of "Separation between policy and mechanism". Cryptography is traditionally a "mechanism" for the protection of information, whereas access control focuses on the models and solutions for the representation of "policies". While the separation between authorization-based access control and cryptographic protection has been beneficial, we maintain that in the data outsourcing scenario such a combination can prove successful.

In this chapter we present an approach merging permissions and encryption and allowing access control to be outsourced together with the data. The significant advantage is that the data owner, while specifying the policy, need not to be involved in its enforcement. The owner only defines access permissions and generates the corresponding encryption keys, tuning the protection on sensitive data. To give users different access rights, all the owner has to do is to ensure that each user can compute the right set of decryption keys needed to access the objects she is authorized to see.

The idea of using different encryption keys for different objects is in itself not new [12, 70, 79, 94], but the problem of applying it in the data outsourced scenario introduces several challenges that have not been investigated in previous proposals. First of all, it is desiderable to define an approach to generate and distribute to each user a single encryption key, supporting fast and secure derivation of the set of keys needed to access the set of data the user is authorized to access. Our basic technique fulfills this requirement and is independent from any specific data model; also, it does not rely on any specific authorization language, as the translation of the access control policy into a key derivation scheme is completely transparent to the owners.

Building on the base model we propose a two-layer approach to enforce selective encryption without requesting the owner to re-encrypt the objects every time there is a change in the authorization policy. The first layer of encryption is applied by the data owner at initialization time (when releasing the data for outsourcing), the second layer of encryption is applied by the service provider itself to take care of dynamic policy changes. Intuitively, the two-layer encryption allows the owner to outsource, besides the object storage and dissemination, the authorization policy management, while not releasing data to the provider.

Finally, we provide a characterization of the different views of the objects by different users and characterize potential risks of information exposures due to dynamic policy changes. The investigation allows us to conclude that, while an exposure risk may exist, it is identifiable. This allows the owner to address the problem and minimize it at design time.

An important strength of our solution is that it does not substitute the current proposals [35, 55, 58], rather it complements them, enabling them to support encryption in a selective form and easily enforce dynamic policy changes.

### 3.1.1 Chapter Outline

The remainder of this chapter is organized as follows. Section 3.2 presents preliminary concepts on relational databases that will be used in the following of the book. Section 3.3 proposes an access control system based on selective encryption and key derivation techniques. Section 3.4 introduces the definition of minimal encryption policy and shows that the problem of computing a minimal encryption policy is NP-hard, while Sect. 3.5 presents a heuristic algorithm for solving this problem in polynomial time. Section 3.6 illustrates a solution for efficiently manage policy updates in the model previously introduced. Section 3.7 proposes a solution based on two layers of encryption for managing policy updates without resorting to re-encryption. Section 3.8 illustrates the management of policy updates in this scenario. Section 3.9 presents an evaluation of the collusion risk to which data are exposed. Section 3.10 presents the experimental results obtained by the implementation of the heuristic algorithm proposed for computing a minimal encryption policy. Finally, Sect. 3.11 presents our concluding remarks.

## 3.2 Relational Model

In the rest of this book, for simplicity, we will refer our discussion to the well known *relational database* model, while noting that all the discussions and results proposed also apply to other models (e.g., XML). We note also that the emphasis on relational databases must not be considered a limitation. First, relational database technology currently dominates the management of data in most scenarios where collections of sensitive information have to be integrated over a network; even if a system offers access to the data using Web technology, the data offered by the system are extracted from a relational database and a description of the access policy in terms of the underlying relational structure offers a high degree of flexibility. Second, for integrated solutions based on Web technology, particularly systems relying on the use of Web services, it is always possible to model the structure of the exported data in terms of a relational representation, and in this situation a description of the access policy according to our model, rather than using a policy description on services invocations, typically provides a more robust and flexible identification of the security requirements of the application.

### 3.2.1 Basic Concepts and Notation

We use the standard notations of the relational database model. Formally, let $\mathscr{A}$ be a set of attributes and $\mathscr{D}$ be a set of domains. At the schema level, a relation is characterized by a name $R$ and a set $\{a_1, \ldots, a_n\}$ of attributes, where each $a_i$ is defined on a domain $D_i \in \mathscr{D}, i = 1, \ldots, n$. Notation $R(a_1, \ldots, a_n)$ represents a relation schema $R$ over the set $\{a_1, \ldots, a_n\}$ of attributes; $R.*$ refers to the set $\{a_1, \ldots, a_n\}$ of attributes in the relation. At the schema level, a database is characterized by a name $\mathscr{R}$ and a set $\{R_1, \ldots, R_m\}$ of relation schemas. At the instance level, a relation $r$ over schema $R(a_1, \ldots, a_n)$ is a set of *tuples* over set $\{a_1, \ldots, a_n\}$. A tuple $t$ over a set of attributes $\{a_1, \ldots, a_n\}$ is a function that associates with each attribute $a_i$ a value $v \in D_i$. Given an attribute $a$ and a set $A$ of attributes, $t[a]$ denotes the value of attribute $a$ in $t$ and $t[A]$ the sub-tuple composed of all values of attributes in $A$.

Each relation has a *primary key* which is the attribute, or the set of attributes, that uniquely identifies each tuple in the relation. Given a relation $R_i$, $K_i \subseteq R_i.*$ denotes $R_i$'s primary key attributes. Primary key attributes cannot assume NULL values and two tuples in the relation cannot assume the same value for the primary key. This latter condition implies the existence of a *functional dependency* between the primary key of a relation and any other attribute in the relation. Given a relation $R(a_1, \ldots, a_n)$ and two non-empty subsets $A_i$ and $A_j$ of the attributes $\{a_1, \ldots, a_n\}$, there is a *functional dependency* on $R$ between $A_i$ and $A_j$ if for each pair of tuples $t_l$, $t_m$ of $r$ with the same values on attributes in $A_i$, $t_l$ and $t_m$ have also the same values on attributes in $A_j$. Without loss of generality, we assume that only functional dependencies given by the primary key hold in the relations. This assumption does not limit the applicability of our solution since it is similar to the common database schema requirement that the relations satisfy the *Boyce-Codd Normal Form* (BCNF), to avoid redundancies and undesirable side-effects during update operations, and it is usually achievable using adequate decomposition procedures [49].

The primary key $K_i$ of a relation $R_i$ can also appear, or more precisely, be *referenced* by a set of attributes $FK_j$, in another relation $R_j$. In such a case, $FK_j$, called *foreign key*, can assume only values that appear for $K_i$ in the instance of $R_i$. This is formalized by the definition of *referential integrity* constraint which, assuming for simplicity absence of NULL values for the foreign key, is as follows.

**Definition 3.1 (Referential integrity).** Given two relation schemas $R_i, R_j \in \mathscr{R}$ and a set of attributes $FK_j \subseteq R_j.*$, there is a *referential integrity* constraint from $FK_j$ to

$K_i$ if and only if for any possible instance $r_i$ of $R_i$ and $r_j$ of $R_j$, $\forall t_j \in r_j$ there exists a tuple $t_i \in r_i$ such that $t_j[FK_j] = t_i[K_i]$.

In the following, we use $\langle FK_j, K_i \rangle$ to denote a referential integrity constraint between $FK_j$ and $K_i$. Also, $\mathscr{I}$ denotes the set of all referential integrity constraints defined over $\mathscr{R}$.

## 3.3 Access Control and Encryption Policies

Considering the data outsourcing scenario described in Sect. 2.2, we present a formal model for representing access control and encryption polices along with the public catalog necessary for users to compute the encryption keys necessary to access data and interacting with the server.

### 3.3.1 Access Control Policy

We assume that the data owner defines a discretionary access control policy to regulate access to the distributed objects, which may be defined at different granularity (i.e., an object can be a cell, a tuple, an attribute, or even a whole relation) without the need of any adaptation to the model proposed in the following, which assumes that each tuple represents a distinct object. Consistently with the scenario described, we assume access by users to the outsourced objects to be read-only while write operations are to be performed at the owner's site (typically by the owner itself). Permissions that need to be enforced through encryption are of the form $\langle user, object \rangle$.[2] Give a set $\mathscr{U}$ of users and a set $\mathscr{O}$ of objects (i.e., resources), we define an authorization policy over $\mathscr{U}$ and $\mathscr{O}$ as follows.

**Definition 3.2 (Authorization policy).** Let $\mathscr{U}$ and $\mathscr{O}$ be the set of users and objects in the system, respectively. An *authorization policy* over $\mathscr{U}$ and $\mathscr{O}$, denoted $\mathscr{A}$, is a triple $\langle \mathscr{U}, \mathscr{O}, \mathscr{P} \rangle$, where $\mathscr{P}$ is a set of permissions of the form $\langle u, o \rangle$, with $u \in \mathscr{U}$ and $o \in \mathscr{O}$, stating the accesses to be allowed.

The set of permissions can be represented through an access matrix $\mathscr{M}_{\mathscr{A}}$, with a row for each user $u \in \mathscr{U}$ and a column for each object $o \in \mathscr{O}$ [84]. Each entry $\mathscr{M}_{\mathscr{A}}[u, o]$ is set to 1 if $u$ can access $o$; 0 otherwise. Given an access matrix $\mathscr{M}_{\mathscr{A}}$ over sets $\mathscr{U}$ and $\mathscr{O}$, $acl(o)$ denotes the *access control list* of $o$ (i.e., the set of users that can access $o$).

We model an authorization policy as a directed and bipartite graph $\mathscr{G}_{\mathscr{A}}$ having a vertex for each user $u \in \mathscr{U}$ and for each object $o \in \mathscr{O}$, and an edge from $u$ to $o$ for

---

[2] For the sake of simplicity, we do not deal with the fact that permissions can be specified for groups of users and groups of objects. Our approach supports dynamic grouping, thus subsuming any statically defined group.

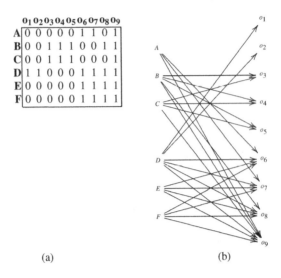

|   | $o_1$ | $o_2$ | $o_3$ | $o_4$ | $o_5$ | $o_6$ | $o_7$ | $o_8$ | $o_9$ |
|---|---|---|---|---|---|---|---|---|---|
| **A** | 0 | 0 | 0 | 0 | 0 | 1 | 1 | 0 | 1 |
| **B** | 0 | 0 | 1 | 1 | 1 | 0 | 0 | 1 | 1 |
| **C** | 0 | 0 | 1 | 1 | 1 | 0 | 0 | 0 | 1 |
| **D** | 1 | 1 | 0 | 0 | 0 | 1 | 1 | 1 | 1 |
| **E** | 0 | 0 | 0 | 0 | 0 | 1 | 1 | 1 | 1 |
| **F** | 0 | 0 | 0 | 0 | 0 | 1 | 1 | 1 | 1 |

(a)                                      (b)

**Fig. 3.1**  An example of access matrix (a) and authorization policy graph (b)

each permission $\langle u, o \rangle \in \mathscr{P}$ to be enforced. Since our modeling of the problem and its solution will exploit graphs, we explicitly define $\mathscr{G}_{\mathscr{A}}$ as follows.

**Definition 3.3 (Authorization policy graph).** Let $\mathscr{A} = \langle \mathscr{U}, \mathscr{O}, \mathscr{P} \rangle$ be an authorization policy. The *authorization policy graph* over $\mathscr{A}$, denoted $\mathscr{G}_{\mathscr{A}}$, is a graph $\langle V_{\mathscr{A}}, E_{\mathscr{A}} \rangle$, where $V_{\mathscr{A}} = \mathscr{U} \cup \mathscr{O}$ and $E_{\mathscr{A}} = \{(u, o) : \langle u, o \rangle \in \mathscr{P}\}$.

In the following, we will use $\xrightarrow{\mathscr{A}}$ to denote reachability of vertices in graph $\mathscr{G}_{\mathscr{A}}$. Consequently, we will use $u \xrightarrow{\mathscr{A}} o$ and $\langle u, o \rangle \in \mathscr{P}$ indistinguishably to denote that user $u$ is authorized to access object $o$ according to policy $\mathscr{A}$.

It is easy to see that the access matrix $\mathscr{M}_{\mathscr{A}}$ corresponds to the adjacency matrix[3] of the authorization policy graph $\mathscr{G}_{\mathscr{A}}$. Figure 3.1 illustrates an example of authorization policy with 6 users, 9 objects, and 26 permissions, reporting the access matrix and the corresponding authorization policy graph.

### 3.3.2 Encryption Policy

Our goal is to represent the authorization policy by means of proper object encryption and key distribution. We assume, for efficiency reasons, to adopt symmetric encryption. A naive solution to our goal would consist in encrypting each object with a different key and assigning to each user the set of keys used to encrypt the

---

[3] Being the graph bipartite and directed, we consider the adjacency matrix to report only rows and columns that correspond to users and objects, respectively.

objects she can access. Such a solution is clearly unacceptable, since it would require each user to manage as many keys as the number of objects she is authorized
to view.

To avoid users having to store and manage a huge number of (secret) keys, we
exploit a *key derivation method*. Among all the key derivation methods, the proposal
in [8] minimizes the amount of re-encrypting and re-keying that must be done following any change in the authorization policy. The method is based on the definition
and computation of *public tokens*. Let $\mathcal{K}$ be the set of symmetric encryption keys in
the system. Given two keys $k_i$ and $k_j$ in $\mathcal{K}$, a token $t_{i,j}$ is defined as $t_{i,j}=k_j\oplus h(k_i,l_j)$,
where $l_j$ is a publicly available label associated with $k_j$, $\oplus$ is the bitwise xor operator, and $h$ is a deterministic cryptographic function. The existence of a public token
$t_{i,j}$ allows a user knowing $k_i$ to derive key $k_j$, through token $t_{i,j}$ and public label $l_j$.
Since keys need to remain secret, while tokens are public, the use of tokens greatly
simplifies key management. Key derivation via tokens can be applied in chains: a
*chain of tokens* is a sequence $t_{i,l}\ldots t_{n,j}$ of tokens such that $t_{c,d}$ directly follows $t_{a,b}$ in
the chain only if $b = c$.

A major advantage of using tokens is that they are public and allow the user to derive multiple encryption keys, while having to worry about a single one. Exploiting
tokens, the release to the user of a set of keys $K = \{k_1,\ldots,k_n\}$ can be equivalently
obtained by the release to each user of a single key $k_i\in K$ and the publication of a
set of tokens allowing the (direct or indirect) derivation of all keys $k_j\in K, j \neq i$. In
the following, we use $\mathcal{K}$ to denote the set of symmetric keys in the system, $\mathcal{T}$ to
denote the set of tokens defined in the system, and $\mathcal{L}$ to denote the set of labels
associated with the keys in $\mathcal{K}$ and used for computing the tokens in $\mathcal{T}$.

Since tokens are public information, we assume to store them on the remote
server (just like the encrypted data), so any user can access them. We model the
relationships between keys through tokens allowing derivation of one key from another, via a graph, called *key and token graph*. The graph has a vertex for each pair
$\langle k,l\rangle$ denoting key $k$ and corresponding label $l$. There is an edge from a vertex $\langle k_i,l_i\rangle$
to a vertex $\langle k_j,l_j\rangle$ if there exists a token $t_{i,j}$ allowing the derivation of $k_j$ from $k_i$.
The graph is formally defined as follows.

**Definition 3.4 (Key and token graph).** Let $\mathcal{K}$ be a set of keys, $\mathcal{L}$ be a set of
publicly available labels, and $\mathcal{T}$ be a set of tokens defined on them. A *key and to-
ken graph* over $\mathcal{K}$, $\mathcal{L}$, and $\mathcal{T}$, denoted $\mathcal{G}_{\mathcal{K},\mathcal{T}}$, is a graph $\langle V_{\mathcal{K},\mathcal{T}},E_{\mathcal{K},\mathcal{T}}\rangle$, where
$V_{\mathcal{K},\mathcal{T}}=\{\langle k_i,l_i\rangle : k_i \in \mathcal{K},l_i \in \mathcal{L}$ is the label associated with $k_i\}$ and $E_{\mathcal{K},\mathcal{T}} =
\{(\langle k_i,l_i\rangle,\langle k_j,l_j\rangle)) : t_{i,j} \in \mathcal{T}\}$.

The graphical representation of keys and tokens nicely captures the derivation
relationship existing between keys, which can be either direct, by means of a single
token, or indirect, via a chain of tokens, corresponding to a path in the key and token
graph.

The definition of tokens allows us to easily support the assumption that each user
can be released only a single key and that each object can be encrypted by using a
single key. Note that these are not simplifying or limiting assumptions, rather they

are desiderata that we impose our solution to satisfy. We then require our solution
to operate under the following assumption.

**Assumption 3.1** *Each object can be encrypted with only one key. Each user can be
released only one key.*

We also assume that each key is uniquely identified through the label associated
with it. A *key assignment and encryption schema* $\phi$ determines the labels of the
keys assigned to users and of the keys used for encrypting objects and is defined as
follows.

**Definition 3.5 (Key assignment and encryption schema).** Let $\mathcal{U}, \mathcal{O}, \mathcal{K}, \mathcal{L}$ be the
set of users, objects, keys, and labels in the system, respectively. A *key assignment
and encryption schema* over $\mathcal{U}, \mathcal{O}, \mathcal{K}, \mathcal{L}$ is a function $\phi : \mathcal{U} \cup \mathcal{O} \to \mathcal{L}$ that associates with each user $u \in \mathcal{U}$ the label $l \in \mathcal{L}$ identifying the (single) key $k$ in $\mathcal{K}$
released to her and with each object $o \in \mathcal{O}$ the label $l \in \mathcal{L}$ identifying the (single)
key $k$ in $\mathcal{K}$ with which the object is encrypted.

We are now ready to introduce the definition of *encryption policy* as follows.

**Definition 3.6 (Encryption policy).** Let $\mathcal{U}$ and $\mathcal{O}$ be the set of users and objects
in the system, respectively. An *encryption policy* over $\mathcal{U}$ and $\mathcal{O}$, denoted $\mathcal{E}$, is a
6-tuple $\langle \mathcal{U}, \mathcal{O}, \mathcal{K}, \mathcal{L}, \phi, \mathcal{T} \rangle$, where $\mathcal{K}$ is the set of keys defined in the system, $\mathcal{L}$
is the set of corresponding labels, $\phi$ is a key assignment and encryption schema, and
$\mathcal{T}$ is a set of tokens defined on $\mathcal{K}$ and $\mathcal{L}$.

The encryption policy can be conveniently represented via a graph by extending
the key and token graph to include a vertex for each user and each object, and adding
an edge from each user vertex $u$ to the vertex $\langle k, l \rangle$ such that $\phi(u)=l$ and from each
vertex $\langle k, l \rangle$ to each object $o$ such that $\phi(o)=l$. We can think of the encryption policy
graph as a graph obtained by merging $\mathcal{G}_{\mathcal{A}}$ with $\mathcal{G}_{\mathcal{K},\mathcal{T}}$, where instead of directly
linking each user $u$ with each object $o$ she can access, we pass through the vertex
$\langle k_i, l_i \rangle$ such that $l_i = \phi(u)$, the vertex $\langle k_j, l_j \rangle$ such that $l_j = \phi(o)$, and possibly a chain
of keys/tokens connecting them. The encryption policy graph is formally defined as
follows.

**Definition 3.7 (Encryption policy graph).** Let $\mathcal{E} = \langle \mathcal{U}, \mathcal{O}, \mathcal{K}, \mathcal{L}, \phi, \mathcal{T} \rangle$ be an
encryption policy. The encryption policy graph over $\mathcal{E}$, denoted $\mathcal{G}_{\mathcal{E}}$, is a graph
$\langle V_{\mathcal{E}}, E_{\mathcal{E}} \rangle$ where:

- $V_{\mathcal{E}} = V_{\mathcal{K},\mathcal{T}} \cup \mathcal{U} \cup \mathcal{O}$;
- $E_{\mathcal{E}} = E_{\mathcal{K},\mathcal{T}} \cup \{(u, \langle k, l \rangle) : u \in \mathcal{U} \wedge l = \phi(u)\} \cup \{(\langle k, l \rangle, o) : o \in \mathcal{O} \wedge l = \phi(o)\}$,

where $V_{\mathcal{K},\mathcal{T}}$ and $E_{\mathcal{K},\mathcal{T}}$ are as in Definition 3.4, that is, $V_{\mathcal{K},\mathcal{T}} = \{\langle k_i, l_i \rangle : k_i \in \mathcal{K} \wedge
l_i \in \mathcal{L} \text{ is the label associated with } k_i\}$ and $E_{\mathcal{K},\mathcal{T}} = \{(\langle k_i, l_i \rangle, \langle k_j, l_j \rangle) : t_{i,j} \in \mathcal{T}\}$.

Figure 3.2 illustrates an example of encryption policy graph, where dotted edges
represent the key assignment and encryption schema (function $\phi$) and solid edges
represent the tokens (set $\mathcal{T}$).

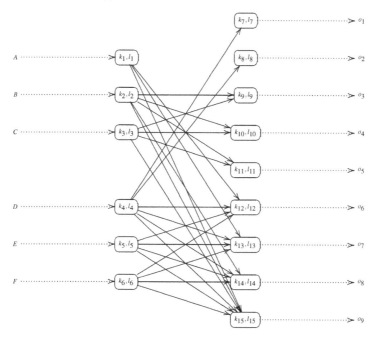

**Fig. 3.2** An example of encryption policy graph

In the following, we will use $\xrightarrow{\mathcal{E}}$ to denote the reachability of vertices in graph $\mathcal{G}_{\mathcal{E}}$ (e.g., $A \xrightarrow{\mathcal{E}} o_6$). By the definition of tokens, a user can retrieve (via her own key and the set of public tokens) all the keys of the vertices reachable from the vertex whose label $l$ is equal to $\phi(u)$. The objects accessible to a user according to an encryption policy are therefore all and only those reachable from $u$ in the encryption policy graph $\mathcal{G}_{\mathcal{E}}$. Our goal is then to translate an authorization policy $\mathcal{A}$ into an equivalent encryption policy $\mathcal{E}$, meaning that $\mathcal{A}$ and $\mathcal{E}$ allow exactly the same accesses, as formally defined in the following.

**Definition 3.8 (Policy equivalence).** Let $\mathcal{A} = \langle \mathcal{U}, \mathcal{O}, \mathcal{P} \rangle$ be an authorization policy and $\mathcal{E} = \langle \mathcal{U}, \mathcal{O}, \mathcal{K}, \mathcal{L}, \phi, \mathcal{T} \rangle$ be an encryption policy. $\mathcal{A}$ and $\mathcal{E}$ are *equivalent*, denoted $\mathcal{A} \equiv \mathcal{E}$, iff the following conditions hold:

- $\forall u \in \mathcal{U}, o \in \mathcal{O} : u \xrightarrow{\mathcal{E}} o \implies u \xrightarrow{\mathcal{A}} o$
- $\forall u \in \mathcal{U}, o \in \mathcal{O} : u \xrightarrow{\mathcal{A}} o \implies u \xrightarrow{\mathcal{E}} o$

For instance, it is easy to see that the authorization policy in Fig. 3.1 and the encryption policy represented by the encryption policy graph in Fig. 3.2 are equivalent.

| LABELS | | | TOKENS | | |
| :---: | :---: | | :---: | :---: | :---: |
| **obj_id** | **label** | | **source** | **destination** | **token_value** |
| $o_1$ | $l_7$ | | $l_1$ | $l_{12}$ | $k_{12} \oplus h(k_1, l_{12})$ |
| $o_2$ | $l_8$ | | $l_1$ | $l_{13}$ | $k_{13} \oplus h(k_1, l_{13})$ |
| $o_3$ | $l_9$ | | $l_1$ | $l_{15}$ | $k_{15} \oplus h(k_1, l_{15})$ |
| $o_4$ | $l_{10}$ | | $l_2$ | $l_9$ | $k_9 \oplus h(k_2, l_9)$ |
| $o_5$ | $l_{11}$ | | $l_2$ | $l_{10}$ | $k_{10} \oplus h(k_2, l_{10})$ |
| $o_6$ | $l_{12}$ | | $l_2$ | $l_{11}$ | $k_{11} \oplus h(k_2, l_{11})$ |
| $o_7$ | $l_{13}$ | | $l_2$ | $l_{14}$ | $k_{14} \oplus h(k_2, l_{14})$ |
| $o_8$ | $l_{14}$ | | $l_2$ | $l_{15}$ | $k_{15} \oplus h(k_2, l_{15})$ |
| $o_9$ | $l_{15}$ | | $l_3$ | $l_9$ | $k_9 \oplus h(k_3, l_9)$ |
| | | | $l_3$ | $l_{10}$ | $k_{10} \oplus h(k_3, l_{10})$ |
| | | | $l_3$ | $l_{11}$ | $k_{11} \oplus h(k_3, l_{11})$ |
| | | | $l_3$ | $l_{15}$ | $k_{15} \oplus h(k_3, l_{15})$ |
| | | | $l_4$ | $l_7$ | $k_7 \oplus h(k_4, l_7)$ |
| | | | $l_4$ | $l_8$ | $k_8 \oplus h(k_4, l_8)$ |
| | | | $l_4$ | $l_{12}$ | $k_{12} \oplus h(k_4, l_{12})$ |
| | | | $l_4$ | $l_{13}$ | $k_{13} \oplus h(k_4, l_{13})$ |
| | | | $l_4$ | $l_{14}$ | $k_{14} \oplus h(k_4, l_{14})$ |
| | | | $l_4$ | $l_{15}$ | $k_{15} \oplus h(k_4, l_{15})$ |
| | | | $l_5$ | $l_{13}$ | $k_{12} \oplus h(k_5, l_{12})$ |
| | | | $l_5$ | $l_{14}$ | $k_{13} \oplus h(k_5, l_{13})$ |
| | | | $l_5$ | $l_{15}$ | $k_{14} \oplus h(k_5, l_{14})$ |
| | | | $l_5$ | $l_{15}$ | $k_{15} \oplus h(k_5, l_{15})$ |
| | | | $l_6$ | $l_{12}$ | $k_{12} \oplus h(k_6, l_{12})$ |
| | | | $l_6$ | $l_{13}$ | $k_{13} \oplus h(k_6, l_{13})$ |
| | | | $l_6$ | $l_{14}$ | $k_{14} \oplus h(k_6, l_{14})$ |
| | | | $l_6$ | $l_{15}$ | $k_{15} \oplus h(k_6, l_{15})$ |

**Fig. 3.3**  Catalog for the encryption policy represented in Fig. 3.2

### 3.3.3 Token Management

To allow users to access the outsourced data, a portion of the encryption policy $\mathcal{E}$ must be made publicly available and therefore stored on the server. The only component of the encryption policy $\mathcal{E}$ that cannot be publicly released is the set $\mathcal{K}$ of keys while all the other components can be released without compromising the protection of the outsourced data. The set $\mathcal{T}$ of tokens, the set $\mathcal{L}$ of labels, and the key assignment and encryption schema $\phi(o)$ over $\mathcal{O}$ are therefore stored on the server in the form of a *catalog* composed of two tables: LABELS and TOKENS. Table LABELS corresponds to the key assignment and encryption schema $\phi$ over $\mathcal{O}$. For each object $o$ in $\mathcal{O}$, table LABELS maintains the correspondence between the identifier of $o$ (attribute *obj_id*) and the label $\phi(o)$ (attribute *label*) associated with the key used for encrypting $o$. Table TOKENS corresponds to the set $\mathcal{T}$ of tokens. For each token $t_{i,j}$ in $\mathcal{T}$, table TOKENS includes a tuple characterized by three attributes: *source* and *destination* are the labels $l_i$ and $l_j$ associated with $k_i$ and $k_j$, respectively, and *token_value* is the token value computed as $t_{i,j} = k_j \oplus h(k_i, l_j)$. Figure 3.3 illustrates tables LABELS and TOKENS corresponding to the encryption

**INPUT**
object $o$ to be accessed
user's key $k$
label $\phi(u)$ of the user's key

**OUTPUT**
key $k_{dest}$ with which $o$ is encrypted

**MAIN**
/* server-side query */
$chain := $ **FindPath**$(\phi(u),o)$
/* client-side computation */
$k_{source} := k$
**if** $chain \neq \emptyset$ **then** /* user $u$ is authorized to access $o$ */
  $t := $ POP($chain$)
  **repeat**
    $k_{dest} := t[token\_value]\oplus h(k_{source},t[destination])$
    $k_{source} := k_{dest}$
    $t := $ POP($chain$)
  **until** $t$=NULL
  **return**($k_{dest}$)


**FINDPATH**($from,o$)
Let $t \in$ LABELS $: t[obj\_id]=o$
$to := t[label]$
Topologically sort $V_{\mathscr{K},\mathscr{T}}$ in $\mathscr{G}_{\mathscr{K},\mathscr{T}}$
**for each** $v \in V_{\mathscr{K},\mathscr{T}}$ **do**
  $dist[v] := \infty$
  $pred[v] := $ NULL
$dist[from] := 0$
**for each** $v_i \in V_{\mathscr{K},\mathscr{T}}$ **do** /* visit vertices in topological order */
  **for each** $(v_i,v_j) \in E_{\mathscr{K},\mathscr{T}}$ **do** /* the weight of each arc is 1 */
    **if** $dist[v_j]>dist[v_i]+1$ **then**
      $dist[v_j] := dist[v_i]+1$
      $pred[v_j] := v_i$
$chain := \emptyset$
$current := to$
**while** $current \neq from \wedge current \neq$ NULL **do**
  Let $t \in$ TOKENS $: t[source]=pred[current] \wedge t[destination]=current$
  PUSH($chain,t$)
  $current := pred[current]$
**if** $current=$NULL **then**
  **return**($\emptyset$)
**else**
  **return**($chain$)

**Fig. 3.4** Key derivation process


policy represented in Fig. 3.2. Note that the information about the key assignment and encryption schema $\phi(u)$ over $\mathscr{U}$ does not need to be outsourced since each user knows the label associated with her key.

Whenever a user wishes to access an object $o$, she queries the catalog to follow a chain of tokens that, starting from her own key $k$, allows the user to derive the key associated with the object. Figure 3.4 illustrates the algorithm that receives as input the object identifier $o$, the key $k$ of $u$, and the label $\phi(u)$ associated with $k$, and computes the key $k_{dest}$ with which object $o$ is encrypted. The algorithm is basically composed of two steps.

The first step is performed server-side and consists in executing function **Find-Path** that, given a label $\phi(u)$ and an object $o$, retrieves the shortest token chain from

$\phi(u)$ to $\phi(o)$ by querying table TOKENS. Function **FindPath** first determines $\phi(o)$ by querying table LABELS and then computes the shortest path in the key and token graph through a shortest path algorithm (an improved version of Dijkstra working on DAGs), which exploits the topological order of vertices. The function then builds backward the path from $current=\phi(o)$ to $\phi(u)$. At each iteration of the **while** loop, the function follows *pred*[*current*], which is an array that contains the label of the predecessor of vertex *current* in the path previously computed, and adds to stack *chain* the token in TOKENS from *pred*[*current*] to *current*.

The second step is evaluated client-side and consists in deriving keys following the chain of tokens (if not empty) returned by **FindPath** and stored in stack *chain*, and terminating with the computation of the key used for encrypting object $o$. For instance, consider the catalog in Fig. 3.3 and suppose that $C$, with $\phi(C)=l_3$, wants to access $o_4$. Function **FindPath**$(l_3,o_4)$ first queries table LABELS for retrieving the label associated with object $o_4$, which is $\phi(o_4)=l_{10}$, and then finds the shortest path from $l_3$ to $l_{10}$. The returned *chain* is composed of one token only, corresponding to tuple $(l_3,l_{10},k_{10}\oplus h(k_3,l_{10}))$ of table TOKENS. The algorithm then derives key $k_{10}$ (i.e., the key used for encrypting $o_4$) through user's secret key $k_3$ and the unique token extracted from *chain*.

## 3.4 Minimal Encryption Policy

A straightforward approach for translating an authorization policy $\mathcal{A}$ into an equivalent encryption policy $\mathcal{E}$ consists in associating with each user a different key, encrypting each object with a different key, and producing and publishing a token $t_{u,o}$ for each permission $\langle u,o \rangle \in \mathcal{P}$. The encryption policy graph in Fig. 3.2 has been generated by translating the authorization policy in Fig. 3.1 with this approach. While simple, this translation generates as many keys as the number of users and objects, and as many tokens as the number of permissions in the system. Even if tokens, being public, need not to be remembered or stored by users, producing and managing a token for each single permission can be unfeasible in practice. Indeed, each access to an encrypted object requires a search across the catalog (see Sect. 3.3.3) and therefore the total number of tokens is a critical factor for the efficiency of accesses to remotely stored data.

This simple solution can be improved by grouping users with the same access privileges and by encrypting each object with the key associated with the set of users that can access it. To this purpose, we can exploit the hierarchy among sets of users induced by the partial order relationship based on set containment ($\subseteq$) to create an encryption policy graph $\mathcal{G}_{\mathcal{E}}=\langle V_{\mathcal{E}},E_{\mathcal{E}}\rangle$, with $V_{\mathcal{E}}=V_{\mathcal{K},\mathcal{T}} \cup \mathcal{U} \cup \mathcal{O}$, where $V_{\mathcal{K},\mathcal{T}}$ includes a vertex for each possible subset $U$ of $\mathcal{U}$, and $E_{\mathcal{E}}$ includes:

- an edge $(v_i,v_j)$ for each possible pair of vertices $v_i,v_j \in V_{\mathcal{K},\mathcal{T}}$ such that the set $U_i$ of users represented by $v_i$ is a subset of the set $U_j$ of users represented by $v_j$ and the containment relationship is direct;

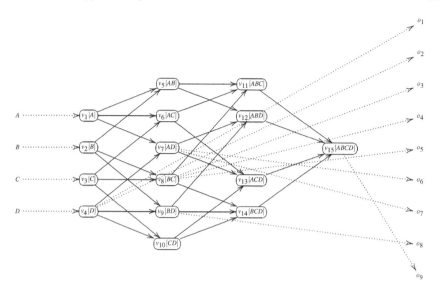

**Fig. 3.5** An example of encryption policy graph over $\{A,B,C,D\}$

- an edge $(u_i,v_i)$ for each user $u_i \in \mathcal{U}$ such that $v_i \in V_{\mathcal{K},\mathcal{F}}$ and the set of users represented by $v_i$ is $\{u_i\}$;
- an edge $(v_j,o_j)$ for each object $o_j \in \mathcal{O}$ such that $v_j \in V_{\mathcal{K},\mathcal{F}}$ and the set of users represented by $v_j$ is $acl(o_j)$.

As an example, consider the portion of the authorization policy in Fig. 3.1 that is defined on the set $\{A, B, C, D\}$ of users. Figure 3.5 illustrates the encryption policy graph over $\{A, B, C, D\}$ defined as previously described, where each vertex $v_i$ is marked with the set of users, denoted $v_i.acl$, that represents. It is interesting to note that the subgraph induced by $V_{\mathcal{K},\mathcal{F}}$ has the particularity of being a $n$-stratified graph, where $n$ is the number of users in the system (i.e., $n = |\mathcal{U}|$). Each strata, which we call *level*, contains all vertices that represent a set of users with the same cardinality. For instance, in the encryption policy graph in Fig. 3.5 the vertices at level 1 are $v_1$, $v_2$, $v_3$, and $v_4$. In the following, the level of a vertex $v \in V_{\mathcal{K},\mathcal{F}}$ will be denoted $level(v)$, equal to $|v.acl|$.

By assigning to each vertex $v \in V_{\mathcal{K},\mathcal{F}}$ of the graph a pair $\langle v.key,v.label \rangle$, corresponding to a key and label, the authorization policy can be enforced by encrypting each object with the key of the vertex corresponding to its access control list (e.g., object $o_5$ should be encrypted with the key associated with the vertex representing $\{B, C\}$) and by assigning to each user the key associated with the vertex representing the user in the graph. This means that the encryption policy corresponding to this graph is such that the sets $\mathcal{K}$ and $\mathcal{L}$ of keys and labels, respectively, include all keys and labels associated with vertices in $V_{\mathcal{K},\mathcal{F}}$. The key assignment and encryption schema $\phi$ is such that for each user $u \in \mathcal{U}$, $\phi(u) = v.label$, where $v$ is the vertex representing the user, (i.e., $v.acl = \{u\}$) and for each object $o \in \mathcal{O}$, $\phi(o) =$

*v.label*, where *v* is the vertex representing $acl(o_j)$ (i.e., $v.acl = acl(o_j)$). Finally, for each edge $(v_i,v_j)$ in $E_{\mathscr{E}}$, with $v_i,v_j \in V_{\mathscr{K},\mathscr{T}}$, there is a token in $\mathscr{T}$ that allows the derivation of key $v_j.key$ from key $v_i.key$.

The advantage of this solution, with respect to the trivial one above-mentioned, is that potentially a key can be used to encrypt more than one object. The disadvantage is that it defines more keys than actually needed and requires the publication of a great amount of information on the remote server, thus causing an expensive key derivation process at the user-side. For instance, in the encryption policy graph in Fig. 3.5 vertex $v_{10}$ is not need for enforcing the authorization policy since its key is not used for encrypting any object. The presence of such a vertex only increases the size of table TOKENS stored on the server without giving any benefit. We are then interested in finding a *minimal encryption policy* equivalent to a given authorization policy and that minimizes the number of tokens to be maintained by the server.

**Definition 3.9 (Minimal encryption policy).** Let $\mathscr{A} = \langle \mathscr{U}, \mathscr{O}, \mathscr{P} \rangle$ be an authorization policy and $\mathscr{E} = \langle \mathscr{U}, \mathscr{O}, \mathscr{K}, \mathscr{L}, \phi, \mathscr{T} \rangle$ be an encryption policy such that $\mathscr{A} \equiv \mathscr{E}$. $\mathscr{E}$ is *minimal* with respect to $\mathscr{A}$ iff $\nexists \mathscr{E}' = \langle \mathscr{U}, \mathscr{O}, \mathscr{K}', \mathscr{L}', \phi', \mathscr{T}' \rangle$ such that $\mathscr{A} \equiv \mathscr{E}'$ and $|\mathscr{T}'| \leq |\mathscr{T}|$.

Given an authorization policy $\mathscr{A}$, different minimal encryption policies may exist and our goal is to compute one of them, as stated by the following problem definition.

**Problem 3.1 (Min-EP).** Given an authorization policy $\mathscr{A} = \langle \mathscr{U}, \mathscr{O}, \mathscr{P} \rangle$, determine a *minimal encryption policy* $\mathscr{E} = \langle \mathscr{U}, \mathscr{O}, \mathscr{K}, \mathscr{L}, \phi, \mathscr{T} \rangle$.

Unfortunately, it turns out that Problem 3.1 is *NP-hard*, as the following theorem states.

**Theorem 3.1.** *The Min-EP problem is NP-hard.*

*Proof.* The considered problem is NP-hard since it can be reduced to the *Minimum Set Cover* (MSC) problem, which can be formulated as follows: *given a universal set Uset* $= \{a_1,\ldots,a_n\}$ *and a set of subsets of Uset,* $\mathscr{S} = \{S_1,\ldots,S_m\}$, *find the smallest subset C of* $\mathscr{S}$ *such that* $\bigcup_{i=1}^{m} S_i \in \mathscr{C} = Uset$.

Given a universal set *Uset* and a set $\mathscr{S}$ of its subsets, we define a corresponding authorization policy $\mathscr{A} = \langle \mathscr{U}, \mathscr{O}, \mathscr{P} \rangle$ in polynomial time. For each item $a_i$ in *Uset*, there is a user $u_i$ in $\mathscr{U}$. For each subset $S_j = \{a_{j,1},\ldots,a_{j,m_j}\}$ in $\mathscr{S}$, there is an object $o_j$ with $acl(o_j)=S_j$ and a set $R_j$ of $m_j - 1$ objects $o_{j,k}$, $k = 1,\ldots,m_j - 1$, with $acl(o_{j,k})=\{a_{j,1},\ldots,a_{j,k}\}$. Finally, a further object $o_{\perp}$ with $acl(o_{\perp})=Uset$ is added to $\mathscr{O}$.

As an example, let *Uset*$=\{A,B,C,D,E\}$ and $\mathscr{S} = \{S_1 = \{A,B,C\}, S_2 = \{B,D\}, S_3 = \{B,D,E\}\}$. The corresponding authorization policy is characterized by 5 users, *A*, *B*, *C*, and *D*. Initially, 3 objects, $o_1$ with $acl(o_1)=\{A,B,C\}$, $o_2$ with $acl(o_2)=\{B,D\}$, and $o_3$ with $acl(o_3)=\{B,D,E\}$, are added to $\mathscr{O}$, followed by $o_{1,1}$ with $acl(o_{1,1})=\{A\}$, $o_{1,2}$ with $acl(o_{1,2})=\{A,B\}$, and $o_{2,1}$ with $acl(o_{1,1})=\{B\}$, since duplicates are removed.

An encryption policy $\mathcal{E} = \langle \mathcal{U}, \mathcal{O}, \mathcal{K}, \mathcal{L}, \phi, \mathcal{T} \rangle$ equivalent to $\mathcal{A}$ is characterized by a key and token graph with a vertex for each user, which key is known to the user itself, and a vertex for each *acl* value, which key is used to encrypt the objects characterized by the represented *acl*. Therefore, there is a path in the graph from each vertex representing a user $u$ to each vertex representing an *acl* value containing $u$. To this purpose, each vertex $v \in \mathcal{G}_{\mathcal{K},\mathcal{T}}$, besides vertices $v$ such that $\phi(u) = v.label$, must have at least two incoming edges in the graph (i.e., tokens). Specifically, the staring point of these tokens must cover all users represented by $v$. By construction, for each vertex $v$ representing a set $\{u_1, \ldots, u_k\}$ of user, but the vertex representing $\mathcal{U}$, there is a vertex $v'$ representing $\{u_1, \ldots, u_{k-1}\}$. Therefore, $v$ is covered by $v'$ and with the vertex representing $\{u_k\}$. The encryption policy minimal with respect to $\mathcal{T}$ is the encryption policy minimizing the number of incoming tokens in vertex $v_\perp$ representing $\mathcal{U}$, since the addition of vertices would not produce benefits.

The solution to the corresponding minimum set covering problem is obtained from the solution to the corresponding Min-EP problem as follows. For each edge $(v, v_\perp)$ ending in $v_\perp$, $v$ can either represent a subset of $\mathcal{U}$ belonging to $\mathcal{S}$ or not. In the latter case, $v$ is substituted with its nearest descendant representing a subset belonging to $\mathcal{S}$. Such a descendant must exist since, by construction, we generate additional vertices representing only subsets of items appearing in $\mathcal{S}$. Since the set of direct ancestors of $v_\perp$ represents a cover for $\mathcal{U}$, then the subsets they represent are a minimum set cover for *Uset*.

We then propose a heuristic approach for solving Problem 3.1 that tries to reduce the user's overhead in deriving keys through a simplification of the encryption policy graph that consists in removing non necessary vertices, while ensuring a correct key derivability. A further important observation is that, beside the vertices needed for the enforcement of the authorization policy, other vertices can be included if they are useful for reducing the size of the catalog, even if their keys are not used for encrypting objects. We now discuss more in the details these two basic observations.

## 3.4.1 Vertices and Edges Selection

From the previous discussion, it is immediate to see that the vertices in $V_{\mathcal{K},\mathcal{T}}$ strictly needed for the enforcement of the authorization policy are the vertices representing: *i)* singleton sets of users, whose keys are needed to derive all the other keys used for decrypting objects in the users' capabilities; and *ii)* the *acl*s of the objects, whose keys are needed for decrypting such objects. In the following, we refer to these vertices as *material*. The material vertices must then be connected in the graph in such a way that each user $u \in \mathcal{U}$ is able to derive the keys of all objects she is entitled to access. This means that the encryption policy graph must include at least one path from the vertex $v_i$ representing user $u$ (i.e., vertex $v_i$ such that $v_i.acl = \{u\}$) to all material vertices $v_j$ such that $u \in v_j.acl$. Since our main goal is to keep at minimum the number of tokens managed by the server and since each edge in the encryption policy graph corresponds to a token, our problem is then to connect the material vertices, thus creating an encryption policy equivalent to a given authorization policy and with the minimum number of edges/tokens. To solve this problem, we observe that the direct ancestors of a vertex must form a set covering for it. Indeed, since for each user $u$ the encryption policy graph must include a path from the vertex representing it and all vertices $v_j$ such that $u \in v_j.acl$ and, by construction, there is an edge $(v_i, v_j)$ iff $v_i.acl \subset v_j.acl$, vertex $v_j$ must have at least a direct ancestor $v_k$ such that $u \in v_k.acl$. An encryption policy graph corresponding to an encryption policy equivalent to a given authorization policy satisfies therefore the following *local cover* property.

**Theorem 3.2 (Local cover).** *Let $\mathscr{A}$ be an authorization policy and $\mathscr{E}$ be an encryption policy. If $\mathscr{E}$ is equivalent to $\mathscr{A}$, the encryption policy graph $\mathscr{G}_{\mathscr{E}} = \langle V_{\mathscr{E}}, E_{\mathscr{E}} \rangle$ over $\mathscr{E}$, with $V_{\mathscr{E}} = V_{\mathscr{K},\mathscr{T}} \cup \mathscr{U} \cup \mathscr{O}$, satisfies the* local cover property *stating that $\forall v_i \in V_{\mathscr{K},\mathscr{T}}$, with $|v_i.acl| > 1$, $v_i.acl = \bigcup_j \{v_j.acl : (v_j, v_i) \in E_{\mathscr{E}}\}$.*

*Proof.* By induction, we prove that $\forall v_i \in V_{\mathscr{K},\mathscr{T}}$ the local cover property is satisfied.

- For all $v_i$ such that $|v_i.acl| = 1$, $v_i$ is correctly covered by definition.
- Let us suppose that for all $v_i$ such that $|v_i.acl| \leq n$, $v_i$ is correctly covered. We now prove that also all vertices $v_j$ with $|v_i.acl| = n + 1$ are correctly covered.

  By definition, $\forall \langle u, R \rangle \in p$, $u \xrightarrow{\mathscr{E}} R$, that is there exists a path in $\mathscr{G}_{\mathscr{E}}$ from $u$ to $R$. This means that there exists a path from the vertex $v_i$, such that $v_i.acl = \{u\}$, to the vertex $v_j$, such that $v_j.acl = acl(R)$. Therefore, there exists an edge $(v, v_j) \in E_{\mathscr{K},\mathscr{T}}$ such that $u \in v.acl$. Also, by construction, $v.acl \subseteq v_j.acl$. As a consequence $|v.acl| \leq n$. By hypothesis, $v$ is correctly covered. We then conclude that $v_j$ is correctly covered.

Our approach to create an encryption policy graph works bottom up, starting from the vertices at the highest level to the vertices at the lowest level. For each vertex $v$ at level $l$, its possible direct ancestors are first searched among the material vertices at level $l - 1$, then at level $l - 2$, and so on, until all the material vertices directly connected to $v$ form a set covering for $v$. The rationale behind this bottom up strategy is that, in principle[4], by searching first among the vertices at higher levels, the number of direct ancestors and therefore of edges for connecting them to $v$ should be less than the number of direct ancestors needed for covering vertex $v$ when such vertices are chosen according to other approaches. As an example, consider the authorization policy in Fig. 3.1. Here, we have ten material vertices representing the following sets of users: $\{A\}$, $\{B\}$, $\{C\}$, $\{D\}$, $\{E\}$, $\{F\}$, $\{BC\}$, $\{ADEF\}$, $\{BDEF\}$, and $\{ABCDEF\}$. Consider now the material vertex representing $\{ABCDEF\}$ and suppose to compute a set covering for it by choosing the appropriate direct ancestors from the given material vertices. If we apply the bottom up strategy previously described, the possible direct ancestors for $\{ABCDEF\}$ are first chosen among the vertices at level: 5, which is empty; 4, where there are two

---

[4] Since this bottom up strategy is a heuristic that we apply for solving a NP-hard problem, the solution computed through it may not be always the optimal solution. However, we will see in Sect. 3.10 that this heuristic produces good results.

material vertices (i.e., $\{ADEF\}$, $\{BDEF\}$) that can be chosen as direct ancestors for $\{ABCDEF\}$; 3, which is empty; and then 2, where vertex $\{BC\}$ is chosen. The final set covering for $\{ABCDEF\}$ is $\{\{ADEF\}, \{BDEF\}, \{BC\}\}$, which requires three edges for connecting the vertices in the set covering to the vertex representing $\{ABCDEF\}$. Another possible set covering for $\{ABCDEF\}$ is, for example, $\{\{A\}, \{B\}, \{C\}, \{D\}, \{E\}, \{F\}\}$, which instead requires six edges.

This simple approach for computing a set covering may however introduce redundant edges. For instance, with respect to the previous example, since $\{ADEF\}$ and $\{BDEF\}$ are selected before $\{BC\}$, it is easy to see that the edge from the vertex representing $\{BDEF\}$ to the vertex representing $\{ABCDEF\}$ is redundant since each user in $\{BDEF\}$ is also a member of at least one of the other two direct ancestors of the vertex representing $\{ABCDEF\}$. The redundant edges increase the number of tokens and are not useful for the enforcement of the authorization policy. We are then interested in computing a *non-redundant* encryption policy graph defined as follows.

**Definition 3.10 (Non-redundant encryption policy graph).** Let $\mathscr{A} = \langle \mathscr{U}, \mathscr{O}, \mathscr{P} \rangle$ be an authorization policy and $\mathscr{E} = \langle \mathscr{U}, \mathscr{O}, \mathscr{K}, \mathscr{L}, \phi, \mathscr{T} \rangle$ be an equivalent encryption policy. The encryption policy graph $\mathscr{G}_{\mathscr{E}} = \langle V_{\mathscr{E}}, E_{\mathscr{E}} \rangle$, with $V_{\mathscr{E}} = V_{\mathscr{K}, \mathscr{T}} \cup \mathscr{U} \cup \mathscr{O}$, over $\mathscr{E}$ is *non-redundant* if $\forall v_i \in V_{\mathscr{K}, \mathscr{T}}$, with $|v_i.acl| > 1$, $\forall (v_j, v_i) \in E_{\mathscr{E}}$, $\exists\, u \in v_j.acl$: $\forall (v_l, v_i) \in E_{\mathscr{E}}$, with $v_l \neq v_j$, $u \notin v_l.acl$.

Sect. 3.5 will present in more details a heuristic algorithm for computing a non-redundant encryption policy graph equivalent to a given authorization policy.

### 3.4.2 Vertices Factorization

In addition to the material vertices, other vertices can be inserted into the graph whenever they can reduce the number of tokens in the catalog. Consider, for example, the authorization policy in Fig. 3.1 and, in particular, the two material vertices representing $\{ADEF\}$ and $\{BDEF\}$. The sets covering these two material vertices can only be the sets including the vertices representing singleton sets of users, since there are no material vertices representing subsets of $\{ADEF\}$ or of $\{BDEF\}$. The number of edges needed for connecting the vertices in the sets covering to $\{ADEF\}$ and $\{BDEF\}$ are then eight. Suppose now to add a non material vertex representing $\{DEF\}$. In this case, the set covering for $\{ADEF\}$ is $\{\{DEF\}, \{A\}\}$ and the set covering for $\{BDEF\}$ is $\{\{DEF\}, \{B\}\}$, which require four edges for connecting them to $\{ADEF\}$ and $\{BDEF\}$, respectively, and three edges for covering $\{DEF\}$ through $\{\{D\}, \{E\}, \{F\}\}$ for a total of seven edges against the eight edges of the previous case. Generalizing, it is easy to see that whenever there are $m$ vertices $v_1, \ldots, v_m$ that share $n$, with $n > 2$, ancestors $v'_1, \ldots, v'_n$, it is convenient to factorize the common ancestors by inserting an intermediate vertex $v'$, with $v'.acl = \bigcup_{i=1}^{n} v'_i.acl$, and to connect each vertex $v'_i, i = 1, \ldots, n$, to $v'$, and $v'$ to $v_j, j = 1, \ldots, m$, for saving tokens in the catalog. In this way, the encryption policy graph includes $n + m$, instead

---

**INPUT**
authorization policy $\mathscr{A} = \langle \mathscr{U}, \mathscr{O}, \mathscr{P} \rangle$

**OUTPUT**
encryption policy $\mathscr{E}$ such that $\mathscr{A} \equiv \mathscr{E}$

**MAIN**
$V_{\mathscr{K},\mathscr{T}} := \emptyset$
$E_{\mathscr{K},\mathscr{T}} := \emptyset$
/* Initialization */
$ACL := \{acl(o){:}o{\in}\mathscr{O}\} \cup \{\{u\}{:}u{\in}\mathscr{U}\}$
**for** $acl{\in}ACL$ **do**
  create vertex $v$
  $v.acl := acl$
  $v.label :=$ NULL
  $v.key :=$ NULL
  **for each** $u{\in}v.acl$ **do** $v.counter[u] := 0$
  $V_{\mathscr{K},\mathscr{T}} := V_{\mathscr{K},\mathscr{T}} \cup \{v\}$
/* Phase 1: cover vertices without redundancies */
**for** $l:=|\mathscr{U}|\ldots 2$ **do**
  **for each** $v_i{\in}\{v{:}v{\in}V_{\mathscr{K},\mathscr{T}} \wedge level(v){=}l\}$ **do**
    **CoverVertex**$(v_i,v_i.acl)$
/* Phase 2: factorize common ancestors */
**for** $l:=|\mathscr{U}|\ldots 2$ **do**
  **for each** $v_i{\in}\{v{:}v{\in}V_{\mathscr{K},\mathscr{T}} \wedge level(v){=}l\}$ **do**
    **Factorize**$(v_i)$
/* Phase 3: generate encryption policy */
**GenerateEncryptionPolicy**()

---

**Fig. 3.6** Algorithm for computing an encryption policy $\mathscr{E}$ equivalent to $\mathscr{A}$

of $n \cdot m$, edges for correctly covering vertices $v_1, \ldots, v_m$. The advantage may appear small in this example, but the experiments in Sect. 3.10 show that this optimization can produce significant gains in scenarios with complex policies.

The factorization process is enforced during the construction of an encryption policy graph by applying a bottom up strategy, starting from vertices at the highest level to the vertices at the lowest level, and by comparing pairs of vertices at each time. The bottom up strategy guarantees that the vertex added in the graph (if any) will appear at a level lower than the level of the current pair of vertices and therefore it will be compared to the other vertices in the graph when the vertices at that level will be analyzed. To limit the number of pairs of vertices analyzed, we consider only pairs of vertices that have at least one common direct ancestor; the adaptation of the analysis in [10] demonstrates that it is sufficient to consider these pairs, with a significant reduction in the number of comparisons.

## 3.5 $\mathscr{A}2\mathscr{E}$ Algorithm

Our heuristic method for computing a minimal encryption policy is illustrated in Fig. 3.6. The algorithm takes an authorization policy $\mathscr{A} = \langle \mathscr{U}, \mathscr{O}, \mathscr{P} \rangle$ as input and returns an encryption policy $\mathscr{E}$ equivalent to $\mathscr{A}$ and that satisfies Definition 3.10. To this purpose, the algorithm first computes a key and token graph $\langle V_{\mathscr{K},\mathscr{T}}, E_{\mathscr{K},\mathscr{T}} \rangle$

---

**COVERVERTEX**(*v*,*tocover*)
*Eadded* := ∅
*l* := *level*(*v*) − 1
/* find a correct cover for users in *tocover* */
**while** *tocover* ≠ ∅ **do**
    $V_l := \{v_i : v_i \in V_{\mathscr{K},\mathscr{T}} \wedge level(v_i)=l \wedge v_i.acl \subset v.acl\}$
    **while** *tocover* ≠ ∅ ∧ $V_l$ ≠ ∅ **do**
        extract $v_i$ from $V_l$
        **if** $v_i.acl \cap tocover \neq \emptyset$ **then**
            *tocover* := *tocover* \ $v_i.acl$
            *Eadded* := *Eadded* ∪ {($v_i$,*v*)}
            **for each** $u \in v_i.acl$ **do**
                *v.counter*[*u*] := *v.counter*[*u*] + 1
    *l* := *l* − 1
/* remove redundant edges */
**for each** ($v_i$,*v*) ∈ *Eadded* **do**
    **if** ( $\not\exists u : u \in v_i.acl \wedge v.counter[u]$= 1) **then**
        *Eadded* := *Eadded* \ {($v_i$,*v*)}
        **for each** $u \in v_i.acl$ **do**
            *v.counter*[*u*] := *v.counter*[*u*] − 1
$E_{\mathscr{K},\mathscr{T}} := E_{\mathscr{K},\mathscr{T}} \cup Eadded$

---

**Fig. 3.7** Procedure for covering material vertices and removing redundant edges

and then generates the corresponding encryption policy, by computing the set $\mathscr{T}$ of tokens and by defining the key assignment and encryption schema $\phi$. Each vertex $v$ in $V_{\mathscr{K},\mathscr{T}}$ is associated with four variables: *v.key* represents the key of the vertex; *v.label* represents the publicly available label associated with *v.key*; *v.acl* represents the set of users who can derive *v.key*; *v.counter*[] is an array with one component for each user $u$ in *v.acl* such that *v.counter*[*u*] is equal to the number of direct ancestors of $v$ whose *acl* contains user $u$ (as we will see, this information will be used to detect redundant edges).

The algorithm starts by creating the material vertices and by appropriately initializing the variables associated with them. The algorithm is logically partitioned in three phases: *i) cover vertices* that adds edges to the graph satisfying both local cover (Theorem 3.2) and non-redundancy (Definition 3.10), *ii) factorize common ancestors* that adds non material vertices for reducing the number of edges in the graph, and *iii) generate encryption policy*. We now describe these three phases more in details.

**Phase 1: Cover Vertices**

To grant local cover and non redundancy in the key and token graph, the algorithm proceeds bottom up, starting from level $l = |\mathscr{U}|$ to 2, and for each material vertex $v$ at level $l$, calls procedure **CoverVertex**. Procedure **CoverVertex** takes a vertex $v$ and a set *tocover* of users, corresponding to *v.acl*, as input. The procedure first initializes two local variables: *Eadded*, representing the set of edges that need to be added to the graph, is set to the empty set; and $l$, representing the level of candidates direct ancestors for $v$, is set to *level*(*v*)−1.

At each iteration of the outermost **while** loop, the procedure computes the set $V_l$ of vertices at level $l$ whose *acl* is a subset of *v.acl* and the innermost **while** loop checks if there are vertices in $V_l$ that can be covered by $v$. To this purpose, the procedure randomly extracts a vertex $v_i$ from $V_l$ and if $v_i.acl$ has at least a user in common with *tocover*, it removes from *tocover* the set of users appearing in $v_i.acl$ and adds edge $(v_i,v)$ to *Eadded*. Also, for each user $u$ in $v_i.acl$, the procedure increases *v.counter*[$u$] by one. The innermost **while** loop terminates when *tocover* becomes empty or when all vertices in $V_l$ have been processed. Local variable $l$ is then decreased by one and the process is repeated, until *tocover* or $V_l$ become empty.

The procedure then checks if *Eadded* contains redundant edges. For each edge $(v_i,v)$ in *Eadded*, if for all users in $v_i.acl$, *v.counter*[$u$] is greater than one (remember that *v.counter*[$u$] keeps track of the number of ancestors of $v$ that include user $u$ in their *acls*), then edge $(v_i,v)$ is redundant and can be removed from *Eadded*. If this is the case, for each user $u$ in $v_i.acl$, the procedure decreases *v.counter*[$u$] by one. The set *Eadded* of non redundant edges is then added to $E_{\mathcal{K},\mathcal{T}}$.

### Phase 2: Factorize Acls

As a result of the previous phase, we have a key and token graph that guarantees that each user is able to derive the keys of the objects she is authorized to access. The goal of this phase is to verify if it is possible to add some additional vertices to reduce the number of edges in the graph. To this purpose, the algorithm works bottom up, starting from level $l = |\mathcal{U}|$ to 2. For each vertex $v_i$ at level $l$, the algorithm calls procedure **Factorize** on $v_i$. For each vertex $v_j$ having at least a common direct ancestor with $v_i$ (first **for** loop), procedure **Factorize** first initializes two local variables: *Eadded* and *Eremoved*, representing the set of edges that need to be added to and removed from the graph, respectively, are both set to the empty set. Procedure **Factorize** then determines the set *CommonAnc* of direct ancestors common to $v_i$ and $v_j$. If *CommonAnc* contains more than two vertices, it means that $v_i$ and $v_j$ can conveniently be factorized by a vertex $v$ covering both $v_i$ and $v_j$ instead of the vertices in *CommonAnc*. Vertex $v$ is covered, if it does not satisfy local cover property, by the vertices in *CommonAnc*. Therefore, $2 \cdot |CommonAnc|$ edges are removed from the graph, while at most $2 + |CommonAnc|$ edges need to be added to the graph. Procedure **Factorize** computes the union $U$ among the *acls* associated with vertices in *CommonAnc*. The procedure checks if the graph already includes a vertex $v$ whose *acl* is equal to $U$ and possibly detects the set of edges that has to be added and removed from the graph. Three cases may then occur. First, vertex $v$ already exists and coincides neither with $v_i$ nor with $v_j$. The two edges from $v$ to $v_i$ and from $v$ to $v_j$ are inserted in *Eadded*, and all edges from the common ancestors in *CommonAnc* to $v_i$ and to $v_j$ are inserted in *Eremoved*. Second, vertex $v$ coincides with $v_i$ ($v_j$, resp.). The procedure inserts a new edge from $v_i$ to $v_j$ (from $v_j$ to $v_i$, resp.) in *Eadded* and all edges from the common ancestors in *CommonAnc* to $v_j$ ($v_i$, resp.) are inserted in *Eremoved*. Third, vertex $v$ does not exist in the graph. The procedure creates a new vertex $v'$ and initializes $v'.acl$ to $U$ and both $v'.label$ and $v'.key$

---

FACTORIZE($v_i$)
**for each** $v_j \in \{v : \exists v_a, (v_a, v_i) \in E_{\mathcal{K}, \mathcal{T}} \wedge (v_a, v) \in E_{\mathcal{K}, \mathcal{T}}\}$ **do** /* children of $v_i$'s direct ancestors */
    *Eadded* := ∅
    *Eremoved* := ∅
    *CommonAnc* := $\{v_a : (v_a, v_i) \in E_{\mathcal{K}, \mathcal{T}} \wedge (v_a, v_j) \in E_{\mathcal{K}, \mathcal{T}}\}$ /* common direct ancestors */
    **if** $|CommonAnc| > 2$ **then**
        /* create a new common ancestor for $v_i$ and $v_j$ */
        $U := \bigcup \{v_a.acl : v_a \in CommonAnc\}$
        find the vertex $v \in V_{\mathcal{K}, \mathcal{T}}$ with $v.acl = U$
        **case** $v$ **of**
            $\neq v_i \wedge \neq v_j$:  *Eadded* := *Eadded* ∪ $\{(v, v_i), (v, v_j)\}$
                    **for each** $v_a \in CommonAnc$ **do**
                        *Eremoved* := *Eremoved* ∪ $\{(v_a, v_i), (v_a, v_j)\}$
            $= v_i$:        *Eadded* := *Eadded* ∪ $\{(v_i, v_j)\}$
                    **for each** $v_a \in CommonAnc$ **do**
                        *Eremoved* := *Eremoved* ∪ $\{(v_a, v_j)\}$
            $= v_j$:        *Eadded* := *Eadded* ∪ $\{(v_j, v_i)\}$
                    **for each** $v_a \in CommonAnc$ **do**
                        *Eremoved* := *Eremoved* ∪ $\{(v_a, v_i)\}$
            UNDEF:     create vertex $v'$
                    $v'.acl := U$
                    $v'.label :=$ NULL
                    $v'.key :=$ NULL
                    **for each** $u \in v'.acl$ **do**
                        $v'.counter[u] := 0$
                    $V_{\mathcal{K}, \mathcal{T}} := V_{\mathcal{K}, \mathcal{T}} \cup \{v'\}$
                    *Eadded* := *Eadded* ∪ $\{(v', v_i), (v', v_j)\}$
                    **for each** $v_a \in CommonAnc$ **do**
                        *Eadded* := *Eadded* ∪ $\{(v_a, v')\}$
                        *Eremoved* := *Eremoved* ∪ $\{(v_a, v_i), (v_a, v_j)\}$
    /* update counters */
    **for each** $(v_l, v_h) \in$ *Eadded* **do**
        **for each** $u \in v_l.acl$ **do**
            $v_h.counter[u] := v_h.counter[u] + 1$
    **for each** $(v_l, v_h) \in$ *Eremoved* **do**
        **for each** $u \in v_l.acl$ **do**
            $v_h.counter[u] := v_h.counter[u] - 1$
    $E_{\mathcal{K}, \mathcal{T}} := E_{\mathcal{K}, \mathcal{T}} \cup$ *Eadded* \ *Eremoved*

---

**Fig. 3.8** Procedure for factorizing the common ancestors between vertices

to NULL. The new vertex is then inserted in the graph and the edges from the common ancestors in *CommonAnc* to $v'$ are inserted in *Eadded* along with the two edges from the new vertex $v'$ to $v_i$ and to $v_j$. The edges from all the common ancestors in *CommonAnc* to $v_i$ and to $v_j$ are instead inserted in *Eremoved*. The procedure then appropriately updates variables $v_h.counter[u]$ for all edges $(v_l, v_h)$ in *Eadded* and *Eremoved*. Finally, the set $E_{\mathcal{K}, \mathcal{T}}$ of edges is updated by adding edges in *Eadded* and by removing edges in *Eremoved*.

## Phase 3: Generate ℰ

The last phase of the algorithm generates the encryption policy corresponding to the key and token graph computed during the previous phases. To this purpose, the algorithm calls procedure **GenerateEncryptionPolicy**. First, the procedure initializes the set $\mathcal{K}$ of keys, the set $\mathcal{L}$ of labels, and the set $\mathcal{T}$ of tokens to the empty

**GENERATEENCRYPTIONPOLICY()**
$\mathcal{K} := \emptyset$
$\mathcal{L} := \emptyset$
$\mathcal{T} := \emptyset$
/* generate keys */
**for each** $v \in V_{\mathcal{K},\mathcal{T}}$ **do**
   generate key $k$
   $v.key := k$
   generate label $l$
   $v.label := l$
   $\mathcal{K} := \mathcal{K} \cup \{v.key\}$
   $\mathcal{L} := \mathcal{L} \cup \{v.label\}$
/* compute tokens */
**for each** $(v_i, v_j) \in E_{\mathcal{K},\mathcal{T}}$ **do**
   $t_{i,j} := v_j.key \oplus h(v_i.key, v_j.label)$
   $\mathcal{T} := \mathcal{T} \cup \{t_{i,j}\}$
   upload token $t_{i,j}$ on the server by adding it to table TOKENS
/* define key assignment and encryption schema */
**for each** $u \in \mathcal{U}$ **do**
   find the vertex $v \in V_{\mathcal{K},\mathcal{T}}$ with $v.acl = \{u\}$
   $\phi(u) := v.label$
**for each** $o \in \mathcal{O}$ **do**
   find the vertex $v \in V_{\mathcal{K},\mathcal{T}}$ with $v.acl = acl(o)$
   encrypt $o$ with key $v.key$
   upload the encrypted version $o^k$ of $o$ on the server
   $\phi(o) := v.label$
   update table LABELS on the server

**Fig. 3.9** Procedure for creating an encryption policy

set. Then, for each vertex $v$ in $V_{\mathcal{K},\mathcal{T}}$, the procedure generates a key $k$ and a label $l$ and inserts them in $\mathcal{K}$ and $\mathcal{L}$, respectively. Also, for each edge $(v_i, v_j)$ in $E_{\mathcal{K},\mathcal{T}}$, procedure **GenerateEncryptionPolicy** computes token $t_{i,j}$, which is inserted in $\mathcal{T}$ and uploaded on the server by inserting a corresponding tuple in table TOKENS. Finally, the procedure defines the key assignment and encryption schema $\phi$ based on the labels previously generated. For each user $u$, $\phi(u)$ is defined as the label of the vertex representing the singleton set $\{u\}$, and for each object $o$, $\phi(o)$ is defined as the label of the vertex representing $acl(o)$ in the graph. Also, each object $o$ is encrypted with the key of the vertex corresponding to $\phi(o)$ and uploaded on the server; table LABELS in the catalog is updated accordingly.

*Example 3.1.* Figure 3.10 presents the execution, step by step, of the algorithm in Fig. 3.6, applied to the authorization policy in Fig. 3.1. The algorithm first generates 10 material vertices: $v_1, \ldots, v_6$ represent the singleton sets of users $A, \ldots, F$, respectively; $v_7$ represents $BC$; $v_8$ represents $ADEF$; $v_9$ represents $BDEF$; and $v_{10}$ represents $ABCDEF$.

Figure 3.10($a$) illustrates the key and token graph obtained after the first phase of the algorithm. Each vertex satisfies the local cover property and the graph does not include redundant edges. As an example of how this graph has been obtained, consider vertex $v_{10}$. Procedure **CoverVertex** first inserts in *Eadded* edges $(v_8, v_{10})$, $(v_9, v_{10})$, and $(v_7, v_{10})$. Then, it removes edge $(v_9, v_{10})$, since all users in $v_9.acl$ can derive $v_{10}.key$ through $v_7$ or $v_9$.

Figure 3.10($b$) illustrates the graph obtained after the second phase of the algorithm.

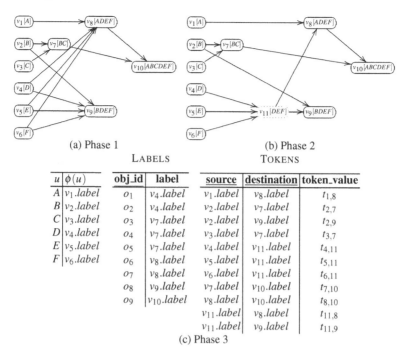

(a) Phase 1      (b) Phase 2

| $u$ | $\phi(u)$ |
|---|---|
| A | $v_1.label$ |
| B | $v_2.label$ |
| C | $v_3.label$ |
| D | $v_4.label$ |
| E | $v_5.label$ |
| F | $v_6.label$ |

LABELS

| obj_id | label |
|---|---|
| $o_1$ | $v_4.label$ |
| $o_2$ | $v_4.label$ |
| $o_3$ | $v_7.label$ |
| $o_4$ | $v_7.label$ |
| $o_5$ | $v_7.label$ |
| $o_6$ | $v_8.label$ |
| $o_7$ | $v_8.label$ |
| $o_8$ | $v_9.label$ |
| $o_9$ | $v_{10}.label$ |

TOKENS

| source | destination | token_value |
|---|---|---|
| $v_1.label$ | $v_8.label$ | $t_{1,8}$ |
| $v_2.label$ | $v_7.label$ | $t_{2,7}$ |
| $v_2.label$ | $v_9.label$ | $t_{2,9}$ |
| $v_3.label$ | $v_7.label$ | $t_{3,7}$ |
| $v_4.label$ | $v_{11}.label$ | $t_{4,11}$ |
| $v_5.label$ | $v_{11}.label$ | $t_{5,11}$ |
| $v_6.label$ | $v_{11}.label$ | $t_{6,11}$ |
| $v_7.label$ | $v_{10}.label$ | $t_{7,10}$ |
| $v_8.label$ | $v_{10}.label$ | $t_{8,10}$ |
| $v_{11}.label$ | $v_8.label$ | $t_{11,8}$ |
| $v_{11}.label$ | $v_9.label$ | $t_{11,9}$ |

(c) Phase 3

**Fig. 3.10** An example of algorithm execution

Note that the graph has a new vertex, $v_{11}$, which is inserted by procedure **Factorize** since vertices $v_8$ and $v_9$ in the graph in Fig. 3.10($a$) have three common direct ancestors (i.e., $v_4$, $v_5$, and $v_6$). Here, material vertices are represented with solid lines, while non material vertices are represented with dotted lines.

Finally, Fig. 3.10($c$) illustrates the key assignment and encryption schema for users in $\mathcal{U}$ and tables LABELS and TOKENS uploaded on the server by procedure **GenerateEncryptionPolicy**.

### 3.5.1 Correctness and Complexity

We first introduce some lemmas necessary to prove that the encryption policy created by the algorithm in Fig. 3.6 is equivalent to a given authorization policy.

First, we prove that users do not share encryption keys.

**Lemma 3.1 (User key uniqueness).** *Given an authorization policy* $\mathcal{A} = \langle \mathcal{U}, \mathcal{O}, \mathcal{P} \rangle$, *the algorithm in Fig. 3.6 creates a key and token graph* $\mathcal{G}_{\mathcal{K},\mathcal{T}} = \langle V_{\mathcal{K},\mathcal{T}}, E_{\mathcal{K},\mathcal{T}} \rangle$ *and the corresponding encryption policy* $\mathcal{E} = \langle \mathcal{U}, \mathcal{O}, \mathcal{K}, \mathcal{L}, \phi, \mathcal{T} \rangle$ *such that* $\forall u_i, u_j \in \mathcal{U}, i \neq j \implies \phi(u_i) \neq \phi(u_j)$.

*Proof.* During the initialization phase, for each user $u$ in the system, the algorithm creates a unique vertex $v$ and assigns $\{u\}$ to $v.acl$. Since the algorithm never removes vertices from the graph, when the algorithm calls procedure **GenerateEncryptionPolicy** the graph contains one vertex for each user. Also, since we assume that procedure **GenerateEncryptionPolicy** correctly generates keys (i.e., avoiding duplicates), at each iteration of the first **for** loop the procedure assigns a unique key and a unique label to each vertex $v$ in the graph, and therefore also to vertices representing singleton sets of users. The key assignment and encryption schema function $\phi$ is then defined based on the keys associated with the vertices representing singleton sets of users. For each user $u$, the procedure sets $\phi(u)$ to $v.key$, where $v$ is the unique vertex in the graph such that $v.acl=\{u\}$. Consequently, we have the guarantee that different users are associated with different labels and, also, with different keys.

We also need to prove that both Theorem 3.2 and Definition 3.10 are satisfied by the encryption policy graph generated by the algorithm in Fig. 3.6.

**Lemma 3.2 (Local cover and non-redundancy).** *Given an authorization policy $\mathscr{A}=\langle \mathscr{U},\mathscr{O},\mathscr{P}\rangle$, the algorithm in Fig. 3.6 creates a key and token graph $\mathscr{G}_{\mathscr{K},\mathscr{T}}=\langle V_{\mathscr{K},\mathscr{T}},E_{\mathscr{K},\mathscr{T}}\rangle$ and the corresponding encryption policy $\mathscr{E}=\langle \mathscr{U},\mathscr{O},\mathscr{K},\mathscr{L},\phi,\mathscr{T}\rangle$ such that $\mathscr{G}_{\mathscr{E}}$ satisfies local cover (Theorem 3.2) and is non redundant (Definition 3.10).*

*Proof.* We first prove that procedure **CoverVertex**($v$,*tocover*) terminates and grants both Theorem 3.2 and Definition 3.10. Then, we prove that procedure **Factorize**($v_i$) terminates and preserves both local cover and non redundancy with respect to vertex $v$.

During the initialization phase, for each material vertex $v$ created, the algorithm sets variable $v.counter[u]$ to 0 for each user $u$ in $v.acl$.

Procedure **CoverVertex**.    For each material vertex $v_i$ in $V_{\mathscr{K},\mathscr{T}}$ the algorithm calls procedure **CoverVertex** with $v_i$ and $v_i.acl$ as parameters, respectively.
The procedure is composed of two phases: the first phase finds a correct cover for $v$, and the second removes redundant edges.
The first phase is composed of two nested **while** loops that in the worst case terminate when variable *tocover* is empty. Variable *tocover* initially contains users in $v.acl$ and no user is inserted in *tocover* by the procedure. Also, the set of users in $v_i.acl$, where vertex $v_i$ is randomly extracted from the set $V_l$ of vertices at level $l$ such that $v_i.acl\subseteq v.acl$, is removed from *tocover* only if $v_i.acl\cap tocover\neq\emptyset$. Since $l$ is decreased by one at each iteration of the outermost **while** loop, $l$ assumes also the value 1. When $l$ becomes 1, $V_l$ contains the set of vertices $v_i$ in $V_{\mathscr{K},\mathscr{T}}$ such that $v_i.acl=\{u_i\}$, for all $u_i$ in $\mathscr{U}$. Since $v.acl\subseteq\mathscr{U}$, in the worst case *tocover* becomes empty when $l=1$ and the two **while** loops terminate. Since any time $v_i.acl$ is removed from *tocover* an edge $(v_i,v)$ is inserted in *Eadded* (and consequently in $E_{\mathscr{K},\mathscr{T}}$), when the two loops terminate (i.e., *tocover* becomes empty) vertex $v$ is correctly covered. Indeed, for each user $u$ in $v.acl$ there exists an edge $(v_i,v)$ such that $u$ belongs to $v_i.acl$. Also, for each edge $(v_i,v)$ inserted in *Eadded*,

$v.counter[u]$ is increased by one for each $u$ in $v_i.acl$, meaning that $v.counter[u]$ represents the number of edges $(v_i,v)$ in *Eadded* such that $u$ belongs to $v_i.acl$.

The second phase is composed of a **for each** loop that processes each edge $(v_i,v)$ in *Eadded*. Since the first phase of the procedure terminates, *Eadded* contains a finite number of edges and also this second phase terminates. Edge $(v_i,v)$ is removed from *Eadded* (and therefore not inserted in $E_{\mathcal{K},\mathcal{T}}$) only if $v.counter[u]$ is greater than 1 for each user $u$ belonging to $v_i.acl$, since there is at least another direct ancestor $v_j$ of $v$ (besides $v_i$) such that $u$ belongs to $v_j.acl$. When $(v_i,v)$ is removed from *Eadded*, $v.counter[u]$ is decreased by one for each user $u$ belonging to $v_i.acl$, to keep $v.counter[u]$ consistent with edges in *Eadded*. Since edge $(v_i,v)$ is not removed if $v.counter[u]$ is equal to 1 for at least a user, local cover of vertex $v$ is preserved. Also, since all edges incoming in $v$ belong to *Eadded* and each edge in *Eadded* is evaluated by the procedure, Definition 3.10 is satisfied for $v$.

Finally, *Eadded* is inserted in $E_{\mathcal{K},\mathcal{T}}$, which were empty. Therefore both local cover and non redundancy are satisfied for vertex $v$.

Procedure **Factorize**.   For each material vertex $v_i$ in $V_{\mathcal{K},\mathcal{T}}$ the algorithm calls procedure **Factorize** with $v_i$ as parameter.

The first **for each** loop composing the procedure evaluates each vertex $v_j$ in $V_{\mathcal{K},\mathcal{T}}$ having at least a common direct ancestor with $v_i$. Also, the nested **for each** loops process each vertex $v_a$ in the set *CommonAnc* of the direct ancestors common to $v_i$ and $v_j$. Since the number of vertices in $V_{\mathcal{K},\mathcal{T}}$ and then also in *CommonAnc* is finite, the loops terminates. Analogously, the **for each** loops operating on *Eadded* and *Eremoved* sets of edges terminate, since both *Eadded* and *Eremoved* are initially set to the empty set and the finite **for each** loops on vertices in *CommonAnc* insert edges in the two sets. Given a pair of vertices $v_i$ and $v_j$, procedure **Factorize** changes the set of direct ancestors of $v_i$ and $v_j$ iff they have at least three or more common ancestors. In this case, the edges from the common ancestors, say $v_1,\ldots,v_m$, to $v_i$ and $v_j$ are removed and replaced by two edges from $v'$ to $v_i$ and $v_j$, where $v'$ is a vertex such that $v'.acl = v_1.acl \cup \ldots \cup v_m.acl$. It immediately follows that local cover, limited to vertices $v_i$ and $v_j$, is satisfied. The same observation applies to vertex $v'$, which is covered by $v_1,\ldots,v_m$ that, by definition, form a cover for $v'$. Note that the same discussion applies when vertex $v'$ coincides with $v_i$ or $v_j$.

We note here that variables $v.counter[u]$ are updated according to inserted and removed edges.

We conclude that, since both **CoverVertex** and **Factorize** procedures are called on each vertex $v$ in $V_{\mathcal{K},\mathcal{T}}$, $\mathcal{G}_{\mathcal{E}}$ satisfies both Theorem 3.2 and Definition 3.10.

By combining the results proved in Lemma 3.1 and in Lemma 3.2, we can conclude that the encryption policy generated by the algorithm in Fig. 3.6 is equivalent to a given authorization policy.

**Theorem 3.3 (Policy   equivalence).**   *Given   an   authorization   policy* $\mathscr{A} = \langle \mathscr{U},\mathscr{O},\mathscr{P} \rangle$, *the   algorithm   in   Fig.   3.6   creates   a   key   and   token*

graph   $\mathcal{G}_{\mathcal{K},\mathcal{T}}=\langle V_{\mathcal{K},\mathcal{T}},E_{\mathcal{K},\mathcal{T}}\rangle$   and   the   corresponding   encryption   policy
$\mathcal{E}=\langle \mathcal{U},\mathcal{O},\mathcal{K},\mathcal{L},\phi,\mathcal{T}\rangle$ such that $\mathcal{A}\equiv\mathcal{E}$.

*Proof.*

$\mathcal{E}\Longrightarrow\mathcal{A}$

Procedure **GenerateEncryptionPolicy** defines an encryption policy $\mathcal{E}$ that is
based on the key and token graph created by the first two phases of the algorithm
in Fig. 3.6. In particular, the procedure defines an encryption policy such that:
for each user $u$, $\phi(u)$ corresponds to the label of vertex $v_i$ representing the
singleton set $\{u\}$ (i.e., $v_i.acl=\{u\}$); and for each object $o$, $\phi(o)$ corresponds to
the label of vertex $v_j$ representing $acl(o)$ (i.e., $v_j.acl=acl(o)$). Consider now
the encryption policy graph corresponding to the encryption policy $\mathcal{E}$ created
by procedure **GenerateEncryptionPolicy**, and suppose that $u\overset{\mathcal{E}}{\longrightarrow}o$. This is
equivalent to say that the key and token graph includes a path from the vertex $v$
with label equal to $\phi(u)$ to the vertex $v_j$ with label equal to $\phi(o)$. Also, since the
key and token graph satisfies Theorem 3.2 (Lemma 3.2), we know that $u$ belongs
to $v_j.acl=acl(o)$ and therefore the authorization policy $\mathcal{A}$ includes permission
$\langle u,o\rangle$.

$\mathcal{E}\Longleftarrow\mathcal{A}$

Suppose that $u\overset{\mathcal{A}}{\longrightarrow}o$. During the initialization phase, the algorithm inserts in the
key and token graph a vertex for each users in the systems and for each *acl* value
for the objects in the systems. Therefore, there is a material vertex $v_i$ such that
$v_i.acl=\{u\}$, and there is a material vertex $v_j$ such that $v_j.acl=acl(o)$ in the key
and token graph. Since the algorithm never removes vertices and it creates a key
and token graph that satisfies Theorem 3.2 (Lemma 3.2), it is immediate to conclude that the key and token graph includes a path from $v_i$ to $v_j$ and that the encryption policy graph obtained by defining an encryption policy complementing
the key and token graph, generated by procedure **GenerateEncryptionPolicy**,
includes a path from $u$ to $o$.

The following theorem proves that the encryption policy generated by the algorithm in Fig. 3.6 presents a total number of keys and tokens that is less than
the number of users, resources, and permissions composing a given authorization
policy, thus greatly reducing the overhead on the users in deriving the keys of the
resources they are entitled to access (as also the experiments in Sect. 3.10 show).

**Theorem 3.4.** *Given an authorization policy $\mathcal{A}=\langle\mathcal{U},\mathcal{O},\mathcal{P}\rangle$, the algorithm in
Fig. 3.6 creates a key and token graph $\mathcal{G}_{\mathcal{K},\mathcal{T}}=\langle V_{\mathcal{K},\mathcal{T}},E_{\mathcal{K},\mathcal{T}}\rangle$ and the correspond-
ing encryption policy $\mathcal{E}=\langle\mathcal{U},\mathcal{O},\mathcal{K},\mathcal{L},\phi,\mathcal{T}\rangle$ such that $|\mathcal{K}\cup\mathcal{T}|<|\mathcal{U}\cup\mathcal{O}\cup\mathcal{P}|$.*

*Proof.* Since all the sets involved in the union operations are disjoint, we need to
prove that $|\mathcal{K}|+|\mathcal{T}|<|\mathcal{U}|+|\mathcal{O}|+|\mathcal{P}|$.

The number of keys created by the algorithm is equal to the number of vertices in
the key and token graph while the number of tokens is equal to the number of edges.
With respect to the vertices, the algorithm creates a vertex for each user in $\mathcal{U}$, for

each *acl* associated with objects in $\mathcal{O}$, plus some additional vertices inserted during
Phase 2. Since two or more objects may share the same *acl*, it is easy to see that what
we need to prove is that the number of vertices inserted in Phase 2 plus the number
of tokens is less than the number of permissions. First, consider the graph created
after Phase 1, where there is no additional vertex besides the material vertices. In
this case, it is easy to see that the number of edges (i.e., tokens) in the graph is less
than the number of permissions. Indeed, if there are *m* objects that share the same
*acl* that is composed by *n* users, the graph will include *n* tokens instead of $n \cdot m$
tokens. Consider now Phase 2. Here, procedure **Factorize** adds a vertex iff the pair
of vertices currently analyzed have $n > 2$ common parents. In this case, $2 \cdot n$ edges
are removed from the graph and at most $n + 2$ edges are inserted. This means that at
least the number of tokens in the catalog decreases by one and therefore the number
of additional vertices plus the number of tokens remains lower than the number of
permissions.

Finally, we prove that the time complexity of the proposed algorithm is polynomial in time.

**Theorem 3.5 (Complexity).** *Given an authorization policy $\mathcal{A} = \langle \mathcal{U}, \mathcal{O}, \mathcal{P} \rangle$, the
algorithm in Fig. 3.6 generates an encryption policy $\mathcal{E} = \langle \mathcal{U}, \mathcal{O}, \mathcal{K}, \mathcal{L}, \phi, \mathcal{T} \rangle$, with
$\mathcal{A} \equiv \mathcal{E}$, in $O((|\mathcal{O}| + |V_{\mathcal{K},\mathcal{T}}|^2) \cdot |\mathcal{U}|)$.*

*Proof.* The complexity of the algorithm is obtained by evaluating the complexity of
the operations performed during the initialization and of the two phases composing
it.

Initialization.   The **for** loop composing the initialization phase requires time
   proportional to $|\mathcal{U}| + |\mathcal{O}| \cdot |\mathcal{U}|$, since the inner most **for** loop has constant
   cost for vertices representing singleton sets of users.

Phase 1.   The algorithm calls procedure **CoverVertex** for each material vertex $v$
   in $V_{\mathcal{K},\mathcal{T}}$. In the worst case, the two nested **while** loops check all vertices $v_i$
   in $V_{\mathcal{K},\mathcal{T}}$ such that $level(v_i) < level(v)$, with a computational cost proportional to
   $|V_{\mathcal{K},\mathcal{T}}|^2 \cdot |\mathcal{U}|$.
   The following **for each** loop checks each edge $(v_i, v) \in Eadded$ and evaluates
   and possibly updates the value of variable $v.counter[u]$ for each $u$ belonging to
   $acl(v_i)$. In the worst case, the cost of this loop is proportional to $|E_{\mathcal{K},\mathcal{T}}| \cdot |\mathcal{U}|$.
   Since $|E_{\mathcal{K},\mathcal{T}}|$ is upperbounded by $|V_{\mathcal{K},\mathcal{T}}|^2$ in any graph, the overall complexity
   of the first phase of the algorithm is proportional to $|V_{\mathcal{K},\mathcal{T}}|^2 \cdot |\mathcal{U}|$.

Phase 2.   The algorithm calls procedure **Factorize** for each vertex $v_i$ in $V_{\mathcal{K},\mathcal{T}}$. The
   first **for each** loop checks all vertices with at least a common ancestor with $v_i$,
   which in the worst case are all vertices in $V_{\mathcal{K},\mathcal{T}}$. The procedure then finds the
   common direct ancestors by considering the edges incident in $v_i$ and $v_j$. Since
   the maximum number of direct ancestors of a vertex $v_i$ is equal to $|v_i.acl|$, the
   costs of this operation is proportional to $|\mathcal{U}|$. The **for each** loops nested in the
   **case** instruction evaluate all the vertices in *CommonAnc*, which are at most $|\mathcal{U}|$.

Since both *Eadded* and *Eremoved* are filled in by these loops, they contain a number of elements linear in $|\mathcal{U}|$.

The overall complexity of the second phase of the algorithm is therefore proportional to $|V_{\mathcal{K},\mathcal{T}}|^2 \cdot |\mathcal{U}|$.

Phase 3.  The algorithm finally calls procedure **GenerateEncryptionPolicy**, which is composed of four **for each** loops, checking vertices, edges, users, and objects in the order.

The overall complexity of the third phase of the algorithm is therefore proportional to $|V_{\mathcal{K},\mathcal{T}}|^2 + |\mathcal{U}| + |\mathcal{O}|$.

Overall, the time complexity is proportional to $(|\mathcal{O}| + |V_{\mathcal{K},\mathcal{T}}|^2) \cdot |\mathcal{U}|$. If we assume that all operations performed by procedures **CoverVertex**, **Factorize** and **GenerateEncryptionPolicy** have a constant cost and $c_{max}$ is the maximum cost, the time complexity is in $O(c_{max}((|\mathcal{O}| + |V_{\mathcal{K},\mathcal{T}}|^2) \cdot |\mathcal{U}|)) = O((|\mathcal{O}| + |V_{\mathcal{K},\mathcal{T}}|^2) \cdot |\mathcal{U}|)$.

## 3.6 Policy Updates

Since the authorization policy is likely to change over time, the corresponding encryption policy needs to be re-arranged accordingly. The possible policy update operations are: *1)* insertion/deletion of a user; *2)* insertion/deletion of an object; and *3)* grant/revoke of an permission. We note that the insertion/deletion of users has an impact on the encryption policy only when the user gains permissions. In this case, inserting (deleting, resp.) a user implies granting (revoking, resp.) all the permissions in which the user is involved. Analogously, the insertion/deletion of objects has an impact on the encryption policy only when the object is made accessible to users. Therefore, inserting (deleting, resp.) an object implies granting (revoking, resp.) all the permissions in which the object is involved. For this reason, we focus on the grant and revoke operations. Also, we assume that each operation always refers to a single user $u$ and a single object $o$; extension to sets of users and objects is immediate.

The grant and revoke operations on the authorization policy $\mathcal{A}$ are translated into operations that appropriately update the encryption policy graph, to guarantee that $\mathcal{E}$ is equivalent to $\mathcal{A}$ also after grant/revoke operations. Creating from scratch the encryption policy graph any time a grant or revoke operation is executed obviously grants policy equivalence, but is too expensive, since it requires to re-generate the whole set of keys and tokens and to re-encrypt all the objects in the system. Therefore, we propose a strategy that updates the existing encryption policy graph, changing only the portions of the graph that are affected by the grant or revoke operation.

---

**GRANTREVOKE**($u$,$o$,*operation*)
/* update the access control list of $o$ */
find the vertex $v_{old}$ with $v_{old}.label = \phi(o)$
**case** *operation* **of**
    'grant': $acl(o) := v_{old}.acl \cup \{u\}$
    'revoke':$acl(o) := v_{old}.acl \setminus \{u\}$
find the vertex $v_{new}$ with $v_{new}.acl = acl(o)$
**if** $v_{new}$=UNDEF **then**
    $v_{new} := $ **CreateNewVertex**($acl(o)$)
$\phi(o) := v_{new}.label$
/* re-encrypt object $o$ */
download the encrypted version $o^k$ of $o$ from the server
decrypt $o^k$ with key $v_{old}.key$ to retrieve the original object $o$
encrypt $o$ with key $v_{new}.key$
upload the new encrypted version $o^k$ of $o$ on the server
update LABELS on the server
**DeleteVertex**($v_{old}$)

---

**Fig. 3.11**  Procedure for granting or revoking permission $\langle u,o \rangle$

### 3.6.1  Grant and Revoke

Any grant/revoke request for a user $u$ on an object $o$ has the effect of changing the set of users that can access $o$ and always requires the data owner to decrypt and to re-encrypt the object with a new key that should be (directly or indirectly) derivable only by the users that belong to the new access control list. Figure 3.11 illustrates procedure **GrantRevoke** that implements both grant and revoke operations. The procedure takes as input a user $u$, an object $o$, and the type of operation that has to be executed, which can be either 'grant' or 'revoke', and modifies the encryption policy accordingly. First, the procedure retrieves vertex $v_{old}$ whose *acl* corresponds to the current *acl* of $o$ and sets $acl(o)$ to the old *acl* to which is added (grant) or removed (revoke) user $u$. Since, according to our approach (see Sect. 3.4), each object has to be encrypted with the key associated with the vertex that represents its *acl*, the procedure checks the existence of a vertex $v_{new}$ in the encryption policy graph representing the new value of $acl(o)$. If such a vertex does not exist, vertex $v_{new}$ is created and inserted in the graph (procedure **CreateNewVertex**). The procedure then downloads the object from the server, decrypts it through $v_{old}.key$, re-encrypts it through $v_{new}.key$, and uploads the new encrypted version of $o$ on the server. Finally, the procedure calls **DeleteVertex** on vertex $v_{old}$ that checks if vertex $v_{old}$ is still needed or if it can be removed from the graph.

The insertion and removal of vertices in the encryption policy graph are realized through function **CreateNewVertex** in Fig. 3.12 and procedure **DeleteVertex** in Fig. 3.13. Note that function **CreateNewVertex** and procedure **DeleteVertex** are based on the same operations (i.e., **CoverVertex** and **Factorize**) used by the algorithm in Fig. 3.6 for initially creating the encryption policy graph, but they operate locally to the vertex inserted in or removed from the graph.

Function **CreateNewVertex** receives as input a set $U$ of users and returns the vertex $v$ inserted in the graph and representing $U$. The function first copies the current sets $V_{\mathcal{K},\mathcal{T}}$ of vertices and $E_{\mathcal{K},\mathcal{T}}$ of edges in two local variables $V_0$ and $E_0$,

**CREATENEWVERTEX**($U$)
/* initial key and token graph vertices and edges */
$V_0 := V_{\mathcal{K},\mathcal{T}}$
$E_0 := E_{\mathcal{K},\mathcal{T}}$
/* create the new vertex */
create vertex $v$
$v.acl := U$
$v.key :=$ NULL
$v.label :=$ NULL
**for each** $u \in v.acl$ **do** $v.counter[u] := 0$
/* connect $v$, remove redundancies, and factorize common ancestors */
**CoverVertex**($v$,$v.acl$)
**Factorize**($v$)
/* update encryption policy */
**UpdateEncryptionPolicy**($V_0$,$E_0$)
**for each** $v_i \in \{v_j : (v_j,v_h) \in (E_0 \setminus E_{\mathcal{K},\mathcal{T}})\}$ **do**
   **DeleteVertex**($v_i$)
**return**($v$)

**Fig. 3.12** Function that inserts a new vertex representing $U$

**DELETEVERTEX**($v$)
**if** $(|v.acl| > 1) \wedge (\not\exists o \in \mathcal{O} : \phi(o) = v.label)$ **then**
  /* direct ancestors and descendants of $v$ */
  $Anc := \{v_i : (v_i,v) \in E_{\mathcal{K},\mathcal{T}}\}$
  $Desc := \{v_i : (v,v_i) \in E_{\mathcal{K},\mathcal{T}}\}$
  **if** $(|Desc| \cdot |Anc|) \leq (|Desc| + |Anc|)$ **then**
    /* initial key and token graph vertices and edges */
    $V_0 := V_{\mathcal{K},\mathcal{T}}$
    $E_0 := E_{\mathcal{K},\mathcal{T}}$
    /* update the key and token graph */
    $E_{\mathcal{K},\mathcal{T}} := E_{\mathcal{K},\mathcal{T}} \setminus (\{(v,v_i) \in E_{\mathcal{K},\mathcal{T}}\} \cup \{(v_i,v) \in E_{\mathcal{K},\mathcal{T}}\})$
    **for each** $(v,v_i) \in E_0$ **do**
      **for each** $u \in v.acl$ **do**
        $v_i.counter[u] := v_i.counter[u] - 1$
      $tocover := \{u : u \in v_i.acl \wedge v_i.counter[u] = 0\}$
      **CoverVertex**($v_i$,$tocover$)
      **Factorize**($v_i$)
    $V_{\mathcal{K},\mathcal{T}} := V_{\mathcal{K},\mathcal{T}} - \{v\}$
    /* update encryption policy */
    **UpdateEncryptionPolicy**($V_0$,$E_0$)
    **for each** $v_i \in \{v_j : (v_j,v_h) \in (E_0 \setminus E_{\mathcal{K},\mathcal{T}})\}$ **do**
      **DeleteVertex**($v_i$)

**Fig. 3.13** Procedure for deleting vertex $v$

respectively. This copy is needed to determine the updates in the set of vertices and edges in the graph in such a way to modify the encryption policy accordingly. Indeed, the presence of a new vertex requires the generation of a new key and label and the removal of a vertex requires the deletion of the corresponding key and label. Analogously, a new edge requires the generation of the corresponding token, which is then stored in table TOKENS, and the removal of an edge requires the deletion of the corresponding token from table TOKENS. Function **CreateNewVertex** creates a new vertex $v$ whose variable $v.acl$ is set to $U$ while $v.key$ and $v.label$ are both set to NULL. This new vertex is appropriately covered by other vertices in the graph by calling: procedure **CoverVertex** on $v$ and $v.acl$, thus ensuring that the vertex is inserted without introducing redundant edges and in such a way that local cover

---

**UPDATEENCRYPTIONPOLICY**($V,E$)
**for each** $v \in (V_{\mathcal{K},\mathcal{T}} \setminus V)$ **do** /* new vertices */
    generate key $k$
    $v.key := k$
    generate label $l$
    $v.label := l$
    $\mathcal{K} := \mathcal{K} \cup \{v.key\}$
    $\mathcal{L} := \mathcal{L} \cup \{v.label\}$
**for each** $(v_i,v_j) \in (E_{\mathcal{K},\mathcal{T}} \setminus E)$ **do** /* new edges */
    $t_{i,j} := v_j.key \oplus h(v_i.key, v_j.label)$
    $\mathcal{T} := \mathcal{T} \cup \{t_{i,j}\}$
    upload token $t_{i,j}$ on the server by adding it to table TOKENS
**for each** $v \in (V \setminus V_{\mathcal{K},\mathcal{T}})$ **do** /* vertices removed */
    $\mathcal{K} := \mathcal{K} \setminus \{v.key\}$
    $\mathcal{L} := \mathcal{L} \setminus \{v.label\}$
**for each** $(v_i,v_j) \in (E \setminus E_{\mathcal{K},\mathcal{T}})$ **do** /* edges removed */
    $\mathcal{T} := \mathcal{T} \setminus \{t_{i,j}\}$
    remove $t_{i,j}$ from the table TOKENS on the server

---

**Fig. 3.14** Procedure for updating the encryption policy

(Theorem 3.2) is satisfied; and procedure **Factorize**, which determines whether the new vertex has more than two direct ancestors in common with other vertices in the graph. Function **CreateNewVertex** then calls procedure **UpdateEncryptionPolicy** in Fig. 3.14. This procedure takes as input the copies of the old sets of vertices and edges stored in $V_0$ and $E_0$, respectively, and updates the encryption policy by generating and adding the new keys and labels associated with the new vertices, by computing and adding the new tokens corresponding to the new edges, and by removing the keys, labels, and tokens that are not anymore needed. Finally, for each vertex $v_i$ that appears as starting point of a removed edge, **CreateNewVertex** calls procedure **DeleteVertex** to check whether vertex $v_i$ can be removed from the graph. Note that we do not call procedure **DeleteVertex** on the vertices appearing as ending point of removed edges since, by definition, they correspond to material vertices or have at least two incoming edges and therefore are always useful (or, in the worst case, ineffective) for reducing the number of tokens in the encryption policy graph.

Procedure **DeleteVertex** receives as input a vertex $v$ and removes it from the graph if it is neither necessary for policy enforcement nor useful for reducing the size of $\mathcal{T}$. Indeed, if the key associated with $v$ is no more used for encrypting any object and is no more needed for factorizing common ancestors, vertex $v$ and all its ingoing and outgoing edges are removed. At this point, the direct descendants of $v$ violate the local cover property since, by construction (see Lemma 3.2), the graph has no redundant edges and therefore the removed edge was need to satisfy such a property. For each direct descendant $v_i$, procedure **DeleteVertex** first calls procedure **CoverVertex** on $v_i$ and on the set of users that do not belong to any other ancestor of $v_i$, and then calls procedure **Factorize** on $v_i$. Like for procedure **CreateNewVertex**, the encryption policy is appropriately updated through procedure **UpdateEncryptionPolicy**. Finally, for each vertex $v_i$ that appears as a starting point of a removed edge, **DeleteVertex** recursively calls itself to check whether or not vertex $v_i$ can be removed from the graph.

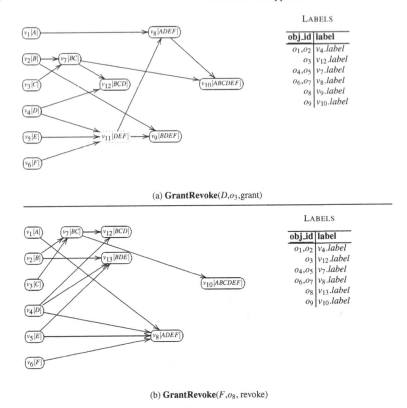

(a) **GrantRevoke**($D,o_3$,grant)

(b) **GrantRevoke**($F,o_8$, revoke)

**Fig. 3.15** Examples of grant and revoke operations

*Example 3.2.* Consider the encryption policy depicted in Fig. 3.10($b$) and ($c$). Figure 3.15 illustrates the key and token graph and table LABELS resulting from granting $D$ access to $o_3$ and revoking $F$ access to $o_8$. (Note that for all users $u$ in $\mathcal{U}$, we do not report $\phi(u)$ since grant/revoke operations do not change it.)

- **GrantRevoke**($D,o_3$,grant): first the procedure identifies the vertex whose key is necessary for decrypting $o_3$, that is, $v_7$. Then, $acl(o_3)$ is updated by inserting $D$. Since there is not a vertex with $acl=\{BCD\}$, procedure **CreateNewVertex** is called with $U=\{BCD\}$ as a parameter. It creates and inserts in the graph a new vertex $v_{12}$, where $v_{12}.acl=\{BCD\}$. Then, $o_3$ is downloaded from the server, decrypted through $v_7.key$, encrypted with $v_{12}.key$, and then uploaded on the server. Finally, procedure **DeleteVertex** is called with $v_7$ as a parameter and, since $v_7.key$ is used to encrypt $o_4$ and $o_5$, vertex $v_7$ is not removed from the graph.
- **GrantRevoke**($F,o_8$,revoke): first the procedure identifies the vertex whose key is necessary for decrypting $o_8$, that is, $v_9$. Then, $acl(o_8)$ is updated by removing $F$. Since there is not a vertex with $acl=\{BDE\}$, procedure **CreateNewVertex** is called with $U=\{BDE\}$ as a parameter. It creates and inserts in the graph a new

vertex $v_{13}$, where $v_{13}.acl=\{BDE\}$. Then, $o_8$ is downloaded from the server, decrypted through $v_9.key$, encrypted with $v_{13}.key$, and uploaded on the server. Then, procedure **DeleteVertex** is called with $v_9$ as a parameter. Since $v_9.key$ was only used for encrypting $o_8$, $v_9$ is no more a useful vertex and is removed from the graph. The procedure recursively calls itself with $v_2$ and with $v_{11}$ as a parameter. Vertex $v_2$ is not removed since it corresponds to user $B$ while vertex $v_{11}$ is removed from the graph.

### 3.6.2 Correctness

We now prove that the procedure implementing the grant and revoke operations preserves policy equivalence. To this aim, we first need to show that both vertex insertion and deletion are correct (i.e., they preserve policy equivalence).

First, we prove that the updates to the encryption policy graph made by procedure **DeleteVertex** do not affect policy equivalence.

**Lemma 3.3.** *Let* $\mathscr{A} = \langle \mathscr{U}, \mathscr{O}, \mathscr{P} \rangle$ *be an authorization policy and* $\mathscr{E} = \langle \mathscr{U}, \mathscr{O}, \mathscr{K}, \mathscr{L}, \phi, \mathscr{T} \rangle$ *be an encryption policy, such that* $\mathscr{A} \equiv \mathscr{E}$. *Procedure* **DeleteVertex** *in Fig. 3.13 generates a new encryption policy* $\mathscr{E}' = \langle \mathscr{U}, \mathscr{O}, \mathscr{K}', \mathscr{L}', \phi', \mathscr{T}' \rangle$ *such that* $\mathscr{A} \equiv \mathscr{E}'$.

*Proof.* Since we assume that $\mathscr{A} \equiv \mathscr{E}$ when procedure **DeleteVertex** is called, we will consider only keys and tokens updated by the procedure. Specifically, as already noted when proving Theorem 3.3, the conditions necessary for granting policy equivalence between $\mathscr{A}$ and $\mathscr{E}$ are the following:

1. for each user $u$, $\phi(u)$ corresponds to the label of vertex $v_i$ representing the singleton set $\{u\}$ (i.e., $v_i.acl = \{u\}$);
2. for each object $o$, $\phi(o)$ corresponds to the label of vertex $v_j$ representing $acl(o)$ (i.e., $v_j.acl = acl(o)$);
3. the key and token graph satisfies Theorem 3.2 (local cover) and Definition 3.10 (non redundancy).

We then prove that procedure **DeleteVertex** satisfies all these conditions.

Procedure **DeleteVertex** does not modify the key assignment and encryption schema and does not remove a vertex $v$ if there exists a user $u$ or an object $o$ such that $\phi(u)=v.label$ or $\phi(o)=v.label$. Therefore the first and second conditions are satisfied.

For each descendant $v_i$ of the removed vertex $v$, procedure **DeleteVertex** calls procedures **CoverVertex** on $v_i$ and *tocover*, where *tocover* contains the subset of users in $v_i.acl$ such that $v_i.counter[u]=0$. Since $v_i.counter[u]$ always represents the number of direct ancestors of $v_i$ such that $u$ belongs to their $acl$, it is not necessary to cover other users. Also, variables $v.counter[u]$ are updated on the basis of the edges incident in $v$ removed from the graph. Procedure **UpdateEncryptionPolicy** simply translates the updates on $\mathcal{G}_{\mathcal{K},\mathcal{T}}$ in the equivalent updates on $\mathcal{E}$ components, therefore local cover and non redundancy are preserved by procedure **DeleteVertex**.

We then prove that also the updates to the encryption policy graph made by procedure **CreateNewVertex** do not affect policy equivalence.

**Lemma 3.4.** *Let* $\mathcal{A} = \langle \mathcal{U}, \mathcal{O}, \mathcal{P} \rangle$ *be an authorization policy and* $\mathcal{E} = \langle \mathcal{U}, \mathcal{O}, \mathcal{K}, \mathcal{L}, \phi, \mathcal{T} \rangle$ *be an encryption policy, such that* $\mathcal{A} \equiv \mathcal{E}$. *Function* **CreateNewVertex** *in Fig. 3.12 generates a new encryption policy* $\mathcal{E}' = \langle \mathcal{U}, \mathcal{O}, \mathcal{K}', \mathcal{L}', \phi', \mathcal{T}' \rangle$ *such that* $\mathcal{A} \equiv \mathcal{E}'$.

*Proof.* Since we assume that $\mathcal{A} \equiv \mathcal{E}$ when function **CreateNewVertex** is called, we will consider only keys and tokens updated by the function. We then prove that function **CreateNewVertex** satisfies all the conditions mentioned in the Proof of Lemma 3.3.

Function **CreateNewVertex** does not modify the key assignment and encryption function and removes vertices only through procedure **DeleteVertex**, therefore the first and the second conditions are satisfied.

Also, function **CreateNewVertex** calls procedures **CoverVertex** and **Factorize** on the new vertex $v$, granting then that the key and token graph satisfies Theorem 3.2 and Definition 3.10 (Lemma 3.2). Procedure **UpdateEncryptionPolicy** simply translates the updates on $\mathcal{G}_{\mathcal{K},\mathcal{T}}$ in the equivalent updates on $\mathcal{E}$ components, therefore the two properties are preserved by function **CreateNewVertex**.

By combining the results proved by Lemma 3.3 and by Lemma 3.4, we conclude that the encryption policy modified by procedure **GrantRevoke** in Fig. 3.11 is equivalent to the authorization policy modified by the same procedure, on the basis of a grant or revoke operation.

**Theorem 3.6.** *Let* $\mathcal{A} = \langle \mathcal{U}, \mathcal{O}, \mathcal{P} \rangle$ *be an authorization policy and* $\mathcal{E} = \langle \mathcal{U}, \mathcal{O}, \mathcal{K}, \mathcal{L}, \phi, \mathcal{T} \rangle$ *be an encryption policy, such that* $\mathcal{A} \equiv \mathcal{E}$. *Procedure* **GrantRevoke** *in Fig. 3.11 generates a new authorization policy* $\mathcal{A}' = \langle \mathcal{U}, \mathcal{O}, \mathcal{P}' \rangle$ *and a new encryption policy* $\mathcal{E}' = \langle \mathcal{U}, \mathcal{O}, \mathcal{K}', \mathcal{L}', \phi', \mathcal{T}' \rangle$ *such that* $\mathcal{A}' \equiv \mathcal{E}'$.

*Proof.* Since we assume that $\mathcal{A} \equiv \mathcal{E}$ when procedure **GrantRevoke** is called, we will consider only users and objects for which the encryption and authorization policies change.

Grant.    $\mathcal{E}' \Longrightarrow \mathcal{A}'$

   Consider user $u$ and object $o$. From the procedure, it is easy to see that $o$ is encrypted with a key such that from the key of the vertex with label $\phi'(u)$ it is possible to derive the key of the vertex with label $\phi'(o)$ through $\mathcal{T}'$, since $\phi'(o)$ is set to $v_{new}.key$, which can be reached from vertex $v$ with $v.acl = \{u\}$ (for the correctness of function **CreateNewVertex**, Lemma 3.4). Therefore, we have that $u \xrightarrow{\mathcal{A}'} o$.

   $\mathcal{E}' \Longleftarrow \mathcal{A}'$

Consider user $u$ and object $o$. From the insertion of $u$ in $acl(o)$, we have that $u \xrightarrow{\mathscr{A}'} o$. Also, $o$ is encrypted with a key such that the key of the vertex with label $\phi'(o)$ can be derived from the key of the vertex with label $\phi'(u)$, for the correctness of function **CreateNewVertex** (Lemma 3.4). Therefore, we have that $u \xrightarrow{\mathscr{E}'} o$.

Revoke.  $\mathscr{E}' \Longrightarrow \mathscr{A}'$

Consider user $u$ and object $o$. From the procedure, it is easy to see that $o$ is encrypted with a key such that from the key of the vertex with label $\phi'(u)$ it is not possible to derive the key of the vertex with label $\phi'(o)$ through $\mathscr{T}'$, since $\phi'(o)$ is set to $v_{new}.key$, which can not be reached from vertex $v$ with $v.acl=\{u\}$ (for the correctness of procedure **DeleteVertex**, Lemma 3.3). Therefore, we have that $u \xnrightarrow{\mathscr{A}'} o$.

$\mathscr{E}' \Longleftarrow \mathscr{A}'$

Consider user $u$ and object $o$. From the removal of $u$ from $acl(o)$, we have that $u \xnrightarrow{\mathscr{A}'} o$. Also, $o$ is encrypted with a key such that the key of the vertex with label $\phi'(o)$ can not be derived from the key of the vertex with label $\phi'(u)$, for the correctness of procedure **DeleteVertex** (Lemma 3.3). Therefore, we have that $u \xnrightarrow{\mathscr{E}'} o$.

## 3.7 Two-Layer Encryption for Policy Outsourcing

The model described in previous sections assumes keys and tokens are computed, on the basis of the existing authorization policy, prior to sending the encrypted objects to the server. When permissions are updated by the data owner, as described in Sect. 3.8, the data owner interacts with the service provider for modifying the token catalog and for re-encrypting the objects involved in the update. Even if the computation and communication overhead caused by policy updates is limited, the data owner may not have the computational or bandwidth resource availability for managing policy changes.

To further reduce the data owner's overhead, we put forward the idea of outsourcing to the server, besides the object storage, the authorization management as well. Note that this delegation is possible since the server is considered trustworthy to properly carry out the service. Recall, however, that the server is not trusted with confidentiality (honest-but-curious). For this reason, our solution has been designed taking into account, and therefore minimizing, the risk that the server colludes with users to breach data confidentiality (see Sect. 3.9). The solution we propose enforces policy changes on encrypted objects themselves (without the need of decrypting them), and can then be performed by the server.

## 3.7.1 Two-Layer Encryption

To delegate policy changes enforcement to the server, avoiding re-encryption for the data owner, we adopt a two layer encryption approach. The owner encrypts the objects and sends them to the server in encrypted form; the server can impose another layer of encryption (following directions by the data owner).

We then distinguish two layers of encryption.

- **Base Encryption Layer** (BEL), performed by the data owner before transmitting data to the server. It enforces encryption on the objects according to the policy existing at initialization time.
- **Surface Encryption Layer** (SEL), performed by the server over the objects already encrypted by the data owner. It enforces the dynamic changes over the policy.

Both layers enforce encryption by means of a set of symmetric keys and a set of public tokens between these keys (see Sect. 3.3), although some adaptations are necessary, as explained below.

In terms of efficiency, the use of a double layer of encryption does not appear as a significant computational burden; experience shows that current systems have no significant delay when managing encryption on data coming from either the network or local disks, as also testified by the widespread use of encryption on network traffic and for protecting the storage of data on local file systems [89].

Base Encryption Layer.

Compared with the model presented in previous sections, in the BEL level we distinguish two kinds of keys: *derivation keys* and *access keys*. Access keys are actually used to encrypt objects, while derivation keys are used to provide the derivation capability via tokens, that is, tokens can be defined only with the derivation key as starting point. Each derivation key $k$ is always associated with an access key $k_a$ obtained by applying a secure hash function to $k$, that is, $k_a = h(k)$. In other words, keys at the BEL level always go in pairs $\langle k, k_a \rangle$. Note that both the derivation and the access keys are associated with a unique label $l$ and $l_a$, respectively. The rationale for this evolution is to distinguish the two roles associated with keys, namely: enabling key derivation (applying the corresponding tokens) and enabling object access. The reason for which such a distinction is needed will be clear in Sect. 3.8.

The BEL level is characterized by an encryption policy $\mathcal{E}_b = \langle \mathcal{U}, \mathcal{O}, \mathcal{K}_b, \mathcal{L}_b, \phi_b, \mathcal{T}_b \rangle$, where $\mathcal{U}$, $\mathcal{O}$, and $\mathcal{T}_b$ are as described in Sect. 3.3, $\mathcal{K}_b$ is the set of (derivation and access) keys defined at BEL level, and $\mathcal{L}_b$ is the set of publicly available labels associated with both derivation and access keys. The *key assignment and encryption schema* $\phi_b : \mathcal{U} \cup \mathcal{O} \rightarrow \mathcal{L}_b$ associates with each user $u \in \mathcal{U}$ the label $l$ corresponding to the *derivation* key released to the user by the data owner and with each object $o \in \mathcal{O}$ the label $l_a$ corresponding to the *access* key with which the object is encrypted by the data owner.

Also at BEL level, the set $\mathcal{K}_b$ of keys and the set $\mathcal{T}_b$ of tokens can be graphically represented through the corresponding key and token graph, which now has a vertex $b$ for each pair of encryption and access keys and labels $\langle(k,l),(k_a,l_a)\rangle$ and an edge $(b_i,b_j)$ if there is a token in $\mathcal{T}_b$ allowing the derivation of either $k_j$ or $k_{ja}$ from $k_i$. Graphically, a vertex is simply represented by $b$ and tokens leading to derivation keys are distinguished from tokens leading to access keys by using dotted lines for the latter. Each vertex $b_i$ in the key and token graph is characterized by: a derivation key along with the corresponding label, denoted $b_i.key$ and $b_i.label$, respectively; an access key along with the corresponding label, denoted $b_i.key_a$ and $b_i.label_a$, respectively. The corresponding encryption policy $\mathcal{E}_b$ is graphically represented by an encryption policy graph $\mathcal{G}_{\mathcal{E}_b}$ as described in Sect. 3.3, where notation $u \xrightarrow{\mathcal{E}_b} o$ indicates that there exists a path connecting $u$ to $o$, both following tokens and applying secure hash function $h$. Note that dotted edges can only appear as the last step of a path in the graph (since they allow the derivation of access keys only). Figure 3.16(a) illustrates an example of BEL key and token graph and key assignment and encryption schema enforcing the authorization policy in Fig. 3.1.

### Surface Encryption Layer.

At the SEL level there is no distinction between derivation and access keys (intuitively a single key carries out both functions). The SEL level is therefore characterized by an encryption policy $\mathcal{E}_s = \langle \mathcal{U}, \mathcal{O}, \mathcal{K}_s, \mathcal{L}_s, \phi_s, \mathcal{T}_s \rangle$ that is defined and graphically represented as described in Sect. 3.3. This means that the set $\mathcal{K}_s$ of keys and the set $\mathcal{T}_s$ of tokens can be graphically represented through a key and token graph having a vertex $s$ for each pair $\langle k,l \rangle$ defined at SEL and an edge $(s_i,s_j)$ if there is a token in $\mathcal{T}_s$ allowing the derivation of $k_j$ from $k_i$. Each vertex $s$ in the graph is characterized by: a key, denoted $s.key$, and corresponding label, denoted $s.label$; and the set of users, denoted $s.acl$, who can derive $s.key$. The corresponding encryption policy $\mathcal{E}_s$ is graphically represented by an encryption policy graph as described in Sect. 3.3, where notation $u \xrightarrow{\mathcal{E}_s} o$ indicates that there exists a path connecting $u$ to $o$.

### BEL and SEL combination.

In the two-layer approach, each object can then be encrypted twice: at the BEL level first, and at the SEL level then. Users can access objects only passing through the SEL level. Each user $u$ receives two keys: one to access the BEL and the other to access the SEL.[5] Users will be able to access objects for which they know both the keys (BEL and SEL) used for encryption.

---

[5] To simplify key management, the user key for SEL can be obtained by the application of a secure hash function from the user key for BEL. In this case, the data owner needs to send in the initialization phase to the server the list of SEL keys of each user.

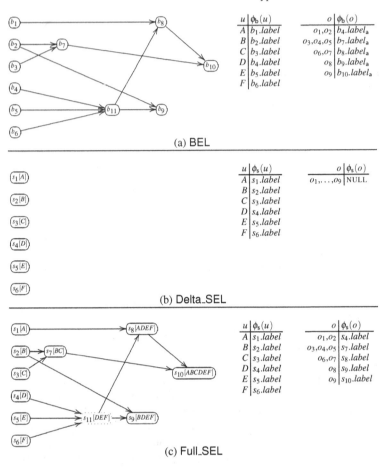

**Fig. 3.16** An example of BEL and SEL combination (Delta_SEL and Full_SEL)

The consideration of the two levels requires to restate the definition of policy equivalence, which is now defined as follows.

**Definition 3.11 (Policy equivalence).** Let $\mathscr{A} = \langle \mathscr{U}, \mathscr{O}, \mathscr{P} \rangle$ be an authorization policy, $\mathscr{E}_b = \langle \mathscr{U}, \mathscr{O}, \mathscr{K}_b, \mathscr{L}_b, \phi_b, \mathscr{T}_b \rangle$ be a BEL level encryption policy, and $\mathscr{E}_s = \langle \mathscr{U}, \mathscr{O}, \mathscr{K}_s, \mathscr{L}_s, \phi_s, \mathscr{T}_s \rangle$ be a SEL level encryption policy. $\mathscr{A}$ and the pair $\langle \mathscr{E}_b, \mathscr{E}_s \rangle$ are *equivalent*, denoted $\mathscr{A} \equiv \langle \mathscr{E}_b, \mathscr{E}_s \rangle$, iff the following conditions hold:

- $\forall u \in \mathscr{U}, o \in \mathscr{O} : (u \xrightarrow{\mathscr{E}_b} o \land u \xrightarrow{\mathscr{E}_s} o) \Longrightarrow u \xrightarrow{\mathscr{A}} o$
- $\forall u \in \mathscr{U}, o \in \mathscr{O} \; u \xrightarrow{\mathscr{A}} o \Longrightarrow (u \xrightarrow{\mathscr{E}_b} o \land u \xrightarrow{\mathscr{E}_s} o)$

In principle, any encryption policy at BEL and SEL can be specified as long as their combination is equivalent to the authorization policy. Let $\mathscr{A}$ be the authorization policy at the initialization time and let $\mathscr{E}_b$ be the encryption policy at the BEL level, which is equivalent to $\mathcal{A}$ (i.e., $\mathcal{A} \equiv \mathcal{E}_b$). We envision two basic approaches that can be followed in the construction of the two levels.

Full_SEL. The SEL encryption policy is initialized to reflect exactly (i.e., to re-
    peat) the BEL encryption policy: for each derivation key in BEL a corresponding
    key is defined in SEL; for each token in BEL, a corresponding token is defined
    in SEL. Note that the set $\mathcal{K}_s$ of keys and the set $\mathcal{T}_s$ of tokens form a key and
    token graph which is isomorphic to the one existing at the BEL level and, there-
    fore, also $\mathcal{G}_{\mathcal{E}_s}$ is isomorphic to $\mathcal{G}_{\mathcal{E}_b}$. The key assignment and encryption pol-
    icy assigns to each user $u$ a unique label $\phi_s(u)=v_s.label$ (and therefore a unique
    key $v_s.key$) corresponding to $\phi_b(u)=v_b.label$. Also, it assigns to each object $o$ a
    unique label $\phi_s(o)=v_s.label$ (and therefore a unique key $v_s.key$) corresponding to
    $\phi_b(o)=v_b.label_a$. The SEL encryption policy models exactly the BEL encryption
    policy, and hence, by definition, is equivalent to the authorization policy (i.e., $\mathcal{A}$
    $\equiv \mathcal{E}_s$).
Delta_SEL. The SEL policy is initialized to not carry out any over-encryption.
    Each user $u$ is assigned a unique label $\phi_s(u)=v_s.label$, and therefore a unique key
    $v_s.key$. No encryption is performed on objects, that is, $\forall o \in \mathcal{O}, \phi_s(o) = \text{NULL}$.
    The SEL level itself does not provide any additional protection at start time, but
    it does not modify the accesses allowed by BEL.

We note that a third approach could be possible, where the permission enforcement is completely delegated at the SEL level and the BEL simply applies a uniform
over-encryption (i.e., with the same key released to all users) to protect the plaintext
content from the server's eyes. We do not consider this approach as it presents a
significant exposure to collusion (see Sect. 3.9).

It is easy to see that all the approaches described produce a correct two layer encryption. In other words, given a correct encryption policy at the BEL level, the ap-
proaches produce a SEL level such that authorization policy $\mathcal{A}$ and the pair $\langle \mathcal{E}_b, \mathcal{E}_s \rangle$
are equivalent.

The reason for considering both the Full_SEL and Delta_SEL approaches is
the different performance and protection guarantees that they enjoy. In particular,
Full_SEL always requires double encryption to be enforced (even when permissions remain unvaried), thus doubling the decryption load of users for each access.
By contrast, the Delta_SEL approach requires double encryption only when actually needed to enforce a change in the permissions. However, as we will see in
Sect. 3.9, the Delta_SEL is characterized by greater information exposure, which
instead does not affect the Full_SEL approach. The choice between one or the other
can then be a trade-off between costs and resilience to attacks.

We close this section with a remark on the implementation. In the illustration of
our approach, we always assume over-encryption to be managed with a direct and
complete encryption and decryption of the object, as needed. We note however that
the server can, at the SEL level, apply a *lazy encryption* approach, similar to the
*copy-on-write* (COW) strategy used by most operating systems, and actually over-
encrypt the object when it is first accessed (and then storing the computed encrypted
representation); the server may choose also to always store the BEL representation

and then dynamically apply the encryption driven by the SEL when users access the object.


## 3.8 Policy Updates in Two-Layer Encryption

While in the basic model described in Sect. 3.3, policy updates are demanded and regulated by the owner, the two-layer approach enables the enforcement of policy updates without the need for the owner to re-encrypt, and to resend objects to the server. By contrast, the owner just adds (if necessary) some tokens at the BEL level and delegates policy changes to the SEL level by possibly requesting the server to over-encrypt the objects. The SEL level (enacted by the server) receives over-encryption requests by the BEL level (under the control of the data owner) and operates accordingly, adjusting tokens and possibly encrypting (and/or decrypting) objects.

Before analyzing grant and revoke operations in this new scenario, we first describe the working of over-encryption at the SEL level.


### 3.8.1 Over-encrypt

The SEL level regulates the update process through over-encryption of objects. It receives from the BEL requests of the form **Over-encrypt**$(O, U)$ corresponding to the demand to the SEL to make the set $O$ of objects accessible only to users in $U$. Note here that the semantics is different in the two different encryption modes. In the Full_SEL approach, over-encryption must reflect the actual authorization policy existing at any given time. In other words, it must reflect, besides the - dynamic - policy changes not reflected in the BEL, also the BEL policy itself. In the Delta_SEL approach, over-encryption is demanded only when additional restrictions (with respect to those enforced by the BEL) need to be enforced. As a particular case, here, the set $U$ of users may be ALL when - while processing a grant operation - the BEL determines that its protection is sufficient and therefore requests the SEL not to enforce any restriction and to possibly remove an over-encryption previously imposed.

Let us then see how the procedure works. Procedure **Over-encrypt** takes a set $O$ of objects and a set $U$ of users as input. First, it checks whether there exists a vertex $s$ whose key $s.key$ is used to encrypt objects in $O$ and the set of users that can derive $s.key$ is equal to $U$, that is, $s.acl=U$. If such a vertex exists, objects in $O$ are over-encrypted with a key that reflects the current $acl$ of objects in $O$ and the procedure terminates. Note that since all objects in $O$ share the same key, it is sufficient to check the above condition on any of the objects $o'$ in $O$. Otherwise, if the objects in $O$ are currently over-encrypted, they are first decrypted through the key of the vertex $s$ such that $s.label=\phi_s(o')$. Also, vertex $s$ is possibly removed from $\mathcal{G}_{\mathcal{E}_s}$ by procedure **DeleteVertex**. Then, if the set of users that should be allowed access to

| BEL | SEL |
|---|---|
| **GRANT**($u,o$)<br>$acl(o) := acl(o) \cup \{u\}$<br>find the vertex $b_j$ with $b_j.label_a = \phi_b(o)$<br>**if** $u \xrightarrow{\mathscr{S}_b} o$ **then**<br>  find the vertex $b_i$ with $b_i.label = \phi_b(u)$<br>  $t_{i,j} := b_j.key_a \oplus h(b_i.key, b_j.label_a)$<br>  $\mathscr{T}_b := \mathscr{T}_b \cup \{t_{i,j}\}$<br>  upload token $t_{i,j}$ on the server by storing it in table TOKENS<br>$O' := \{o' : o' \neq o \wedge \phi_b(o')=\phi_b(o) \wedge \exists u \in \mathscr{U} : u \xrightarrow{\mathscr{S}_b} o \wedge u \notin acl(o')\}$<br>**if** $O' \neq \emptyset$ **then**<br>  Partition $O'$ in sets such that each set $S$<br>  contains objects with the same acl $acl_S$<br>  **for each** set $S$ **do**<br>    **Over-encrypt**($acl_S, S$)<br>**case** encryption model **of**<br>  Delta_SEL: **if** $\{u : u \in \mathscr{U} \wedge u \xrightarrow{\mathscr{S}_b} b_i\}=acl(o)$ **then**<br>          **Over-encrypt**(ALL,$\{o\}$)<br>         **else**<br>          **Over-encrypt**($acl(o),\{o\}$)<br>  Full_SEL: **Over-encrypt**($acl(o),\{o\}$)<br><br>**REVOKE**($u,o$)<br>$acl(o) := acl(o) - \{u\}$<br>**Over-encrypt**($acl(o),\{o\}$) | **OVER-ENCRYPT**($U,O$)<br>let $o'$ be an object in $R$<br>**if** ($\exists s : s.label = \phi_s(o') \wedge s.acl=U$) **then**<br>  exit<br>**else**<br>  **if** $\phi_s(o') \neq$ NULL **then**<br>    find the vertex $s$ with $s.label=\phi_s(o')$<br>    **for each** $o \in O$ **do**<br>      decrypt $o$ with $s.key$<br>    **DeleteVertex**($s$)<br>  **if** $U \neq$ ALL **then**<br>    find the vertex $s$ with $s.acl=U$<br>    **if** $s=$UNDEF **then**<br>      $s :=$ **CreateNewVertex**($U$)<br>    **for each** $o \in O$ **do**<br>      $\phi_s(o) := s.label$<br>      encrypt $o$ with $s.key$<br>      update LABELS on the server |

**Fig. 3.17**  Procedures for granting and revoking permission $\langle u,o \rangle$

the objects in $O$ by the SEL is not ALL, over-encryption is necessary. (No operation is executed otherwise, since $U$=ALL is the particular case of Delta_SEL approach discussed above.) The procedure checks then the existence of a vertex $s$ such that the set of users that can derive key $s.key$ (i.e., belonging to $s.acl$) corresponds to $U$. If such a vertex does not exist, it is created and inserted into the encryption policy graph at the SEL level by function **CreateNewVertex**. Then, for each object $o$ in $O$, the procedure encrypts $o$ through $s.key$ and updates $\phi_s(o)$ and table LABELS accordingly.

### 3.8.2  Grant and Revoke

Consider first procedure **Grant** in Fig. 3.17, which handles a request to grant user $u$ access to object $o$. The BEL level starts and regulates the update process as follows. First, $acl(o)$ is updated to include $u$. Then, the procedure retrieves the vertex $b_j$ whose access key $b_j.key_a$ is the key with which $o$ is encrypted. If the object's access key cannot be derived by $u$, then a new token from user's key $b_i.key$, where $b_i$ is a vertex such that $\phi_b(u)=b_i.label$, to $b_j.key_a$ is generated and added to the token catalog. Note that the separation between derivation and access keys for each vertex allows us to add a token only giving $u$ access to the key used to encrypt object $o$, thus limiting the knowledge of each user to the information strictly needed to guarantee equivalence with the authorization policy. Indeed, knowledge of $b_i.key_a$ is a necessary condition to make $o$ accessible by $u$. However, there may be other objects $o'$ that are encrypted with the same key $b_i.key_a$ and which should not be made accessible to $u$. Since releasing $b_i.key_a$ would make them accessible to $u$, they need to be over-encrypted so to make them accessible to users in $acl(o')$ only. Then, the procedure determines if such a set of objects $O'$ exists. If $O'$ is not empty, the procedure partitions $O'$ in sets such that each set $S \subseteq O'$ includes all objects characterized by the same $acl$, denoted $acl_S$. For each set $S$, the procedure calls **Over-encrypt**$(S, acl_S)$ to demand SEL to execute an over-encryption of $S$ for users in $acl_S$. In addition, the procedure requests the SEL level to synchronize itself with the policy change. Here, the procedure behaves differently depending on the encryption model assumed. In the case of Delta_SEL, the procedure first controls whether the set of users that can reach the object's access key (i.e., the set of users $u \in \mathcal{U}$ such that $b_j.key_a$ can be computed knowing $b_i.key$, with $\phi_b(u)=b_i.label$) corresponds to $acl(o)$. If so, the BEL encryption suffices and no protection is needed at the SEL level, and therefore a call **Over-encrypt**$(\{o\}, \text{ALL})$ is requested. Otherwise, a call **Over-encrypt**$(\{o\}, acl(o))$ requests the SEL to make $o$ accessible only to users in $acl(o)$. In the case of Full_SEL, this is done by always calling **Over-encrypt**$(o, acl(o))$, requesting the SEL to synchronize its policy so to make $o$ accessible only by the users in $acl(o)$.

Consider now procedure **Revoke** in Fig. 3.17, which revokes from user $u$ access to object $o$. The procedure updates $acl(r)$ to remove user $u$ and calls **Over-encrypt**$(\{o\}, acl(o))$ to demand SEL to make $o$ accessible only to users in $acl(o)$.

In terms of performance, the grant and revoke procedures only require a direct navigation of the BEL and SEL structures and they produce the identification of the requests to be sent to the server in a time which, in typical scenarios, will be less than the time required to send the messages to the server.

*Example 3.3.* Consider the two layer encryption policy depicted in Fig. 3.16. Figures 3.18 and 3.19 illustrate the evolution of the corresponding key and token graphs and of both $\phi_b(o)$ and $\phi_s(o)$ for objects in $\mathcal{O}$ when the following grant and revoke operations are executed. Note that we do not report $\phi_b(u)$ and $\phi_s(u)$ for users in $\mathcal{U}$ since they never change due to grant/revoke operations. Note also that the key and token graph at SEL level evolves exactly as described in Example 3.2.

- **Grant**$(D,o_3)$: first $acl(o_3)$ is updated by inserting $D$. Then, since access key $b_7.key_a$ used to encrypt $o_3$ cannot be derived from the derivation key of vertex $b_4$ corresponding to $\phi_b(D)$, the data owner adds a BEL token allowing to compute $b_7.key_a$ from $b_4.key$. Since $b_7.key_a$ is also used to encrypt objects $o_4$ and $o_5$, which $D$ is not authorized to view, these objects have to be over-encrypted in such a way that they are accessible only to users $B$ and $C$. In the Delta_SEL scenario, **Over-encrypt** creates a new vertex $s_7$, with $s_7.acl=BC$, for objects $o_4$ and $o_5$. The protection of object $o_3$ at BEL level is instead sufficient and no over-encryption is needed (i.e., procedure **Over-encrypt** is called with $U=\text{ALL}$). In the Full_SEL scenario objects $o_4$ and $o_5$ are already correctly protected, $o_3$ is

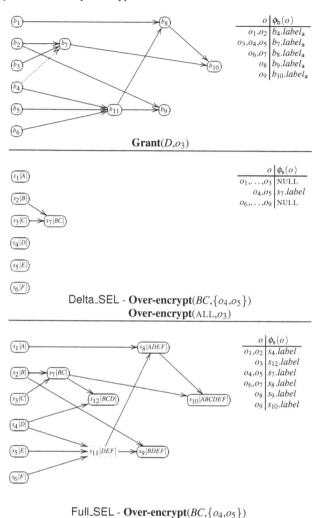

**Fig. 3.18** An example of grant operation

instead over-encrypted with the key of vertex $s_{12}$, which is created and inserted in the graph by function **CreateNewVertex**. Finally, procedure **DeleteVertex** is called with $s_7$ as a parameter and, since $s_7.key$ is used to encrypt $o_4$ and $o_5$, vertex $s_7$ is not removed from the graph.

- **Revoke**$(F,o_8)$: first $acl(o_8)$ is updated by removing $F$. Since now $acl(o_8)$ becomes $\{BEF\}$, object $o_8$ has to be over-encrypted with a key that only this set of users can compute. Consequently, both in the Delta_SEL and in the Full_SEL scenario, a new vertex $s_{13}$ representing $BEF$ is created and its key is used to protect $o_8$. Also, in the Full_SEL scenario, procedure **DeleteVertex** is called with $s_9$

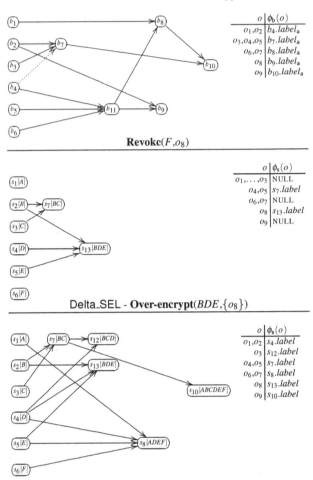

**Fig. 3.19** An example of revoke operation

as a parameter. Since $s_9$ is no more a useful vertex, it is removed from the graph. The procedure recursively calls itself with $s_2$ and with $s_{11}$ as a parameter. Vertex $s_2$ is not removed since it corresponds to user $B$ while vertex $s_{11}$ is removed from the graph.

### *3.8.3 Correctness*

We now prove that the procedures implementing the grant and revoke operations preserve policy equivalence.

**Theorem 3.7.** *Let* $\mathscr{A} = \langle \mathscr{U}, \mathscr{O}, \mathscr{P} \rangle$ *be an authorization policy,* $\mathscr{E}_b = \langle \mathscr{U}, \mathscr{O}, \mathscr{K}_b, \mathscr{L}_b, \phi_b, \mathscr{T}_b \rangle$ *be an encryption policy at the* BEL *level, and* $\mathscr{E}_s = \langle \mathscr{U}, \mathscr{O}, \mathscr{K}_s, \mathscr{L}_s, \phi_s, \mathscr{T}_s \rangle$ *be an encryption policy at the* SEL *level such that* $\mathscr{A} \equiv \langle \mathscr{E}_b, \mathscr{E}_s \rangle$. *Procedures in Fig. 3.17 generate a new* $\mathscr{E}_b' = \langle \mathscr{U}, \mathscr{O}, \mathscr{K}_b', \mathscr{L}_b', \phi_b', \mathscr{T}_b' \rangle$, $\mathscr{E}_s' = \langle \mathscr{U}, \mathscr{O}, \mathscr{K}_s', \mathscr{L}_s', \phi_s', \mathscr{T}_s' \rangle$, *and* $\mathscr{A}'$ *such that* $\mathscr{A}' \equiv \langle \mathscr{E}_b', \mathscr{E}_s' \rangle$.

*Proof.* Since we assume that $\mathscr{A} \equiv \langle \mathscr{E}_b, \mathscr{E}_s \rangle$ when procedures **Grant** and **Revoke** are called, we will consider only users and objects for which the encryption and authorization policies change. Grant and revoke are based on the correctness of over-encryption operations. We then examine it first.

Over-encrypt. We need to prove that **over-encrypt**($O,U$) possibly encrypts all objects in $O$ with a key in such a way that a user $u'$ can derive such a key if and only if $u' \in U$. The only case we need to consider is when the set of users $U$ is different from ALL (when $U$=ALL, objects in $O$ are not needed to be over-encrypted). Then, if the condition in the first **if** statement is evaluated to true, objects in $O$ are already correctly protected and since the procedure terminates, the result is correct. Otherwise, objects in $O$ are first possibly decrypted and then encrypted with the correct key *s.key* or with a key assigned to vertex $s$ created through function **CreateNewVertex**($U$). The correctness is guaranteed by the correctness of both function **CreateNewVertex** and procedure **DeleteVertex** (Lemmas 3.4 and 3.3).

Grant. $\langle \mathscr{E}_b', \mathscr{E}_s' \rangle \Longrightarrow \mathscr{A}'$

Consider user $u$ and object $o$. From the procedures in Fig. 3.17, it is easy to see that $\phi_b'(o) = \phi_b(o)$ and also that there is a (set of) token allowing to derive the key of the vertex with label $\phi_b'(o)$ by knowing the vertex with label $\phi_b'(u)$. From the **case** instruction and by the correctness of **Over-encrypt**, either $\phi_s'(o) = $ NULL or $o$ is over-encrypted with a key such that from the key of the vertex with label $\phi_s'(o)$ it is possible to derive the key of the vertex with label $\phi_s'(o)$ through $\mathscr{T}_s'$ (user $u$ is included in the current $acl(o)$). Since the key of the vertex with label $\phi_b'(o)$ can be derived from the key of the vertex with label $\phi_b'(u)$ and the key of the vertex with label $\phi_s'(o)$ can be derived from the key of the vertex with label $\phi_s'(u)$, we have that $u \xrightarrow{\mathscr{A}'} o$.

Consider now the set of objects $O'$ and suppose that $O'$ is not empty. For each subset $S$ of $O'$, user $u$ can now derive the key used to encrypt such a set of objects. This implies that $\forall o' \in S$, $\phi_b'(o') = \phi_b(o')$, which corresponding key can be computed starting from the key of the vertex with label $\phi_b'(u)$. However, by the correctness of **Over-encrypt**, a call **over-encrypt**($S,acl_S$) guarantees that all objects $o'$ in $S$ are over-encrypted with a key such that $\forall o' \in S$, the key of the vertex with label $\phi_s'(o')$ is not derivable from the key of the vertex with label

$\phi_s'(u)$ because $acl_S$ does not include user $u$.

$\langle \mathscr{E}_b{}', \mathscr{E}_s{}' \rangle \Longleftarrow \mathscr{A}'$
Consider user $u$ and object $o$. From the first instruction in procedure **Grant**, we have that $u \xrightarrow{\mathscr{A}'} o$. From the pseudocode in Fig. 3.17, it is easy to see that $\phi_b'(o) = \phi_b(o)$ and that the corresponding key can be computed knowing the key of the vertex with label $\phi_b'(u)$. Also, from the **case** instruction and by the correctness of **Over-encrypt**, either $\phi_s'(o) = \text{NULL}$ or $o$ is over-encrypted with the key of the vertex with label $\phi_s'(o)$ such that it can be derived from the key of the vertex with label $\phi_s'(u)$.

Revoke.   $\langle \mathscr{E}_b{}', \mathscr{E}_s{}' \rangle \Longrightarrow \mathscr{A}'$
Consider user $u$ and object $o$. A call **Over-encrypt**($\{o\}, acl(o)$) is requested to demand the SEL to make $o$ accessible only to users in the current $acl(o)$. We know that $u \xrightarrow{\mathscr{E}_b'} o$. Also, from the correctness of **Over-encrypt**, it is easy to see that the key of the vertex with label $\phi_s'(o)$ cannot be computed from the key of the vertex with label $\phi_s'(u)$.

$\langle \mathscr{E}_b{}', \mathscr{E}_s{}' \rangle \Longleftarrow \mathscr{A}'$
Consider user $u$ and object $o$. From the first instruction in the procedure we have that $u \xrightarrow{\mathscr{A}'} o$. The subsequent call **over-encrypt**($\{o\}, acl(o)$) makes object $o$ no more accessible to user $u$ because $o$ is over-encrypted with a key that is no more derivable by $u$ (this property is a consequence of the correctness of **Over-encrypt**), that is, the key of the vertex with label $\phi_b'(o)$ is still derivable from the key of the vertex with label $\phi_b'(u)$ but the key of the vertex with label $\phi_s'(o)$ is not derivable from the key of the vertex with label $\phi_s'(u)$.

## 3.9 Protection Evaluation

Since the BEL and SEL encryption policies are equivalent to the authorization policy at initialization time, the correctness of the procedures in Fig. 3.17 ensures that the authorization policy $\mathscr{A}$ and the pair $\langle \mathscr{E}_b, \mathscr{E}_s \rangle$ are equivalent. In other words, at any point in time, users will be able to access only objects for which they have - directly or indirectly - the necessary keys both at the BEL and at the SEL level.

The key derivation function adopted is proved to be secure [8]. We also assume that all the encryption functions and the tokens are robust and cannot be broken, even combining the information available to many users. Moreover, we assume that each user correctly manages her keys, without the possibility for a user to steal keys from another user.

It still remains to evaluate whether the approach is vulnerable to attacks from users who access and store all information offered by the server, or from *collusion* attacks, where different users (or a user and the server) combine their knowledge to

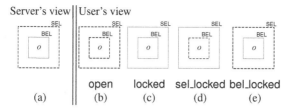

**Fig. 3.20** Possible views on object $o$

access objects they would not otherwise be able to access. Note that for collusion to exist, both parties should gain in the exchange (as otherwise they will not have any incentive in colluding).

To model exposure, we first examine the different views that one can have on an object $o$ by exploiting a graphical notation with object $o$ in the center and with fences around $o$ denoting the barriers to the access imposed by the knowledge of the keys used for $o$'s encryption at the BEL (inner fence) and at the SEL (outer fence). The fence is continuous if there is no knowledge of the corresponding key (the barrier cannot be passed) and it is discontinuous otherwise (the barrier can be passed). Figure 3.20 illustrates the different views that can exist on the object. On the left, Fig. 3.20(a), there is the view of the server itself, which knows the key at the SEL level but does not have access to the key at the BEL level. On the right, there are the different possible views of users, for whom the object can be:

- open: the user knows the key at the BEL level as well as the key at the SEL level (Fig. 3.20(b));
- locked: the user knows neither the key at the BEL level nor the key at the SEL level (Fig. 3.20(c));
- sel_locked: the user knows only the key at the BEL level but does not know the key at the SEL level (Fig. 3.20(d));
- bel_locked: the user knows only the key at the SEL level but does not know the one at the BEL level (Fig. 3.20(e)). Note that this latter view corresponds to the view of the server itself.

By the authorization policy and the encryption policy equivalence (Theorem 3.7), the open view corresponds to the view of authorized users, while the remaining views correspond to the views of non authorized users.

We now discuss possible information exposure, with the conservative assumption that users are not oblivious (i.e., they have the ability to store and keep indefinitely all information they were entitled to access).

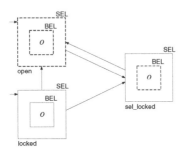

**Fig. 3.21** View transitions in the Full_SEL

## 3.9.1 Exposure Risk: Full_SEL

In the Full_SEL approach, at initialization time, BEL and SEL are completely syn-
chronized. For each user, an object is then protected by both keys or by neither:
authorized users will have the open view, while non authorized users will have the
locked view. Fig. 3.21 summarizes the possible view transitions starting from these
two views.

Let us first examine the evolution of the open view. Since objects at the BEL
level are not re-encrypted, the view of an authorized user can change only if the
user is revoked the permission. In this case, the object is over-encrypted at the SEL
level, then becoming sel_locked for the user. The view could be brought back to be
open if the user is granted the permission again (i.e., over-encryption is removed).

Let us now examine the evolution of the locked view. For how the SEL is con-
structed and maintained in the Full_SEL approach, it cannot happen that the SEL
grants a user an access that is blocked at the BEL level, and therefore the bel_locked
view can never be reached. The view can instead change to open, in case the user
is granted the permission to access the object; or to sel_locked, in case the user is
given the access key at the BEL level but she is not given that at the SEL level. This
latter situation can happen if the release of the key at the BEL level is necessary
to make accessible to the user another object $o'$ that is, at the BEL level, encrypted
with the same key as $o$. To illustrate, suppose that at initialization time objects $o$
and $o'$ are both encrypted with the same key and they are not accessible by user $u$
(see the leftmost view in Fig. 3.22). Suppose then that $u$ is granted the permission
for $o'$. To make $o'$ accessible at the BEL level, a token is added to make the key
corresponding to label $\phi_b(o)$ derivable by $u$, where however $\phi_b(o)=\phi_b(o')$. Hence,
$o'$ will be over-encrypted at the SEL level and the key corresponding to label $\phi_s(o')$
made derivable by $u$. The resulting situation is illustrated in Fig. 3.22, where $o'$ is
open and $o$ results sel_locked.

We now analyze what are the possible views of users that may collude. Users
having the open and the locked view need not be considered as they have nothing
to gain in colluding. Also, recall that in the Full_SEL approach, for what said previously, nobody (but the server) can have a bel_locked view. This leaves us only with

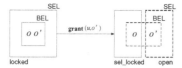

**Fig. 3.22** From locked to sel_locked views

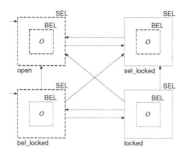

**Fig. 3.23** View transitions in the Delta_SEL

users having the sel_locked view. Since users having the same views will not gain anything in colluding, the only possible collusion can happen between the server (who has a bel_locked view) and a user who has a sel_locked view. In this situation, the knowledge of the server allows lowering the outer fence, while the knowledge of the user allows lowering the inner fence: merging their knowledge, they would then be able to bring down both fences and enjoy the open view on the object. The risk of collusion then arises on objects for which a user holds a sel_locked view and the user never had the permission to access the object (i.e., the user never belonged to the *acl* of the object). Indeed, if a user would get access to an object she previously had permission for, the user has no gain in colluding with the server.

Besides collusion between different parties, we also need to consider the risk of exposure due to a single user merging her own views on an object at different points in time. It is easy to see that, in the Full_SEL approach, where all non authorized users start with a locked view on the object (and transitions are as illustrated in Fig. 3.21), there is no risk of exposure. Trivially, if the user is released the key at the SEL level (i.e., it is possible for her to bring down the lower fence) it is because the user has the permission for *o* at some point in time and therefore she is (or has been) authorized for the object. There is therefore no exposure risk.

### 3.9.2 Exposure Risk: Delta_SEL

In the Delta_SEL approach, users not authorized to see an object have, at initial time, the bel_locked view on it. From there, the view can evolve to be open, sel_locked, or locked. The view becomes open in case the user is given the permission for $o$; it becomes sel_locked in the case the user is given the permission for an object $o'$ that is, at the BEL level, encrypted with the same key as $o$; it becomes locked if another user is given the permission for an object $o'$ that is, at the BEL level, encrypted with the same key as $o$, thus implying that both BEL and SEL level keys are not known to the user. View transitions are illustrated in Fig. 3.23. It is easy to see that, in this case, a single user by herself can then hold the two different views: sel_locked and bel_locked. In other words a (planning-ahead) user could retrieve the object at initial time, when she is not authorized, getting and storing at her side $o$'s bel_locked view. If, at a later point in time the user is released the key corresponding to label $\phi_b(o)$ to make accessible to her another object $o'$, she will acquire the sel_locked view on $o$. Merging this with the past bel_locked view, she can enjoy the open view on $o$. Note that the set of objects potentially exposed to a user coincides with the objects exposed to collusion between that user and the server in the Full_SEL approach.

It is important to note that in both cases (Full_SEL and Delta_SEL), exposure is limited to objects that have been involved in a policy split to make other objects, encrypted with the same BEL key, available to the user. Exposure is therefore limited and well identifiable. This allows the owner to possibly counteract it via explicit selective re-encryption or by proper design (as discussed in the next section).

The collusion analysis clarifies why we did not consider the third possible encryption scenario illustrated in Sect. 3.7. In this scenario, all users non authorized to access an object would always have the sel_locked view on it and could potentially collude with the server. The fact that the BEL key is the same for all objects would make all the objects exposed (as the server would need just one key to be able to access them all).

### 3.9.3 Design Considerations

From the analysis above, we can make the following observations on the Delta_SEL and the Full_SEL approaches.

- *Exposure protection.* The Full_SEL approach provides superior protection, as it reduces the risk of exposure, which is limited to collusion with the server. By contrast, the Delta_SEL approach exposes also to single (planning-ahead) users.
- *Performance.* The Delta_SEL approach provides superior performance, as it imposes over-encryption only when required by a change in permissions. By contrast, the Full_SEL approach always imposes a double encryption on the objects, and therefore an additional load.

From these observations we can draw some criteria that could be followed by a data owner when choosing between the use of Delta_SEL or Full_SEL. If the data owner knows that:

- the access policy will be relatively static, or

- sets of objects sharing the same *acl* at initialization time represent a strong semantic relationship rarely split by policy evolution, or
- objects are grouped in the BEL in fine granularity components where most of the BEL vertices are associated with a single or few objects,

then the risk of exposing the data to collusion is limited also in the Delta_SEL approach, which can then be preferred for performance reasons.

By contrast, if permissions have a more dynamic and chaotic behavior, the Full_SEL approach can be preferred to limit exposure due to collusion (necessarily involving the server). Also, the collusion risk can be minimized by a proper organization of the objects to reduce the possibility of policy splits. This could be done either by producing a finer granularity of encryption and/or better identifying object groups characterized by a persistent semantic affinity (in both cases, using in the BEL different keys for objects with identical *acl*).

## 3.10  Experimental Results

An important issue for the success of the presented techniques is their scalability. The potential for their adoption would be greatly compromised if they were not applicable in large-scale scenarios. A natural verification of their adaptability to large configurations could start from the extraction of a complex authorization policy from a large system, with the goal of computing an equivalent encryption policy using the approach presented above. Unfortunately, there is no large scale access control system available today producing a significant test for the techniques presented in this chapter. The most structurally rich access policies are today those that characterize large enterprise scenarios, but these policies typically exhibit a relatively poor structure, which can be represented in our system with a limited number of tokens and almost no effort on the part of the construction algorithm. We then need to follow a different strategy to obtain a robust guarantee on the ability of the proposed system to scale well, building a simulated scenario exhibiting large scale and articulated policies. As we describe later, a single experiment was not sufficient and we designed two series of experiments, covering different configurations that solicited the system in two distinct ways.

The first scenario starts from the premise that data outsourcing platforms are used to support the exchange and dissemination of objects among the members of a user community. The idea then is to use a description of the structure of a large social network to derive a number of object dissemination requests. We identified as a source for the construction of a large social network the coauthor relationship represented within the DBLP bibliography index. DBLP [39] is a well-known bibliographic database that currently indexes more than one million articles. The assumption at the basis of the first series of experiments is that each paper represents an object that must be accessible by all its authors.

The social network of DBLP coauthors has been the subject of several investigations, showing that this network has a structure similar to that of other social

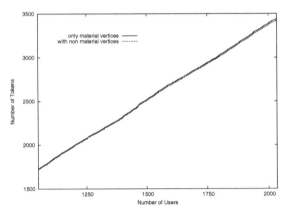

**Fig. 3.24** Number of tokens for the DBLP scenario

networks, synthetically classified as a *power-law* or *self-similar* structure. We implemented a C++ program that starts from a random author and considers all his/her publications and coauthors; then, one of the coauthors is randomly chosen and his/her publications and corresponding coauthors are iteratively retrieved, extending the user population and the set of objects. We then built a token-based encryption policy corresponding to the access policy where every author has access to all the papers that he/she has authored or co-authored.

The first metric we considered in the experiments is the number of tokens required for the representation of the access policy. The graph in Fig. 3.24 presents how the number of tokens increases with the number of users. We observe that the growth is linear and that the number of tokens remains low (with 2000 authors, we have 3369 tokens).

Another important metric was the one evaluating the impact of the identification of candidate non-material vertices. This optimization presented a very limited benefit in the DBLP scenario, as visible from Fig. 3.24 (18 tokens gained out of 3369, thanks to the introduction of 12 non-material vertices). The rationale is that the structure of the social network is relatively sparse. As it has been demonstrated by other investigations on the structure of self-similar networks, they are characterized by a few nodes which present a high level of connectedness, whereas most of the network nodes are loosely connected with a few other nodes and form small strictly connected communities. Then, the construction of a token-based encryption policy for a situation like this produces a relatively simple graph, with relatively few tokens. This is a positive and important property, which demonstrates that our approach is immediately applicable to large social networks, with an efficient construction.

Taking into account the behavior emerging from the above experimental scenario, it became interesting to test the behavior of the system in a more difficult configuration, with a complex access control policy. We were specifically interested in evaluating the benefit produced by the application of the optimization introduced

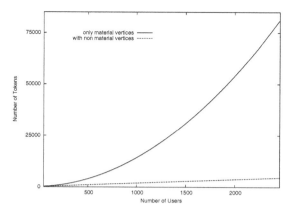

**Fig. 3.25** Number of tokens for the championship scenario

in this chapter. As representative of a potential selective dissemination scenario, we consider the case study, also analyzed in [34, 40], of a sport news database. The chosen service manages a system with *t teams*, where each *team* is composed by *pt players* and is coordinated by one manager. The service is supposed to be used by *s* team supporters, referred in the following as *subscribers*. Moreover, a set of *reporters* follows the league and uses the service to work with *tr* teams. The *reporters* are grouped into sets of *rm* elements, each of which coordinated by one *manager*. In the considered scenario, each subject (team manager, reporter, reporter manager, and subscribers) can subscribe to any number of objects, partitioned between *player news* and *team news*. Consistently with [34, 40], the set of permissions granted to subscribers is modeled to be quite large to evaluate the algorithms in a significant scenario. The number of team news accessed by each subscriber, along with the player news of the same team, follows a *Zipf* distribution that increases with the number *s* of subscribers.

The novel results presented in Fig. 3.24 (continuous line) show the number of tokens required for the representation of the policy. It is immediate to observe that the number of tokens required per user is significantly higher, due to the more intricate structure of the policy in this experimental setup. Still, the number of tokens after the application of the optimization techniques increases linearly with the increase in the number of users, with no sign of divergence for extremely large configurations. The graph in Fig. 3.25 shows the advantage produced by the identification of non-material vertices. It is immediate to observe that the advantage is significant, with a 82% reduction on average on the number of tokens.

Overall, the experiments allow us to express two important claims. First, the approach presented in this chapter is able to manage large scenarios, particularly when the access policy presents a structure analogous to that exhibited by social networks. Second, for complex access policies that present a complex structure and would otherwise require a significant number of tokens per user, the use of the optimization techniques introduced by this chapter is able to provide a significant reduction in the complexity, keeping at a manageable level the total number of tokens required for the representation of the policy.


## 3.11 Chapter Summary

There is an emerging trend towards scenarios where data management is outsourced to an external service providing storage capabilities and high-bandwidth distribution channels. In this context, selective release requires enforcing measures to protect the data confidentiality from both unauthorized users as well as "honest-but-curious" servers. Current solutions provide protection by exploiting encryption in conjunction with proper indexing capabilities, but suffer from limitations requiring the involvement of the owner every time selective access is to be enforced or the access policy is modified. This chapter presents a model that efficiently organizes the use of cryptographic services for the management of an access control policy, while allowing efficient access to data by optimizing the public catalog structure. Since the most important problem arising when using cryptography as a way for enforcing access control is policy updates management, we introduced the idea of enforcing the authorization policy by using a two-layer selective encryption. Our solution offers significant benefits in terms of quicker and less costly realization of authorization policy updates and general efficiency of the system. We believe these benefits to be crucial for the success of emerging scenarios characterized by a huge collection of data that have to be distributed in a selective way to a variety of users.

# Chapter 4
# Combining Fragmentation and Encryption to Protect Data Privacy[1]

Traditional solutions for granting data privacy rely on encryption. However, dealing with encrypted data makes query processing expensive. In this chapter, we propose a solution to enforce privacy over data collections combining *data fragmentation* with *encryption*. We model privacy requirements as confidentiality constraints expressing the sensitivity of the content of single attributes and of their associations. We then use encryption as an underlying (conveniently available) measure for making data unintelligible, while exploiting fragmentation to break sensitive associations among attributes. We introduce both exact and heuristic algorithms computing a fragmentation that tries to minimize the impact of fragmentation on query efficiency.

## 4.1 Introduction

Information is probably today the most important and valued resource. Private and governmental organizations are increasingly gathering vast amounts of data, which are collected and maintained, and often include sensitive personally identifiable information. In such a scenario guaranteeing the privacy of the data, be them stored in the system or communicated to external parties, becomes a primary requirement.

Individuals, privacy advocates, and legislators are today putting more and more attention on the support of privacy over collected information. Regulations are increasingly being established responding to these demands, forcing organizations to provide privacy guarantees over sensitive information when storing, processing or

---

[1] Part of this chapter appeared under V. Ciriani, S. De Capitani di Vimercati, S. Jajodia, S. Foresti, S. Paraboschi, P. Samarati, "Fragmentation and Encryption to Enforce Privacy in Data Storage," in ACM Transactions on Information and System Security (TISSEC), Vol. 13:3, July, 2010 [29] ©2010 ACM, Inc. Reprinted by permission http://doi.acm.org/10.1145/1805974.1805978; and under ©2009 IEEE, reprinted, with permission, from V. Ciriani, S. De Capitani di Vimercati, S. Foresti, S. Jajodia, S. Paraboschi, P. Samarati, "Fragmentation Design for Efficient Query Execution over Sensitive Distributed Databases," in Proc. of the 29th International Conference on Distributed Computing Systems (ICDCS 2009), Montreal, Canada, June 2009 [28].

sharing it with others. Most recent regulations (e.g., see [22] and [78]) require that specific categories of data (e.g., data disclosing health and sex life, or data such as ZIP and date of birth that can be exploited to uniquely identify an individual [83]) to be either *encrypted* or *kept separate* from other personally identifiable information (to prevent their association with specific individuals). Information privacy guarantees may also derive from the need of preventing possible abuses of critical information. For instance, the "Payment Card Industry (PCI) Data Security Standard" [77] forces all the business organizations managing credit card information (e.g., VISA and MasterCard) to apply encryption measures when storing data. The standard also explicitly forbids the use of storage encryption as natively offered by operating systems, requiring access to the encryption keys to be separated from the operating system services managing user identities and privileges.

This demand for encryption is luckily coupled today with the fact that the realization of cryptographic functions presents increasingly lower costs in a computer architecture, where the factor limiting system performances is typically the capacity of the channels that transfer information within the system and among separate systems. Cryptography then becomes an inexpensive tool that supports the protection of privacy when storing or communicating information.

From a data access point of view, however, dealing with encrypted information represents a burden since encryption makes it not always possible to efficiently execute queries and evaluate conditions over the data. In fact, a straightforward approach to guarantee privacy to a collection of data could consist in encrypting all the data. This technique is, for example, adopted in the database outsourcing scenario [35, 55], as discussed in Chaps. 2 and 3. The assumption underlying approaches applying such an encryption wrapper is that all the data are equally sensitive and therefore encryption is a price to be paid to protect them. This assumption is typically an overkill in many scenarios. As a matter of fact, in many situations data are not sensitive per se; what is sensitive is their association with other data. As a simple example, in a hospital the list of illnesses cured or the list of patients could be made publicly available, while the association of specific illnesses to individual patients is sensitive and must be protected. Hence, there is no need to encrypt both illnesses and patients if there are alternative ways to protect the association between them.

A promising approach to protect sensitive data or sensitive associations among data is represented by the combined use of fragmentation and encryption. Fragmentation and encryption provide protection of data in storage or when disseminated ensuring no sensitive information is disclosed neither directly (i.e., present in the database) nor indirectly (i.e., derived from other information present in the database). With this design, the data can be outsourced and stored on an untrusted server, typically obtaining lower costs, greater availability, and more efficient distributed access. The advantage of having only part of the data encrypted is that all the queries that do not require to reconstruct confidential information will be managed more efficiently and securely. Also, the idea that the higher-level privilege is only used when strictly necessary represents a concrete realization of the "least privilege" principle.

We frame our work in the context of relational databases. The reason for this choice is that relational databases are by far the most common solution for the management of the data subject of privacy regulations; also, they are characterized by a clear data model and a simple query language that facilitate the design of a solution. We note, however, that our model could be easily adapted to the protection of data represented with other data models (e.g., records in files or XML documents).

As discussed in Chap. 2, the combined use of fragmentation and encryption to protect confidentiality has been initially proposed in [2], where information is stored on two separate servers and protection relies on the hypothesis that the servers cannot communicate. This assumption is clearly too strong in any practical situation. Our solution overcomes the above limitations: it allows storing data even on a single server and minimizes the amount of data represented only in encrypted format, therefore allowing for efficient query execution.

This chapter, after introducing confidentiality constraints as a simple, yet powerful, way to capture privacy requirements, presents three different approaches for the design of a fragmentation that looks carefully at performance issues. The first approach tries to minimize the number of fragments composing the solution, the second is based on the affinity between pairs of attributes, and the third exploits a complete query workload profile of the system. Then, we introduce a complete search algorithm that computes an optimal fragmentation satisfying confidentiality constraints, which can be adapted to each of the three optimization models. Also, for each cost model considered, we propose an ad hoc heuristic algorithm working in polynomial time. Our approach also manages encrypted indexes, trying to analyze the vulnerability of sensitive data due to their introduction. The experimental results support the quality of the solutions produced by the three heuristics, with respect to the result computed by the complete search strategy.

## 4.1.1 Chapter Outline

The remainder of the chapter is organized as follows. Section 4.2 formally defines confidentiality constraints. Sections 4.3 presents our model for enforcing confidentiality constraints by combining fragmentation and encryption. Section 4.4 introduces the definition of minimal fragmentation and shows that it is a NP-hard problem. Section 4.5 describes a complete search approach that efficiently visits the solution space lattice. Section 4.6 introduces the definition of vector-minimal fragmentation and presents a heuristic algorithm for computing a fragmentation satisfying such a definition. Section 4.7 introduces the concept of attribute affinity. Section 4.8 presents a heuristic algorithm for computing a fragmentation guided by the affinity. Section 4.9 introduces the cost model based on query workload. Section 4.10 presents an algorithm for computing a fragmentation guided by the cost of query execution. Section 4.11 illustrates how queries formulated on the original data are mapped into equivalent queries operating on fragments. Section 4.12 discusses the introduction of indexes on encrypted attributes. Section 4.13 presents the experimental results obtained by the implementation of both complete search and heuristic algorithms. Finally, Sect. 4.14 presents our concluding remarks.

## 4.2 Confidentiality Constraints

We consider a scenario where, consistently with other proposals (e.g., [2, 83]) the data to be protected are represented with a single relation $r$ over a relation schema $R(a_1,\ldots,a_n)$, containing all the information that need to be protected. For simplicity, when clear from the context, we will use $R$ to denote either the relation schema $R$ or the set of attributes in $R$ (instead of using $R.*$).

We model in a quite simple and powerful way the privacy requirements through *confidentiality constraints*, which are sets of attributes, as follows.

**Definition 4.1 (Confidentiality constraint).** Let $\mathscr{A}$ be a set of attributes, a *confidentiality constraint $c$ over $\mathscr{A}$* is:

1. a singleton set $\{a\} \subset \mathscr{A}$, stating that the values of the attribute are sensitive *(attribute visibility)*; or
2. a subset of attributes in $\mathscr{A}$, stating that the association among values of the given attributes is sensitive *(association visibility)*.

While simple, a confidentiality constraint supports the definition of different confidentiality requirements that may need to be expressed, such as the following.

- *The values assumed by some attributes are considered sensitive and therefore cannot be stored in the clear*. For instance, phone numbers or email addresses can be considered sensitive values (even if not associated with any identifying information).
- *The association among values of given attributes is sensitive and therefore should not be released*. For instance, while the list of (names of) patients in a hospital as well as the list of illnesses are by themselves not confidential, the association of patient's names with illnesses is considered sensitive.

Note that constraints specified on the association among attributes can derive from different requirements: they can correspond to an association that explicitly needs protection (as in the case of names and illnesses above) or to associations that could cause inference on other sensitive information. As an example of the latter, consider a hospital database, suppose that the names of patients are considered sensitive, and therefore cannot be stored in the clear, and that the association of the Occupation together with the ZIP code can work as a quasi-identifier (i.e., Occupation and ZIP can be used, possibly in association with external information, to help identifying patients and therefore to infer, or reduce uncertainty about, their names) [30, 83]. This inference channel can be simply blocked by specifying a constraint protecting the association of the Occupation with the ZIP code. As

PATIENT

| SSN | Name | Occupation | Sickness | ZIP |
|-----|------|------------|----------|-----|
| 123-45-6789 | A. Smith | Nurse | Latex al. | 94140 |
| 987-65-4321 | B. Jones | Nurse | Latex al. | 94141 |
| 246-89-1357 | C. Taylor | Clerk | Latex al. | 94140 |
| 135-79-2468 | D. Brown | Lawyer | Celiac | 94139 |
| 975-31-8642 | E. Cooper | Manager | Pollen al. | 94138 |
| 864-29-7531 | F. White | Designer | Nickel al. | 94141 |

$c_0 = \{\texttt{SSN}\}$
$c_1 = \{\texttt{Name,Occupation}\}$
$c_2 = \{\texttt{Name,Sickness}\}$
$c_3 = \{\texttt{Occupation,Sickness,ZIP}\}$

(a)                              (b)

**Fig. 4.1** An example of plaintext relation (a) and its well defined constraints (b)

another example, consider the case where attribute `Name` is not considered sensitive, but its association with `Sickness` is. Suppose again that the `Occupation` together with the `ZIP` code can work as a quasi-identifier (then potentially leaking information on names). In this case, an association constraint will be specified protecting the association among `Occupation`, `ZIP`, and `Sickness`, implying that the three attributes should never be accessible together in the clear.

We are interested in enforcing a set of *well defined* confidentiality constraints, formally defined as follows.

**Definition 4.2 (Well defined constraints).** A set of confidentiality constraints $\mathscr{C} = \{c_1, \ldots, c_m\}$ is said to be *well defined* iff $\forall c_i, c_j \in \mathscr{C}, i \neq j, c_i \not\subset c_j$ and $c_j \not\subset c_i$.

According to this definition, a set of constraints $\mathscr{C}$ over $\mathscr{A}$ cannot contain a constraint that is a subset of another constraint. The rationale behind this property is that, whenever there are two constraints $c_i$, $c_j$ and $c_i$ is a subset of $c_j$ (or vice versa), the satisfaction of constraint $c_i$ implies the satisfaction of constraint $c_j$ (see Sect. 4.3), and therefore $c_j$ is redundant.

*Example 4.1.* Consider the `Patient` relation in Fig. 4.1(a), containing the information about the patients of a hospital. The privacy requirements that the hospital needs to enforce, either due to legislative or internal restrictions, are illustrated in Fig. 4.1(b):

- $c_0$ is a singleton constraint stating that the list of `SSN` of patients is considered sensitive;
- $c_1$ and $c_2$ state that the association between `Name` and `Occupation`, and the association between `Name` and `Sickness`, respectively, are considered sensitive;
- $c_3$ states that the association among `Occupation`, `ZIP`, and `Sickness` is considered sensitive (the rationale for this is that `Occupation` and `ZIP` are a quasi-identifier [83]).

Note that also the association of patients' `Name` and `SSN` is sensitive and should be protected. However, such a constraint is not specified since it is redundant, given that `SSN` by itself has been declared sensitive ($c_0$). As a matter of fact, protecting `SSN` as an individual attribute implies automatic protection of its associations with any other attribute.

## 4.3 Fragmentation and Encryption for Constraint Satisfaction

Our approach to satisfy confidentiality constraints is based on the use of two techniques: encryption and fragmentation.

- *Encryption.* Consistently with how the constraints are specified, encryption applies at the attribute level, that is, it involves an attribute in its entirety. Encrypting an attribute means encrypting (tuple by tuple) all its values. To protect encrypted values from frequency attacks [88], we assume that a *salt*, which is a randomly chosen value, is applied to each encryption (similarly to the use of nonces in the protection of messages from replay attacks).
- *Fragmentation.* Fragmentation, like encryption, applies at the attribute level, that is, it involves an attribute in its entirety. Fragmenting means splitting sets of attributes so that they are not visible together, that is, the associations among their values are not available without access to the encryption key.

It is straightforward to see that attribute visibility constraints can be solved only by encryption. By contrast, an association visibility constraint could be solved by either: *i)* encrypting any (one suffices) of the attributes involved in the constraint, so to prevent joint visibility, or *ii)* fragmenting the attributes involved in the constraint so that they are not visible together. Given a relation $r$ over schema $R$ and a set of confidentiality constraints $\mathscr{C}$ on it, our goal is to fragment $R$ granting constraints satisfaction. However, we must also ensure that no constraint can be violated by re-combining two or more fragments. In other words, there cannot be attributes that can be exploited for linking. Since encryption is differentiated by the use of the salt, the only attributes that can be exploited for linking are the plaintext attributes. Consequently, ensuring that fragments are protected from linking translates into requiring that no attribute appears in clear form in more than one fragment. In the following, we use the term *fragment* to denote any subset of a given set of attributes. A fragmentation is a set of non overlapping fragments, as captured by the following definition.

**Definition 4.3 (Fragmentation).** Let $R$ be a relation schema, a *fragmentation* of $R$ is a set of fragments $\mathscr{F}=\{F_1,\dots,F_m\}$, where $F_i \subseteq R$, for $i = 1,\dots,m$, such that $\forall F_i, F_j \in \mathscr{F}, i \neq j : F_i \cap F_j = \emptyset$ (fragments do not have attributes in common).

In the following, we denote with $F_i^j$ the $i$-th fragment in fragmentation $\mathscr{F}_j$ (the superscript will be omitted when the fragmentation is clear from the context). For instance, with respect to the plaintext relation in Fig. 4.1(a), a possible fragmentation is $\mathscr{F}=\{\{\texttt{Name}\},\{\texttt{Occupation}\},\{\texttt{Sickness},\texttt{ZIP}\}\}$.

At the physical level, a fragmentation translates to a combination of fragmentation and encryption. Each fragment $F$ is mapped into a physical fragment containing all the attributes of $F$ in the clear, while all the other attributes of $R$ are encrypted. The reason for reporting all the original attributes (in either encrypted or clear form) in each of the physical fragments is to guarantee that any query can be executed by querying a single physical fragment (see Sect. 4.11). For the sake of simplicity and

| $\hat{f}_1$ | | |
|---|---|---|
| **salt** | enc | Name |
| $s_1$ | $\alpha$ | A. Smith |
| $s_2$ | $\beta$ | B. Jones |
| $s_3$ | $\gamma$ | C. Taylor |
| $s_4$ | $\delta$ | D. Brown |
| $s_5$ | $\varepsilon$ | E. Cooper |
| $s_6$ | $\zeta$ | F. White |

(a)

| $\hat{f}_2$ | | |
|---|---|---|
| **salt** | enc | Occupation |
| $s_7$ | $\eta$ | Nurse |
| $s_8$ | $\theta$ | Nurse |
| $s_9$ | $\iota$ | Clerk |
| $s_{10}$ | $\kappa$ | Lawyer |
| $s_{11}$ | $\lambda$ | Manager |
| $s_{12}$ | $\mu$ | Designer |

(b)

| $\hat{f}_3$ | | | |
|---|---|---|---|
| **salt** | enc | Sickness | ZIP |
| $s_{13}$ | $\nu$ | Latex al. | 94140 |
| $s_{14}$ | $\xi$ | Latex al. | 94141 |
| $s_{15}$ | $\pi$ | Latex al. | 94140 |
| $s_{16}$ | $\rho$ | Celiac | 94139 |
| $s_{17}$ | $\sigma$ | Pollen al. | 94138 |
| $s_{18}$ | $\tau$ | Nickel al. | 94141 |

(c)

**Fig. 4.2** An example of physical fragments for the relation in Fig. 4.1(a)

efficiency, we assume that all attributes not appearing in the clear in a fragment are encrypted all together (encryption is applied on subtuples). Physical fragments are then defined as follows.

**Definition 4.4 (Physical fragment).** Let $R$ be a relation schema, and $\mathscr{F}=\{F_1,\ldots,F_m\}$ be a fragmentation of $R$. For each $F_i=\{a_{i_1},\ldots,a_{i_n}\} \in \mathscr{F}$, the *physical fragment* of $R$ over $F_i$ is a relation schema $\hat{F}_i(\underline{salt},enc,a_{i_1},\ldots,a_{i_n})$, where *salt* is the primary key, *enc* represents the encryption of all the attributes of $R$ that do not belong to the fragment, XORed (symbol $\oplus$) before encryption with the salt.

At the level of instance, given a fragment $F_i=\{a_{i_1},\ldots,a_{i_n}\}$, and a relation $r$ over schema $R$, the physical fragment $\hat{F}_i$ of $F_i$ is such that each plaintext tuple $t \in r$ is mapped into a tuple $\hat{t} \in \hat{f}_i$ where $\hat{f}_i$ is a relation over $\hat{F}_i$ and:

- $\hat{t}[enc] = E_k(t[R-F_i] \oplus \hat{t}[salt])$
- $\hat{t}[a_{i_j}] = t[a_{i_j}]$, for $j=1,\ldots,n$

Figure 4.2 illustrates an example of physical fragments for the relation schema in Fig. 4.1(a) that does not violate the well defined constraints in Fig. 4.1(b).

The algorithm in Fig. 4.3 shows the construction and population of physical fragments. When the size of the attributes exceeds the size of an encryption block, we assume that encryption of the protected attributes uses a Cipher Block Chaining (CBC) mode [88], with the salt used as the Initialization Vector (IV); in the CBC mode, the clear text of the first block is actually encrypted after it has been combined in binary XOR with the IV. Note that the salts, which we conveniently use as primary keys of physical fragments (ensuring no collision in their generation), need not be secret, because knowledge of the salts does not help in attacking the encrypted values as long as the encryption algorithm is secure and the key remains protected.

## 4.4 Minimal Fragmentation

We first formally discuss the properties we require to candidate fragmentations to ensure efficient query execution.

---

**INPUT**
A relation $r$ over schema $R$
$\mathscr{C} = \{c_1, \ldots, c_m\}$ /* well defined constraints */

**OUTPUT**
A set of physical fragments $\{\hat{F}_1, \ldots, \hat{F}_l\}$
A set of relations $\{\hat{f}_1, \ldots, \hat{f}_l\}$ over schemas $\{\hat{F}_1, \ldots, \hat{F}_l\}$

**MAIN**
$\mathscr{C}_f := \{c \in \mathscr{C} : |c| > 1\}$ /* association visibility constraints */
$\mathscr{A}_f := \{a \in R : \{a\} \notin \mathscr{C}\}$
$\mathscr{F} := \textbf{Fragment}(\mathscr{A}_f, \mathscr{C}_f)$
/* define physical fragments */
**for each** $F = \{a_{i_1}, \ldots, a_{i_l}\} \in \mathscr{F}$ **do**
    define relation $\hat{F}$ with schema: $\hat{F}(\underline{salt}, enc, a_{i_1}, \ldots, a_{i_l})$
/* populate physical fragments instances */
    **for each** $t \in r$ **do**
        $\hat{t}[salt] := \textbf{GenerateSalt}(F, t)$
        $\hat{t}[enc] := E_k(t[a_{j_1} \ldots a_{j_p}] \oplus \hat{t}[salt])$ /* $\{a_{j_1} \ldots a_{j_p}\} = R - F$ */
        **for each** $a \in F$ **do** $\hat{t}[a] := t[a]$
        insert $\hat{t}$ in $\hat{f}$

**Fig. 4.3**  Algorithm that correctly fragments $R$

## 4.4.1 Correctness

Given a schema $R$ and a set of confidentiality constraints $\mathscr{C}$ on it, a fragmentation satisfies all constraints if no fragment contains in the clear all the attributes which visibility is forbidden by a constraint. The following definition formalizes this concept.

**Definition 4.5 (Fragmentation correctness).** Let $R$ be a relation schema, $\mathscr{F}$ be a fragmentation of $R$, and $\mathscr{C}$ be a set of well defined constraints over $R$. $\mathscr{F}$ *correctly enforces* $\mathscr{C}$ iff $\forall F \in \mathscr{F}, \forall c \in \mathscr{C} : c \nsubseteq F$ (each individual fragment satisfies the constraints).

Note that this definition, requiring fragments not to be a superset of any constraint, implies that attributes appearing in singleton constraints do not appear in any fragment (i.e., they are always encrypted). Indeed, as already noted, singleton constraints require the attributes on which they are defined to appear only in encrypted form.

In this chapter, we specifically address the fragmentation problem and therefore focus only on the association visibility (i.e., non singleton) constraints $\mathscr{C}_f \subseteq \mathscr{C}$ and on the corresponding set $\mathscr{A}_f$ of attributes to be fragmented, defined as $\mathscr{A}_f = \{a \in R : \{a\} \notin \mathscr{C}\}$.

## 4.4.2 Maximal Visibility

The availability of plaintext attributes in a fragment allows an efficient execution of queries. Therefore, we aim at minimizing the number of attributes that are not represented in the clear in any fragment, because queries using those attributes will be generally processed inefficiently. In other words, we prefer fragmentation over encryption whenever possible and always solve association constraints via fragmentation.

The requirement on the availability of a plain representation for the maximum number of attributes can be captured by imposing that any attribute not involved in a singleton constraint must appear in the clear in at least one fragment. This requirement is formally represented by the definition of maximal visibility as follows.

**Definition 4.6 (Maximal visibility).** Let $R$ be a relation schema, $\mathscr{F}$ be a fragmentation of $R$, and $\mathscr{C}$ be a set of well defined constraints over $R$. $\mathscr{F}$ *maximizes visibility* iff $\forall a \in \mathscr{A}_f$: $\exists F \in \mathscr{F}$ such that $a \in F$.

Note that the combination of maximal visibility together with the definition of fragmentation (Definition 4.3) imposes that each attribute that does not appear in a singleton constraint must appear in the clear in exactly one fragment (i.e., at least for Definition 4.6, at most for Definition 4.3). In the following, we denote with $\mathfrak{F}$ the set of all possible fragmentations maximizing visibility. Therefore, we are interested in determining a fragmentation in $\mathfrak{F}$ that satisfies all the constraints in the system.

## 4.4.3 Minimum Number of Fragments

Another important aspect to consider when fragmenting a relation to satisfy a set of constraints is to avoid excessive fragmentation. In fact, the availability of more attributes in the clear in a single fragment allows a more efficient execution of queries on the fragment. Indeed, a straightforward approach for producing a fragmentation that satisfies the constraints while maximizing visibility is to define as many (singleton) fragments as the number of attributes not appearing in singleton constraints. Such a solution, unless demanded by the constraints, is however undesirable since it makes any query involving conditions on more than one attribute inefficient.

A simple strategy to find a fragmentation that makes query execution efficient consists in finding a *minimal fragmentation*, that is, a correct fragmentation that maximizes visibility, while minimizing the number of fragments. This problem can be formalized as follows.

**Problem 4.1 (Minimal fragmentation).** Given a relation schema $R$, a set $\mathscr{C}$ of well defined constraints over $R$, find a *fragmentation* $\mathscr{F}$ of $R$ such that all the following conditions hold:

1. $\mathscr{F}$ correctly enforces $\mathscr{C}$ (Definition 4.5);
2. $\mathscr{F}$ maximizes visibility (Definition 4.6);
3. $\nexists \mathscr{F}'$ satisfying the two conditions above such that the number of fragments composing $\mathscr{F}'$ is less than the number of fragments composing $\mathscr{F}$.

The minimal fragmentation problem is *NP-hard*, as formally stated by the following theorem.

**Theorem 4.1.** *The minimal fragmentation problem is NP-hard.*

*Proof.* The proof is a reduction from the NP-hard problem of minimum hypergraph coloring [50], which can be formulated as follows: *given a hypergraph $\mathcal{H}(V,E)$, determine a minimum coloring of $\mathcal{H}$, that is, assign to each vertex in $V$ a color such that adjacent vertices have different colors, and the number of colors is minimized.*

Given a relation schema $R$ and a set $\mathcal{C}$ of well defined constraints, the correspondence between the minimal fragmentation problem and the hypergraph coloring problem can be defined as follows. Any vertex $v_i$ of the hypergraph $\mathcal{H}$ corresponds to an attribute $a_i \in \mathcal{A}_f$. Any edge $e_i$ in $\mathcal{H}$, which connects $v_{i_1}, \ldots, v_{i_c}$, corresponds to a constraint $c_i = \{a_{i_1}, \ldots, a_{i_c}\}$, $c_i \in \mathcal{C}_f$. A fragmentation $\mathcal{F} = \{F_1(a_{1_1}, \ldots, a_{1_k}), \ldots, F_p(a_{p_1}, \ldots, a_{p_l})\}$ of $R$ satisfying all constraints in $\mathcal{C}$ corresponds to a solution $S$ for the corresponding hypergraph coloring problem. Specifically, $S$ uses $p$ colors and $\{v_{1_1}, \ldots, v_{1_k}\}$, corresponding to the attributes in $F_1$, are colored using the first color, vertices $\{v_{i_1}, \ldots, v_{i_j}\}$, corresponding to the attributes in $F_i$, are colored with the $i$-th color, and vertices $\{v_{p_1}, \ldots, v_{p_l}\}$, corresponding to the attributes in $F_p$, are colored using the $p$-th color. As a consequence, any algorithm finding a minimal fragmentation can be exploited to solve the hypergraph coloring problem.

The hypergraph coloring problem has been extensively studied in the literature, reaching interesting theoretical results. In particular, assuming $NP \neq ZPP$, there are no polynomial time approximation algorithms for coloring $k$-uniform hypergraphs with approximation ratio $O(n^{1-\varepsilon})$ for any fixed $\varepsilon > 0$ [60, 65].[2]

## 4.4.4 Fragmentation Lattice

To characterize the space of possible fragmentations and the relationships among them, we first introduce the concept of fragment vector as follows.

**Definition 4.7 (Fragment vector).** Let $R$ be a relation schema, $\mathcal{C}$ be a set of well defined constraints over $R$, and $\mathcal{F} = \{F_1, \ldots, F_m\}$ be a fragmentation of $R$ maximizing visibility. The *fragment vector* $V_{\mathcal{F}}$ of $\mathcal{F}$ is a vector of fragments with an element $V_{\mathcal{F}}[a]$ for each $a \in \mathcal{A}_f$, where the value of $V_{\mathcal{F}}[a]$ is the unique fragment $F_j \in \mathcal{F}$ containing attribute $a$.

*Example 4.2.* Let $\mathcal{F} = \{\{\texttt{Name}\}, \{\texttt{Occupation}\}, \{\texttt{Sickness}, \texttt{ZIP}\}\}$ be a fragmentation of the relation schema in Fig. 4.1(a). The fragment vector is the vector $V_{\mathcal{F}}$ such that:

- $V_{\mathcal{F}}[\texttt{Name}] = \{\texttt{Name}\}$;
- $V_{\mathcal{F}}[\texttt{Occupation}] = \{\texttt{Occupation}\}$;

---

[2] In a minimization framework, an approximation algorithm with approximation ratio $p$ guarantees that the cost $C$ of its solution is such that $C/C^* \leq p$, where $C^*$ is the cost of an optimal solution [50]. On the contrary, we cannot perform any evaluation on the result of a heuristic.

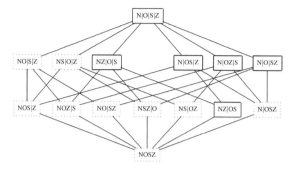

**Fig. 4.4** An example of fragmentation lattice

- $V_{\mathscr{F}}[\text{Sickness}]=V_{\mathscr{F}}[\text{ZIP}]=\{\texttt{Sickness,ZIP}\}$.

Fragment vectors allow us to define a partial order between fragmentations as follows.

**Definition 4.8 (Dominance).** Let $R$ be a relation schema, $\mathscr{C}$ be a set of well defined constraints over $R$, and $\mathscr{F}$, $\mathscr{F}'$ be two fragmentations of $R$ maximizing visibility. We say that $\mathscr{F}'$ *dominates* $\mathscr{F}$, denoted $\mathscr{F} \preceq \mathscr{F}'$, iff $V_{\mathscr{F}}[a] \subseteq V_{\mathscr{F}'}[a]$, $\forall\, a \in \mathscr{A}_f$. We say $\mathscr{F} \prec \mathscr{F}'$ iff $\mathscr{F} \preceq \mathscr{F}'$ and $\mathscr{F} \neq \mathscr{F}'$.

Definition 4.8 states that fragmentation $\mathscr{F}'$ dominates fragmentation $\mathscr{F}$ if $\mathscr{F}'$ can be computed from $\mathscr{F}$ by merging two (or more) fragments composing $\mathscr{F}$.

*Example 4.3.* Let $\mathscr{F}_1=\{\{\texttt{Name,ZIP}\},\ \{\texttt{Occupation,Sickness}\}\}$ and $\mathscr{F}_2=\{\{\texttt{Name}\}, \{\texttt{Occupation,Sickness}\}, \{\texttt{ZIP}\}\}$ be two fragmentations of the relation schema in Fig. 4.1(a). Since $\mathscr{F}_1$ can be obtained from $\mathscr{F}_2$ by merging fragments $\{\texttt{Name}\}$ and $\{\texttt{ZIP}\}$, it results that $\mathscr{F}_2 \prec \mathscr{F}_1$.

The set $\mathfrak{F}$ of all possible fragmentations maximizing visibility, together with the dominance relationship just introduced, form a *lattice*, as formally stated in the following definition.

**Definition 4.9 (Fragmentation lattice).** Let $R$ be a relation schema, and $\mathscr{C}$ be a set of well defined constraints over $R$. The *fragmentation lattice* is a pair $(\mathfrak{F}, \preceq)$, where $\mathfrak{F}$ is the set of all fragmentations of $R$ maximizing visibility and $\preceq$ is the dominance relationship among them, as defined in Definition 4.8.

The top element $\mathscr{F}_\top$ of the lattice represents a fragmentation where each attribute in $\mathscr{A}_f$ appears in a different fragment. The bottom element $\mathscr{F}_\bot$ of the lattice represents a fragmentation composed of a single fragment containing all attributes in $\mathscr{A}_f$. As an example, Fig. 4.4 illustrates the fragmentation lattice for the example in Fig. 4.1, with $\mathscr{A}_f=\{\texttt{Name, Occupation, Sickness, ZIP}\}$. Here, attributes are represented with their initials and fragments are divided by a vertical line. Furthermore, fragmentations that correctly enforce (Definition 4.5) constraints in Fig. 4.1(b) appear as solid boxes, while fragmentations that violate at least a constraint appear as dotted boxes.

An interesting property of the fragmentation lattice is that given a non correct fragmentation $\mathscr{F}_i$, any fragmentation $\mathscr{F}_j$ such that $\mathscr{F}_j \preceq \mathscr{F}_i$ is non correct.

**Theorem 4.2.** *Given a fragmentation lattice* $(\mathfrak{F}, \preceq)$, $\forall \mathscr{F}_i, \mathscr{F}_j \in \mathfrak{F}$ *such that* $\mathscr{F}_j \preceq \mathscr{F}_i$, $\mathscr{F}_i$ *non correct* $\Longrightarrow \mathscr{F}_j$ *non correct.*

*Proof.* If $\mathscr{F}_i$ is not correct, then $\exists c \in \mathscr{C}_f$ and $\exists F^i \in \mathscr{F}_i$ such that $c \subseteq F^i$. Since $\mathscr{F}_j \preceq \mathscr{F}_i$, by Definition 4.8, $\exists F^j \in \mathscr{F}_j$ such that $F^i \subseteq F^j$. Then $c \subseteq F^i \subseteq F^j$, and $\mathscr{F}_j$ is not correct.

By construction, each path in the lattice is characterized by a *locally minimal fragmentation*, which is the fragmentation such that all its descendants in the path correspond to non correct fragmentations. Intuitively, such locally minimal fragmentations can be determined either via a top-down visit or via a bottom-up visit of the lattice. The number of fragmentations at level $i$ (i.e., the solutions composed of $(n-i)+1$ fragments) of the lattice is $\left\{ {n \atop n-i} \right\}$, which is the *number of Stirling of the second kind* [53]. As a consequence, $|\mathfrak{F}| = \sum_i = 0^n \left\{ {n \atop n-i} \right\} = B_n$, which is the *Bell number* [53]. The second level of the lattice then contains a quadratic number of solutions ($O(n^2)$), and an exponential number of fragmentations ($O(2^n)$) resides in the first to last level. The top-down strategy, exploiting the fact that the number of fragments increases while going down in the lattice, seems then to be more convenient. In the following section, we then propose an exact algorithm that performs a top-down tree traversal of the lattice (i.e., each fragmentation is visited at most once) and that generates only a subset of all possible fragmentations.

## 4.5 A Complete Search Approach to Minimal Fragmentation

Although the number of possible fragmentations in $\mathfrak{F}$ is exponential in $|\mathscr{A}_f|$, the set of attributes to be fragmented is usually limited in size and therefore a complete search evaluating the different fragmentations maximizing visibility could be acceptable. To ensure the evaluation of each correct fragmentation maximizing visibility exactly once, we define a *fragmentation tree* as follows.

**Definition 4.10 (Fragmentation tree).** Let $(\mathfrak{F}, \preceq)$ be a fragmentation lattice. A *fragmentation tree* of the lattice is a spanning tree of $(\mathfrak{F}, \preceq)$ rooted in $\mathscr{F}_\top$.

We propose here a method for building a fragmentation tree over a given fragmentation lattice. To this aim, we assume the set $\mathscr{A}_f$ of attributes to be fragmented to be totally ordered, according to a relationship, denoted $<_A$, and assume that in each fragment $F$ attributes are maintained ordered, from the smallest, denoted $F.first$, to the greatest, denoted $F.last$. We then translate the order relationship among attributes into an order relationship among fragments within a fragmentation, by considering fragments to be ordered according to the order dictated by their smallest (.*first*) attribute.

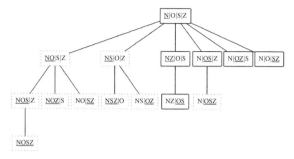

**Fig. 4.5** A fragmentation tree for the fragmentation lattice in Fig. 4.4

Since, within a fragmentation, each attribute appears in exactly one fragment, the fragments in each fragmentation are totally ordered. Each fragmentation $\mathscr{F}$ is then a sequence, denoted $\mathscr{F} = [F_1, \ldots, F_n]$, of fragments, where $\forall i, j = 1, \ldots, n : i < j$, $F_i.first <_A F_j.first$. In this case, we say that fragment $F_i$ *precedes* fragment $F_j$ in fragmentation $\mathscr{F}$. Given two fragments $F_i, F_j$ with $i < j$, we say that $F_i$ *fully precedes* $F_j$ iff all attributes of $F_i$ are smaller than all attributes in $F_j$, that is, $F_i.last <_A F_j.first$. Note that *full precedence* is only a partial ordering.

To ensure tree traversal and therefore to avoid computing a fragmentation twice, we exploit the precedence relationship among fragments and associate with each fragmentation $\mathscr{F} = [F_1, \ldots, F_n]$ a *marker* $F_i$ that is the non singleton fragment such that $\forall j > i$, $F_j$ is a singleton fragment. For the root, the marker is its first fragment. Intuitively, the marker associated with a fragmentation denotes the starting point for fragments to be combined to obtain children of the fragmentation (as a combination with any fragment preceding it will produce duplicate fragmentations). We then define an order-based cover for the lattice as follows.

**Definition 4.11 (Order-based cover).** Let $(\mathfrak{F}, \preceq)$ be a fragmentation lattice. An *order-based cover* of the lattice, denoted $\mathscr{T}(V, E)$, is an oriented graph, where $V = \mathfrak{F}$, and $\forall \mathscr{F}_p, \mathscr{F}_c \in V$, $(\mathscr{F}_p, \mathscr{F}_c) \in E$ iff, being $F_m^p$ the marker of $\mathscr{F}_p$, there exists $i, j$ with $m \leq i$ and $F_i^p$ fully preceding $F_j^p$, such that:

- $\forall l < j, l \neq i, F_l^c = F_l^p$;
- $F_i^c = F_i^p F_j^p$;
- $\forall l \geq j, F_l^c = F_{l+1}^p$.

As an example, consider the order-based cover in Fig. 4.5, where $<_A$ is the lexicographic order. It is built on the fragmentation lattice in Fig. 4.4 and the underlined fragments are the markers. Given fragmentations $\mathscr{F}_p = [\underline{N}|O|S|Z]$ and $\mathscr{F}_c = [N|\underline{OS}|Z]$, edge $(\mathscr{F}_p, \mathscr{F}_c)$ belongs to $\mathscr{T}$ since for $i = 2$ and $j = 3$ we have that $F_1^c = F_1^p = N$; $F_2^c = F_2^p F_3^p = OS$; and $F_3^c = F_{3+1}^p = Z$. The order-based cover so defined corresponds to a fragmentation tree for the lattice, as stated by the following theorem.

**Theorem 4.3.** *The order-based cover $\mathscr{T}$ of a lattice $(\mathfrak{F}, \preceq)$ is a fragmentation tree for $(\mathfrak{F}, \preceq)$ with root $\mathscr{F}_\top$.*

*Proof.* $\mathcal{T}$ is a fragmentation tree for $(\mathfrak{F}, \preceq)$ if: (1) each vertex at level $i$ (but the root $\mathcal{F}_{\top}$) has *exactly one* parent at level $i-1$, and (2) *each edge of $\mathcal{T}$ is an edge in* $(\mathfrak{F}, \preceq)$.

1. *Each vertex has at most one parent.* Suppose, by contradiction, that a vertex $\mathcal{F}=[F_1, \ldots, F_{n-1}]$ is a child of two different vertices in $\mathcal{T}$, say $\mathcal{F}_1=[F_1^1, \ldots, F_n^1]$ and $\mathcal{F}_2=[F_1^2, \ldots, F_n^2]$. Therefore, there exists a fragment $F_{i_1}$ in $\mathcal{F}$ obtained as $F_{i_1}^1 F_{j_1}^1$. Analogously, there exists a fragment $F_{i_2}$ in $\mathcal{F}$ obtained as $F_{i_2}^2 F_{j_2}^2$.
   Suppose also, without loss of generality, $i_1 < i_2$. By Definition 4.11, for each $F_k$ in $\mathcal{F}$, $k \neq i_1$, there exists a fragment $F_{k_1}^1$ in $\mathcal{F}_1$ such that $F_{k_1}^1=F_k$ and $k_1 \geq k$ (either $k_1 = k$ or $k_1 = k+1$). Therefore, there exists a non singleton fragment $F_l^1=F_{i_2}$ with $l \geq i_2$. As a consequence, $l > i_1$, thus the marker for $\mathcal{F}_1$ must be greater than or equal to $i_1$, by definition. This generates the contradiction.
   *Each vertex has at least one parent.* Let $\mathcal{F}$ be a vertex at level $i$ ($i \neq 1$) in $\mathcal{T}$ ($\mathcal{F} \neq \mathcal{F}_{\top}$), $F_m$ be its marker, and $F_m.last$ be the highest attribute in $F_m$. Consider fragmentation $\mathcal{F}_p$, containing all the fragments in $\mathcal{F}$ but $F_m$ and the two fragments obtained by splitting $F_m$ into $F_m - \{F_m.last\}$ and $\{F_m.last\}$. The marker of $\mathcal{F}_p$ precedes $m$, since all the fragments following $F_m$ in $\mathcal{F}$ are singleton in $\mathcal{F}_p$ as well. Also, the additional fragment $\{F_m.last\}$ is singleton and it follows $F_m^p$, according to relationship $<_A$ (since it is the maximum attribute). Therefore, by Definition 4.11, there is an edge $(\mathcal{F}_p, \mathcal{F})$ in $\mathcal{T}$, then $\mathcal{F}_p$ is parent of $\mathcal{F}$ and $\mathcal{F}_p$ has exactly one fragment more than $\mathcal{F}$ (i.e., $\mathcal{F}_p$ is at level $i-1$).
2. *Each edge in $\mathcal{T}$ is an edge in $(\mathfrak{F}, \preceq)$.* Let $(\mathcal{F}_p, \mathcal{F}_c)$ be an edge in $\mathcal{T}$. By Definition 4.11 it follows that $\mathcal{F}_p \preceq \mathcal{F}_c$, then $(\mathcal{F}_p, \mathcal{F}_c)$ is an edge of $(\mathfrak{F}, \preceq)$.

### 4.5.1 Computing a Minimal Fragmentation

Our complete search function, function **Fragment** in Fig. 4.6, performs a *depth first search* on the fragmentation tree $\mathcal{T}$ built as an order-based cover. Besides exploiting the tree structure, our proposal takes advantage of the result of Theorem 4.2 by pruning the fragmentation tree to avoid the visit of subtrees composed only of fragmentations violating constraints (i.e., the children of a non correct parent).

The function takes as input the set $\mathcal{A}_f$ of attributes to be fragmented and the set $\mathcal{C}_f$ of well defined non singleton constraints. The function uses variables: $marker[\mathcal{F}]$, representing the position of the marker within fragmentation $\mathcal{F}$; $Min$, representing the current minimal fragmentation; and $MinNumFrag$, representing the number of fragments composing $Min$. First, the function initializes variable $Min$ to $\mathcal{F}_{\top}$ and variable $MinNumFrag$ to the number of fragments in $\mathcal{F}_{\top}$. Then, it calls function **SearchMin** on $\mathcal{F}_{\top}$ that iteratively builds the children of $\mathcal{F}_{\top}$ according to Definition 4.11. Function **SearchMin**($\mathcal{F}_p$) is then recursively called on each fragmentation $\mathcal{F}_c$, child of $\mathcal{F}_p$, only if $\mathcal{F}_c$ satisfies all the constraints (i.e., if function **SatCon** returns *true*). The function exploits the fact that the number of fragments decreases while going down the lattice and compares $Min$ with a fragmentation only if it does not have correct children (i.e., it is a candidate minimal fragmentation).

---

**FRAGMENT**$(\mathscr{A}_f, \mathscr{C}_f)$
**for each** $a_i \in \mathscr{A}_f$ **do** $F_i^\top := \{a_i\}$ /* root of the search tree $\mathscr{F}_\top$ */
$marker[\mathscr{F}_\top] := 1$
$Min := \mathscr{F}_\top$ /* current minimal fragmentation */
$MinNumFrag :=$ **Evaluate**$(Min)$
**SearchMin**$(\mathscr{F}_\top)$ /* recursive call that builds the search tree */
**return**$(Min)$

**SEARCHMIN**$(\mathscr{F}_p)$
$localmin := true$ /* minimal fragmentation */
**for** $i := marker[\mathscr{F}_p] \ldots (|\mathscr{F}_p| - 1)$ **do**
  **for** $j := (i+1) \ldots |\mathscr{F}_p|$ **do**
    **if** $F_i^p.last <_A F_j^p.first$ **then** /* $F_i^p$ fully precedes $F_j^p$ */
      **for** $l := 1 \ldots |\mathscr{F}_p|$ **do**
        **case**:
          $(l < j \wedge l \neq i)$: $F_l^c := F_l^p$
          $(l > j)$:       $F_{l-1}^c := F_l^p$
          $(l = i)$:       $F_i^c := F_i^p F_j^p$
      $marker[\mathscr{F}_c] := i$
      **if SatCon**$(F_i^c)$ **then**
        $localmin := false$
        **SearchMin**$(\mathscr{F}_c)$ /* recursive call on correct fragmentation */
**if** $localmin$ **then**
  $nf :=$ **Evaluate**$(\mathscr{F}_p)$
  **if** $nf < MinNumFrag$ **then**
    $MinNumFrag := nf$
    $Min := \mathscr{F}_p$

**SATCON**$(F)$
**for each** $c \in \mathscr{C}_f$ **do**
  **if** $c \subseteq F$ **then return**$(false)$
**return**$(true)$

---

**Fig. 4.6**  Function that performs a complete search

It is interesting to note that, by substituting the definition of the **Evaluate** function with any other cost function monotonic with respect to the dominance relationship, the given function **Fragment** can determine the minimum cost/maximum gain fragmentation in $\mathfrak{F}$.

The fragmentation tree generated by function **Fragment** in Fig. 4.6 according to the order-based cover introduced in Definition 4.11 is not balanced. Indeed, the fragmentation tree is built by inserting the vertices in a specific order, starting from $\mathscr{F}_\top$ and inserting, at each level of the tree, the vertices from left to right. This implies that each vertex in the tree at the $i$-th level has, as parent, the leftmost vertex in the $(i-1)$-th level that satisfies Definition 4.11. Consequently, as it is visible from Fig. 4.5 the length of the paths from $\mathscr{F}_\top$ to the leaves of the fragmentation lattice decreases when moving from the left to the right in the tree.

*Example 4.4.* Figure 4.7 illustrates the execution, step by step, of function **Search-Min** applied to Example 4.1. The columns of the table in Fig. 4.7(a) represent the call to **SearchMin** with its parameter $\mathscr{F}_p$; the fragments $F_i^p$ and $F_j^p$ merged; the resulting fragmentation $\mathscr{F}_c$; the value of **SatCon** on $F_i^c$; the possible recursive call to **SearchMin**$(\mathscr{F}_c)$; the result of function **Evaluate**$(\mathscr{F}_p)$ (i.e., the number of fragments in $\mathscr{F}_p$), when computed; the updates to $Min$. Figure 4.7(b) illustrates the tree built by the recursive calls of function **SearchMin** on the considered example, with the number of fragments necessary for comparison with $Min$

| SearchMin($\mathscr{F}_p$) | $F_i^p$ | $F_j^p$ | $\mathscr{F}_c$ | SatCon($F_i^c$) | SearchMin($\mathscr{F}_c$) | Evaluate($\mathscr{F}_p$) | Min |
|---|---|---|---|---|---|---|---|
| N\|O\|S\|Z | N | O | NO\|S\|Z | false | – | | |
| | | S | NS\|O\|Z | false | – | | |
| | | Z | NZ\|O\|S | true | NZ\|O\|S | | |
| | O | S | N\|OS\|Z | true | N\|OS\|Z | | |
| | | Z | N\|OZ\|S | true | N\|OZ\|S | | |
| | S | Z | N\|O\|SZ | true | N\|O\|SZ | | |
| NZ\|O\|S | NZ | O | – | – | – | | |
| | | S | – | – | – | | |
| | O | S | NZ\|OS | true | NZ\|OS | | |
| NZ\|OS | – | – | – | – | – | 2 | NZ\|OS |
| N\|OS\|Z | OS | Z | N\|OSZ | false | | 3 | |
| N\|OZ\|S | OZ | S | – | – | – | 3 | |
| N\|O\|SZ | – | – | – | – | – | 3 | |

(a)

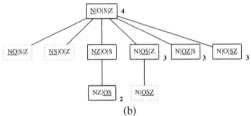

(b)

**Fig. 4.7**  An example of the execution of function **Fragment** in Fig. 4.6

at the right of the corresponding fragmentations. At the beginning, variable *Min* is initialized to [N|O|S|Z] and the corresponding *MinNumFrag* is set to 4. The function then calls function **SearchMin** on [N|O|S|Z]. At the first iteration of the two **for** loops in **SearchMin**([N|O|S|Z]), fragments $F_1^p$=N and $F_2^p$=O are merged, thus generating the fragmentation [NO|S|Z] that violates constraint $c_1$. The second fragmentation generated is [NS|O|Z], which violates $c_3$. The third fragmentation [NZ|O|S] is correct and **SearchMin**([NZ|O|S]) is recursively called, which in turn calls **SearchMin**([NZ|OS]). Since the two fragments in [NZ|OS] cannot be merged ($Z \not<_A O$), **SearchMin** is not further called. Therefore, the function compares the number of fragments composing [NZ|OS], which is 2, with *MinNumFrag* and updates *Min* accordingly. The recursive calls on the other fragmentations are processed in an analogous way. The final minimal fragmentation computed by the function is [NZ|OS] with 2 fragments only.

### 4.5.2 Correctness and Complexity

Before proving the complexity of function **Fragment** in Fig. 4.6, we introduce a lemma, proving that function **Fragment** computes all correct fragmentations, while it never generates more than once the same solution.

**Lemma 4.1.** *Function* **Fragment** *in Fig. 4.6 visits all correct fragmentations in $\mathscr{T}$ exactly once.*

*Proof.* The function starts from the root of $\mathscr{T}$ and recursively visits it with a depth-first strategy. At each call of **SearchMin**($\mathscr{F}_p$) it generates all the children of $\mathscr{F}_p$, according to Definition 4.11, by the first two **for** loops and the following **if** instruction. Since **SearchMin** is recursively called only on correct solutions, the subtrees rooted at non correct children are not visited. However, by Theorem 4.2, no correct solution belongs to these subtrees.

**Theorem 4.4 (Correctness).** *Function* **Fragment** *in Fig. 4.6 terminates and finds a minimal fragmentation (Problem 4.1).*

*Proof.* Function **Fragment** in Fig. 4.6 always terminates since, at each recursive call, it combines two of the fragments in the parent to compute its children. Therefore, the maximum reachable depth is $|\mathscr{A}_f|$.

We now prove that a solution $\mathscr{F}$ computed by this function over $\mathscr{A}_f$ and $\mathscr{C}_f$ is a minimal fragmentation. According to Problem 4.1, a fragmentation $\mathscr{F}$ is *minimal* if and only if (1) it is correct, (2) it maximizes visibility, and (3)$\nexists\mathscr{F}'$ composed of less fragments than $\mathscr{F}$ and satisfying the two conditions above. A fragmentation $\mathscr{F}$ computed by function **Fragment** in Fig. 4.6 satisfies these three properties.

1. The computed fragmentation $\mathscr{F}$ is correct since function **SearchMin** is recursively called only on correct fragmentations $\mathscr{F}_p$ (i.e., when **SatCon** is *true*). Therefore only correct solutions are assigned to the returned solution $\mathscr{F}$ (i.e., *Min*).
2. $\mathscr{F}$ is a fragmentation of $R$ maximizing visibility, since any solution generated by the function is obtained by merging fragments in $\mathscr{F}_\top$. $\mathscr{F}_\top$ is a fragmentation maximizing visibility, since it contains all attributes in $\mathscr{A}_f$ and each $a \in \mathscr{A}_f$ appears exactly in one fragment. The merge operation in the **SearchMin** function simply concatenates two fragments into a single one, thus producing a fragmentation $\mathscr{F}$ such that the condition of maximal visibility is satisfied.
3. $\mathscr{F}$ has minimum number of fragments, since the function visits all the correct solutions in $\mathscr{T}$ and compares *MinNumFrag* with the number of fragments in solutions having only non correct children. By Definition 4.8, the correct solutions that are not compared with $\mathscr{F}$ have a number of fragments greater or equal than $\mathscr{F}$.

Therefore the solution $\mathscr{F}$ computed by function **Fragment** in Fig. 4.6 is a minimal fragmentation.

**Theorem 4.5 (Complexity).** *Given a set $\mathscr{C} = \{c_1, \ldots, c_m\}$ of constraints and a set $\mathscr{A} = \{a_1, \ldots, a_n\}$ of attributes the complexity of function* **Fragment**($\mathscr{A}, \mathscr{C}$) *in Fig. 4.6 is $O(B_n \cdot m)$ in time.*

*Proof.* The proof comes directly from Lemma 4.1. In the worst case, each fragmentation in $\mathfrak{F}$, which are $O(B_n)$ in number, is generated exactly once by function

**Fragment** in Fig. 4.6. Also, function **SatCon** is called once for each solution generated and checks if all constraints, which are $m$ in number, are satisfied. The overall time complexity is therefore $O(B_n \cdot m)$.

## 4.6 A Heuristic Approach to Minimize Fragmentation

In this section, we present a heuristic algorithm for Problem 4.1 to be applied when the number of attributes in the schema does not allow a complete exploration of the solution space. The heuristic is based on the definition of *vector minimality*, which is then exploited to efficiently find a correct fragmentation maximizing visibility.

A *vector-minimal fragmentation* is formally defined as a fragmentation $\mathcal{F}$ that is correct, maximizes visibility, and all fragmentations that can be obtained from $\mathcal{F}$ by merging any two fragments in $\mathcal{F}$ violate at least one constraint.

**Definition 4.12 (Vector-minimal fragmentation).** Let $R$ be a relation schema, $\mathcal{C}$ be a set of well defined constraints, and $\mathcal{F}$ be a fragmentation of $R$. $\mathcal{F}$ is a *vector-minimal fragmentation* iff all the following conditions are satisfied:

1. $\mathcal{F}$ correctly enforces $\mathcal{C}$ (Definition 4.5);
2. $\mathcal{F}$ maximizes visibility (Definition 4.6);
3. $\nexists \mathcal{F}'$ satisfying the two conditions above such that $\mathcal{F} \prec \mathcal{F}'$.

According to this definition of minimality, it easy to see that while a minimal fragmentation is also vector-minimal, the vice versa is not necessarily true.

*Example 4.5.* Consider fragmentations $\mathcal{F}_1$ and $\mathcal{F}_2$ of Example 4.3, and the set of constraints in Fig. 4.1(b). Since $\mathcal{F}_2 \prec \mathcal{F}_1$, $\mathcal{F}_2$ is not vector-minimal. By contrast, $\mathcal{F}_1$ is vector-minimal. As a matter of fact, $\mathcal{F}_1$ contains all attributes of relation schema Patient in Fig. 4.1(a) but SSN (maximal visibility); satisfies all constraints in Fig. 4.1(b) (correctness); and no fragmentation obtained from it by merging any pair of fragments satisfies the constraints.

### 4.6.1 Computing a Vector-minimal Fragmentation

The definition of vector-minimal fragmentation allows us to design a heuristic approach for Problem 4.1 that works in polynomial time and computes a fragmentation that, even if it is not necessarily a minimal fragmentation, it is however near to the optimal solution, as the experimental results show (see Sect. 4.13).

Our heuristic method starts with an empty fragmentation and, at each step, selects the attribute involved in the highest number of unsolved constraints. The rationale behind this selection criterion is to bring all constraints to satisfaction in a few steps. The selected attribute is then inserted into a fragment that is determined in such a way that there is no violation of the constraints involving the attribute. If

---

FRAGMENT($\mathscr{A}_f, \mathscr{C}_f$)

*A_ToPlace* := $\mathscr{A}_f$
*C_ToSolve* := $\mathscr{C}_f$
*Min* := $\emptyset$
**for each** $a \in$ *A_ToPlace* **do** /* initialize arrays *Con*[] and *N_con*[] */
  *Con*[$a$] := $\{ c \in$ *C_ToSolve*: $a \in c \}$
  *N_con*[$a$] := $|$*Con*[$a$]$|$
**repeat**
  **if** *C_ToSolve* $\neq \emptyset$ **then**
    let *attr* be an attribute with the maximum value of *N_con*[]
    **for each** $c \in$ (*Con*[*attr*] $\cap$ *C_ToSolve*) **do**
      *C_ToSolve* := *C_ToSolve* $- \{c\}$ /* adjust the constraints */
      **for each** $a \in c$ **do** *N_con*[$a$] := *N_con*[$a$]$-1$ /* adjust array *N_con*[] */
  **else** /* since all the constrains are satisfied, choose any attribute in *A_ToPlace* */
    let *attr* be an attribute in *A_ToPlace*
  *A_ToPlace* := *A_ToPlace* $- \{attr\}$
  *inserted* := *false* /* try to insert *attr* into the existing fragments */
  **for each** $F \in$ *Min* **do** /* evaluate if $F \cup \{attr\}$ satisfies the constraints */
    *satisfies* := *true*
    **for each** $c \in$ *Con*[*attr*] **do**
      **if** $c \subseteq (F \cup \{attr\})$ **then**
        *satisfies* := *false* /* choose the next fragment */
        **break**
    **if** *satisfies* **then**
      $F := F \cup \{attr\}$ /* *attr* has been inserted into $F$ */
      *inserted* := *true*
      **break**
  **if** NOT *inserted* **then** /* insert *attr* into a new fragment */
    add $\{attr\}$ to *Min*
**until** *A_ToPlace* $= \emptyset$
**return**(*Min*)

---

**Fig. 4.8**  Function that finds a vector-minimal fragmentation

such a fragment does not exist, a new fragment for the selected attribute is created. The process terminates when all attributes have been inserted into a fragment. Figure 4.8 illustrates function **Fragment** that implements this heuristic method. The function takes as input the set $\mathscr{A}_f$ of attributes to be fragmented, and the set $\mathscr{C}_f$ of well defined non singleton constraints, used to initialize variables *A_ToPlace* and *C_ToSolve*, respectively. It computes a vector-minimal fragmentation *Min* of $\mathscr{A}_f$ as follows.

First, the function initializes *Min* to the empty set and creates two arrays *Con*[] and *N_con*[] that contain an element for each attribute $a$ in *A_ToPlace*. Element *Con*[$a$] contains the set of constraints on $a$, and element *N_con*[$a$] is the number of non solved constraints involving $a$ (note that, at the beginning, *N_con*[$a$] coincides with the cardinality of *Con*[$a$]). The function then executes a **repeat until** loop that, at each iteration, places an attribute *attr* into a fragment as follows. If there are constraints still to be solved (*C_ToSolve* $\neq \emptyset$) *attr* is selected as an attribute appearing in the highest number of unsolved constraints. Then, for each constraint $c$ in *Con*[*attr*]$\cap$*C_ToSolve*, the function removes $c$ from *C_ToSolve* and, for each attribute $a$ in $c$, decreases *N_con*[$a$] by one. Otherwise, that is, if all constraints are solved (*C_ToSolve* $= \emptyset$), the function chooses *attr* by randomly extracting an attribute from *A_ToPlace* and removes it from *A_ToPlace*. Then, the function looks for a fragment $F$ in *Min* in which *attr* can be inserted without violating any constraint

|            | $c_1$ | $c_2$ | $c_3$ | $N\_con[a_i]$ |
|------------|:-:|:-:|:-:|:-:|
| Name       | × | × |   | 2 |
| Occupation | × |   | × | 2 |
| Sickness   |   | × | × | 2 |
| ZIP        |   |   | × | 1 |
| *ToSolve*  | yes | yes | yes | |

*Min*=∅
*C_ToSolve*={$c_1,c_2,c_3$}
*A_ToPlace*={Name,Occupation,Sickness,ZIP}

---

*attr* = Name
*Con*[Name]={$c_1,c_2$}

|            | $c_1$ | $c_2$ | $c_3$ | $N\_con[a_i]$ |
|------------|:-:|:-:|:-:|:-:|
| Name       | ✓ | ✓ |   | 0 |
| Occupation | ✓ |   | × | 1 |
| Sickness   |   | ✓ | × | 1 |
| ZIP        |   |   | × | 1 |
| *ToSolve*  | ✓ | ✓ | yes | |

*Min* = {{Name}}
*C_ToSolve* = {$c_3$}
*A_ToPlace* = {Occupation,Sickness,ZIP}

---

*attr* = Occupation
*Con*[Occupation]={$c_1,c_3$}

|            | $c_1$ | $c_2$ | $c_3$ | $N\_con[a_i]$ |
|------------|:-:|:-:|:-:|:-:|
| Name       | ✓ | ✓ |   | 0 |
| Occupation | ✓ |   | ✓ | 0 |
| Sickness   |   | ✓ | ✓ | 0 |
| ZIP        |   |   | ✓ | 0 |
| *ToSolve*  | ✓ | ✓ | ✓ | |

*Min* = {{Name},{Occupation}}
*C_ToSolve* = ∅
*A_ToPlace* = {Sickness,ZIP}

---

*attr* = Sickness
*Con*[Sickness]={$c_2,c_3$}

|            | $c_1$ | $c_2$ | $c_3$ | $N\_con[a_i]$ |
|------------|:-:|:-:|:-:|:-:|
| Name       | ✓ | ✓ |   | 0 |
| Occupation | ✓ |   | ✓ | 0 |
| Sickness   |   | ✓ | ✓ | 0 |
| ZIP        |   |   | ✓ | 0 |
| *ToSolve*  | ✓ | ✓ | ✓ | |

*Min* = {{Name},{Occupation,Sickness}}
*C_ToSolve* = ∅
*A_ToPlace* = {ZIP}

---

*attr* = Z
*Con*[Z]={$c_3$}

|            | $c_1$ | $c_2$ | $c_3$ | $N\_con[a_i]$ |
|------------|:-:|:-:|:-:|:-:|
| Name       | ✓ | ✓ |   | 0 |
| Occupation | ✓ |   | ✓ | 0 |
| Sickness   |   | ✓ | ✓ | 0 |
| ZIP        |   |   | ✓ | 0 |
| *ToSolve*  | ✓ | ✓ | ✓ | |

*Min* = {{Name,ZIP},{Occupation,Sickness}}
*C_ToSolve* = ∅
*A_ToPlace* = ∅

**Fig. 4.9** An example of the execution of function **Fragment** in Fig. 4.8

including *attr*. If such a fragment *F* is found, *attr* is inserted into *F*, otherwise a new fragment {*attr*} is added to *Min*. Note that the search for a fragment terminates as soon as a fragment is found (*inserted=true*). Also, the control on constraint satisfaction terminates as soon as a violation to constraints is found (*satisfies=false*).

*Example 4.6.* Figure 4.9 presents the execution, step by step, of function **Fragment** in Fig. 4.8 applied to the example in Fig. 4.1. The left hand side of Fig. 4.9 illustrates the evolution of variables *attr*, *Min*, *C_ToSolve*, and *A_ToPlace*, while the right hand side graphically illustrates the same information through a matrix with a row for each attribute and a column for each constraint. If an attribute belongs to an unsolved constraint $c_i$, the corresponding cell is set to ×; otherwise, if $c_i$ is solved, the cell is set to ✓. At the beginning, *Min* is empty, all constraints are unsolved, and all attributes need to be placed. In the first iteration, function **Fragment** chooses attribute Name, since it is one of the attributes involved in the highest number of unsolved constraints. The constraints in $Con[\texttt{Name}]$ become now solved, $N\_con[a_i]$ is updated accordingly (for all the attributes in the relation), and fragment $\{\texttt{Name}\}$ is added to $Min$. Function **Fragment** proceeds in an analogous way by choosing attributes Occupation, Sickness, and Zip. The final solution is represented by fragmentation $Min=\{\{\texttt{Name},\texttt{ZIP}\}, \{\texttt{Occupation},\texttt{Sickness}\}\}$, which corresponds to the one computed by the complete search function in Fig. 4.6.

## 4.6.2 Correctness and Complexity

The correctness and complexity of function **Fragment** in Fig. 4.8 are stated by the following theorems.

**Theorem 4.6 (Correctness).** *Function* **Fragment** *in Fig. 4.8 terminates and finds a vector-minimal fragmentation (Definition 4.12).*

*Proof.* Function **Fragment** in Fig. 4.8 terminates since each attribute is considered only once, and the **repeat until** loop is performed till all the attributes are extracted from $A\_ToPlace$ (which is initialized to $\mathscr{A}_f$).

We now prove that a solution $\mathscr{F}$ computed by this function over $\mathscr{A}_f$ and $\mathscr{C}_f$ is a vector-minimal fragmentation. According to Definition 4.12, a fragmentation $\mathscr{F}$ is *vector-minimal* if and only if (1) it is correct, (2) it maximizes visibility, and (3) $\nexists \mathscr{F}':\mathscr{F} \prec \mathscr{F}'$ that satisfies the two conditions above. A fragmentation $\mathscr{F}$ computed by function **Fragment** in Fig. 4.8 satisfies these three properties.

1. Function **Fragment** inserts *attr* into a fragment $F$ if and only if $F \cup \{attr\}$ satisfies the constraints in $Con[attr]$. By induction, we prove that if $F \cup \{attr\}$ satisfies constraints in $Con[attr]$, it satisfies all constraints in $\mathscr{C}$.
   If $\{attr\}$ is the first attribute inserted into $F$, $F \cup \{attr\}=\{attr\}$. Since $attr \in \mathscr{A}_f$, then the set $\{attr\}$ satisfies all constraints in $\mathscr{C}$. Otherwise, if we suppose that $F$ already contains at least one attribute and that it satisfies all constraints in $\mathscr{C}$, then, by adding *attr* to $F$ the constraints that may be violated are only the constraints in $Con[attr]$. Consequently, if $F \cup \{attr\}$ satisfies all these constraints, it satisfies all constraints in $\mathscr{C}$.
   We can therefore conclude that $\mathscr{F}$ is a correct fragmentation.
2. Since each attribute $a$ in $\mathscr{A}_f$ is inserted exactly into one fragment, function **Fragment** produces a fragmentation $\mathscr{F}$ such that the condition of maximal visibility is satisfied.
3. By contradiction, let $\mathscr{F}'$ be a fragmentation satisfying the constraints in $\mathscr{C}_f$, maximizes visibility, and such that $\mathscr{F} \prec \mathscr{F}'$. Let $V_{\mathscr{F}}$ and $V_{\mathscr{F}'}$ be the fragment vectors associated with $\mathscr{F}$ and $\mathscr{F}'$, respectively.
   First, we prove that $\mathscr{F}'$ contains a fragment $V_{\mathscr{F}'}[a_i]$ that is the union of two different fragments, $V_{\mathscr{F}}[a_i]$ and $V_{\mathscr{F}}[a_j]$, of $\mathscr{F}$. Second, we prove that function **Fragment** cannot generate two different fragments whose union does not violate

any constraint. These two results generate a contradiction since $V_{\mathscr{F}'}[a_i]$, which contains $V_{\mathscr{F}}[a_i] \cup V_{\mathscr{F}}[a_j]$, is a fragment of $\mathscr{F}'$, and thus it does not violate the constraints.

a. Since $\mathscr{F} \prec \mathscr{F}'$, there exists a fragment such that $V_{\mathscr{F}}[a_i] \subset V_{\mathscr{F}'}[a_i]$, and then there exists an attribute $a_j$ (with $j \neq i$) such that $a_j \in V_{\mathscr{F}'}[a_i]$ and $a_j \notin V_{\mathscr{F}}[a_i]$. Note that $a_j \neq a_i$ because, by definition, $a_i \in V_{\mathscr{F}}[a_i]$ and $a_i \in V_{\mathscr{F}'}[a_i]$.
$V_{\mathscr{F}}[a_j]$ and $V_{\mathscr{F}'}[a_j]$ are the fragments that contain $a_j$. We now show that, not only $a_j \in V_{\mathscr{F}'}[a_i]$, but also the whole fragment $V_{\mathscr{F}}[a_j] \subset V_{\mathscr{F}'}[a_i]$. Since, $a_j \in V_{\mathscr{F}'}[a_j]$ and $a_j \in V_{\mathscr{F}'}[a_i]$ we have that $V_{\mathscr{F}'}[a_j] = V_{\mathscr{F}'}[a_i]$, but since $V_{\mathscr{F}}[a_j] \subset V_{\mathscr{F}'}[a_j]$ we have that $V_{\mathscr{F}}[a_j] \subset V_{\mathscr{F}'}[a_i]$ and therefore $(V_{\mathscr{F}}[a_i] \cup V_{\mathscr{F}}[a_j]) \subseteq V_{\mathscr{F}'}[a_i]$.

b. Let $F_h$ and $F_k$ be the two fragments computed by function **Fragment**, corresponding to $V_{\mathscr{F}}[a_i]$ and $V_{\mathscr{F}}[a_j]$, respectively. Assume, without loss of generality, that $h < k$ (since the proof in the case $h > k$ immediately follows by symmetry). Let $a_{k_1}$ be the first attribute inserted into $F_k$ by the function. Recall that the function inserts an attribute into a new fragment if and only if the attribute cannot be inserted into the already-existing fragments (e.g., $F_h$) without violating constraints. Therefore, the set of attributes $F_h \cup \{a_{k_1}\}$ violates a constraint as well as the set $V_{\mathscr{F}}[a_i] \cup V_{\mathscr{F}}[a_j]$ that contains $F_h \cup \{a_{k_1}\}$.

This generates a contradiction.

Therefore the solution $\mathscr{F}$ computed by function **Fragment** in Fig. 4.8 is a vector-minimal fragmentation.

**Theorem 4.7 (Complexity).** *Given a set $\mathscr{C} = \{c_1, \ldots, c_m\}$ of constraints and a set $\mathscr{A} = \{a_1, \ldots a_n\}$ of attributes the complexity of function* **Fragment**$(\mathscr{A}, \mathscr{C})$ *in Fig. 4.8 is $O(n^2 m)$ in time.*

*Proof.* To choose attribute *attr* from *A_ToPlace*, in the worst case function **Fragment** in Fig. 4.8 scans array *N_con[]*, and adjusts array *N_con[]* for each attribute involved in at least one constraint with *attr*. This operation costs $O(nm)$ for each chosen attribute. After the choosing phase, each attribute is inserted into a fragment. Note that the number of fragments is $O(n)$ in the worst case. To choose the right fragment that will contain *attr*, in the worst case the function tries to insert it into all fragments $F \in \mathscr{F}$, and compares $F \cup \{attr\}$ with the constraints in *Con[attr]*. Since the sum of the number of attributes in all the fragments is $O(n)$, then $O(n)$ attributes will be compared with the $O(m)$ constraints containing *attr*, giving, in the worst case, a $O(nm)$ complexity for each *attr*. Thus, the complexity of choosing the right fragment is $O(n^2 m)$. We can then conclude that the overall time complexity is $O(n^2 m)$.

## 4.7 Taking Attribute Affinity into Account

The computation of a minimal fragmentation exploits the basic principle according to which the presence of a high number of plaintext attributes permits an efficient execution of queries. Although this principle may be considered acceptable in many situations, other criteria can also be applied for computing a fragmentation. Indeed, depending of the use of the data, it may be useful to preserve the associations among some attributes. As an example, consider the fragmentation in Fig. 4.2 and suppose that the data need to be used for statistical purposes. In particular, suppose that physicians should be able to explore the link between a specific `Sickness` and the `Occupation` of patients. The computed fragmentation however does not make visible the association between `Sickness` and `Occupation`, thus making the required analysis not possible (as it would violate the constraints). In this case, a fragmentation where these two attributes are stored in clear form in the same fragment is preferable to the computed fragmentation. The need for keeping together some specific attributes in the same fragment may not only depend on the use of the data but also on the queries that need to be frequently executed on the data. Indeed, given a query $Q$ and a fragmentation $\mathscr{F}$, the execution cost of $Q$ varies according to the specific fragment used for computing the query. This implies that, with respect to a specific query workload, different fragmentations may be more convenient than others in terms of query performance.

To take into consideration both the use of the data and the query workload in the fragmentation process, we exploit the concept of *attribute affinity* traditionally applied to express the advantage of having pairs of attributes in the same fragment in distributed DBMSs [76] and that is therefore adopted by schema design algorithms using the knowledge of a representative *workload* for computing a suitable partition. In our context, attribute affinity is also a measure of how strong the need of keeping the attributes in the same fragment is. By considering the total order relationship $<_A$ among attributes in $\mathscr{A}_f$ and assuming $a_i$ to denote the $i$-th attribute in the ordered sequence, the affinity between attributes is represented through an *affinity matrix*. The matrix, denoted $M$, has a row and a column for each attribute appearing in non singleton constraints, and each cell $M[a_i, a_j]$ represents the benefit obtained by having attributes $a_i$ and $a_j$ in the same fragment. Clearly, the affinity matrix contains only positive values and is symmetric with respect to its main diagonal. Also, for all attributes $a_i$, $M[a_i, a_i]$ is not defined. The affinity matrix can then be represented as a triangular matrix, where only cells $M[a_i, a_j]$, with $i < j$ (i.e., $a_i <_A a_j$), are represented. Figure 4.10 illustrates an example of affinity matrix for relation `Patient` in Fig. 4.1, where $<_A$ is the lexicographic order.

The consideration of attribute affinity naturally applies to fragments and fragmentations. Fragmentations that maintain together attributes with high affinity are to be preferred. To reason about this, we define the concept of *fragmentation affinity*. Intuitively, the affinity of a fragment is the sum of the affinities of the different pairs of attributes in the fragment; the affinity of a fragmentation is the sum of the affinities of the fragments in it. This is formalized by the following definition.

|     | N  | O  | S  | Z  |
|-----|----|----|----|----|
| N   | 10 | 15 | 5  |    |
| O   |    | 5  | 10 |    |
| S   |    |    | 20 |    |
| Z   |    |    |    |    |

**Fig. 4.10** An example of affinity matrix

**Definition 4.13 (Fragmentation affinity).** Let $R$ be a relation schema, $M$ be an affinity matrix for $R$, $\mathscr{C}$ be a set of well defined constraints over $R$, and $\mathscr{F}=\{F_1,\ldots,F_n\}$ be a correct fragmentation of $R$. The affinity of $\mathscr{F}$, denoted $affinity(\mathscr{F})$, is computed as:

$affinity(\mathscr{F}) = \sum_{k=1}^{n} aff(F_k)$, where $aff(F_k) = \sum_{a_i,a_j \in F_k, i<j} M[a_i,a_j]$ is the affinity of fragment $F_k$, $k = 1 \ldots n$.

As an example, consider the affinity matrix in Fig. 4.10 and fragmentation $\mathscr{F}=\{\{\text{Name,ZIP}\}, \{\text{Occupation,Sickness}\}\}$. Then, $affinity(\mathscr{F}) = aff(\{\text{Name,ZIP}\}) + aff(\{\text{Occupation,Sickness}\}) = M[\text{N,Z}] + M[\text{O,S}] = 5+5 = 10$. With the consideration of affinity, the problem becomes therefore to determine a correct fragmentation that has maximum affinity. This is formally defined as follows.

**Problem 4.2 (Maximum affinity).** Given a relation schema $R$, a set $\mathscr{C}$ of well defined constraints over $R$, and an affinity matrix $M$, find a *fragmentation $\mathscr{F}$* of $R$ such that all the following conditions hold:

1. $\mathscr{F}$ correctly enforces $\mathscr{C}$ (Definition 4.5);
2. $\mathscr{F}$ maximizes visibility (Definition 4.6);
3. $\nexists \mathscr{F}'$ satisfying the conditions above such that $affinity(\mathscr{F}') > affinity(\mathscr{F})$.

Like Problem 4.1, the maximum affinity problem is *NP-hard*, as formally stated by the following theorem.

**Theorem 4.8.** *The maximum affinity problem is NP-hard.*

*Proof.* The proof is a reduction from the NP-hard minimum hitting set problem [50], which can be formulated as follows: *given a collection C of subsets of a set S, find the smallest subset S' of S such that S' contains at least one element from each subset in C.*

The reduction of the hitting set problem to the maximum affinity problem can be defined as follows. Let $S'$ be the solution of the minimum hitting set problem, and let $R = S \cup \{a_c\}$ be a relation, where $a_c$ is an attribute different from any other element in $S$.

We consider only the sets in $C$ with cardinality greater than 1, since any singleton set $s$ in $C$ corresponds to an element that must be inserted into the solution $S'$, and we can directly put it in. Moreover, if $s_i, s_j \in C$ and $s_i \subset s_j$, $s_j$ is redundant and can be removed from $C$, since if $S'$ contains an element of $s_i$, then it also contains an element of $s_j$. Thus, let $\mathscr{C}_f = \{s \in C: |s| > 1$ and $\forall s' \in C, s' \not\subset s\}$ be the set of association constraints, and let $\mathscr{A}_f = \{a \in R: \{a\} \not\in C\}$ be the set of attributes to be fragmented. We note that the construction of the set of constraints $\mathscr{C}_f$ is polynomial in $C$, and that, by construction, $\mathscr{C}_f$ is a set of well defined association constraints. Also, $a_c$ is not contained in any constraint in $\mathscr{C}_f$. Consider now an affinity matrix that contains the value 0 in every cell but the cells corresponding to $a_c$, which are set to 1 (i.e., $M[a_i, a_j] = 1$ iff $a_i = a_c$ or $a_j = a_c$; $M[a_i, a_j] = 0$, otherwise).

Since only the affinity between attribute $a_c$ and any other attribute is greater than 0, a fragmentation algorithm with the goal of maximizing the affinity computes a fragmentation where fragment $F_c$ containing $a_c$ includes the maximum number of attributes that can be inserted into a single fragment without violating the constraints. The affinity of the computed fragmentation corresponds to the cardinality of $F_c$. Since a constraint is violated only if all its attributes belong to the same fragment, a fragment may include all attributes composing a constraint but one. Therefore, maximizing the number of attributes composing $F_c$ is equivalent to minimizing the size of the set $S'$ of attributes that contains at least one attribute from each constraint. $S'$ is the solution of the minimum hitting set problem. Consequently, a maximal affinity fragmentation $\mathscr{F}$ of $R$, with respect to $M$, satisfying all constraints in $\mathscr{C}_f$, corresponds to a solution for the minimum hitting set problem. In particular, given fragment $F_c$ that contains attribute $a_c$, the solution for the minimum hitting set problem is $S' = R - F_c$.

In the following, we describe a heuristic approach for Problem 4.2.

## 4.8  A Heuristic Approach to Maximize Affinity

Our heuristic approach to determine a fragmentation that maximizes affinity exploits a greedy approach that, at each step, combines fragments that have the highest affinity. The heuristic starts by putting each attribute to be fragmented into a different fragment. The affinity between pairs of fragments is the affinity between the attributes contained in their union (as dictated by the affinity matrix). Then, the two fragments with the highest affinity, let call them $F_i$ and $F_j$, are merged together (if this does not violate constraints) and $F_i$ is updated by adding the attributes of $F_j$, while $F_j$ is removed. The affinity of the new version of $F_i$ with respect to any other fragment $F_k$ is the sum of the affinities that $F_k$ had with the old version of $F_i$ and $F_j$. The heuristic proceeds in a greedy way iteratively merging, at each step, the fragments with highest affinity until no more fragments can be merged without violating the constraints. Figure 4.11 gives a graphical representation of our heuristic approach; at each step, light grey boxes denote the pair of fragments with highest affinity. The correctness of the heuristics lies in the fact that, at each step, the affinity of the resulting fragmentation can only increase. As a matter of fact, it is easy to see that affinity is monotonic with respect to the dominance relationship (see Lemma 4.2 in Sect. 4.8.2).

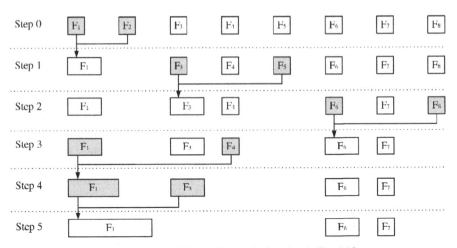

**Fig. 4.11** Graphical representation of the working of the function in Fig. 4.12

The following subsection describes the function implementing this heuristic approach. In the function, instead of controlling constraints to determine whether two fragments can be merged, we exploit the affinity matrix and set to $-1$ the affinity of fragments whose merging would violate the constraints (thus ignoring them in the evaluation of fragments to be merged).

### 4.8.1 Computing a Vector-minimal Fragmentation with the Affinity Matrix

Function **Fragment** in Fig. 4.12 takes as input the set $\mathscr{A}_f$ of attributes to be fragmented and a set $\mathscr{C}_f$ of well defined non singleton constraints. It computes a vector-minimal fragmentation *Max* of $\mathscr{A}_f$, where at each step the fragments to be merged are chosen according to their affinity. In the following, with a slight abuse of notation, we use $M[F_i,F_j]$ to denote the cell in the affinity matrix identified by the smallest attribute in $F_i$ and $F_j$ (i.e., $F_i.first$ and $F_j.first$), according to the order relationship $<_A$ on attributes in $\mathscr{A}_f$.

First, the function initializes the set of constraints *C_ToSolve* to be solved with $\mathscr{C}_f$, *Max* to a fragmentation having a fragment $F_i$ for each of the attributes $a_i$ in $\mathscr{A}_f$, and creates a set *FragmentIndex* that contains the index $i$ of each fragment $F_i \in Max$. The function also checks all constraints in *C_ToSolve* composed of two attributes only, and sets to $-1$ the corresponding cells in the affinity matrix. These constraints are removed from *C_ToSolve*. In general, at each iteration of the algorithm, for each $i < j$, $M[F_i,F_j]$ is equal to $-1$ if the fragment obtained as $F_i \cup F_j$ violates some constraints.

---

**FRAGMENT**$(\mathscr{A}_f, \mathscr{C}_f)$

/* initial solution with a fragment for each attribute */
$C\_ToSolve := \mathscr{C}_f$
$Max := \emptyset$
$FragmentIndex := \emptyset$
**for** $i=1\ldots|\mathscr{A}_f|$ **do**
    $F_i := \{a_i\}$
    $Max := Max \cup \{F_i\}$
    $FragmentIndex := FragmentIndex \cup \{i\}$
/* cells in $M$ corresponding to constraints are invalidated */
**for each** $\{a_x, a_y\} \in C\_ToSolve$ **do**
    $M[F_{min(x,y)}, F_{max(x,y)}] := -1$
    $C\_ToSolve := C\_ToSolve - \{\{a_x, a_y\}\}$
/* extract the pair of fragments with maximum affinity */
Let $[F_i, F_j]$, $i<j$ and $i,j \in FragmentIndex$, be the pair of fragments with maximum affinity
**while** $|FragmentIndex| > 1 \wedge M[F_i, F_j] \neq -1$ **do** /* merge the two fragments */
    $F_i := F_i \cup F_j$
    $Max := Max - \{F_j\}$
    $FragmentIndex := FragmentIndex - \{j\}$
    /* update the affinity matrix */
    **for each** $k \in FragmentIndex : k \neq i$ **do**
        **if** $M[F_{min(i,k)}, F_{max(i,k)}] = -1 \vee M[F_{min(j,k)}, F_{max(j,k)}] = -1$ **then**
            $M[F_{min(i,k)}, F_{max(i,k)}] := -1$
        **else**
            **for each** $c \in C\_ToSolve$ **do**
                **if** $c \subseteq (F_i \cup F_k)$ **then**
                    $M[F_{min(i,k)}, F_{max(i,k)}] := -1$
                    $C\_ToSolve := C\_ToSolve - \{c\}$
            **if** $M[F_{min(i,k)}, F_{max(i,k)}] \neq -1$ **then**
                $M[F_{min(i,k)}, F_{max(i,k)}] := M[F_{min(i,k)}, F_{max(i,k)}] + M[F_{min(j,k)}, F_{max(j,k)}]$
    Let $[F_i, F_j]$, $i<j$ and $i,j \in FragmentIndex$, be the pair of fragments with maximum affinity
**return**$(Max)$

---

**Fig. 4.12**  Function that finds a vector-minimal fragmentation with maximal affinity

Function **Fragment** in Fig. 4.12 then executes a **while** loop that, at each iteration, merges two fragments in *Max* as follows. If there are still pairs of fragments that can be merged, that is, there are still cells in $M$ different from $-1$, the function identifies the cell $[F_i, F_j]$ (with $i<j$) with the maximum value in $M$. Then, $F_i$ is updated to the union of the two fragments and $F_j$ is removed from *Max*. Also, $j$ is removed from *FragmentIndex*, since the corresponding fragment is no more part of the solution. The function, in the end, updates $M$. In particular, for each fragment $F_k$, $k \in (FragmentIndex - \{i\})$, cell $M[F_i, F_k]$ is set to $-1$ if either cell $M[F_i, F_k]$ or cell $M[F_j, F_k]$ is $-1$, or if $F_i \cup F_k$ violates at least one constraint still in *C_ToSolve*. In this latter case, the violated constraints $\{c_x, \ldots, c_y\}$ are removed from *C_ToSolve*. Otherwise, cell $M[F_i, F_k]$ is summed with the value in cell $M[F_j, F_k]$.

*Example 4.7.* Figure 4.13 presents the execution, step by step, of function **Fragment** in Fig. 4.12, applied to the example in Fig. 4.1 and considering the affinity matrix in Fig. 4.10. The left hand side of Fig. 4.13 illustrates the evolution of fragments and of the chosen pair $F_i$, $F_j$. The central part of Fig. 4.13 illustrates the evolution of matrix $M$, where dark grey columns represent fragments merged with other fragments, and thus removed from the set of fragments. The right hand side of Fig. 4.13 illustrates the set *C_ToSolve* of constraints to be solved: if an attribute belongs to constraint $c_i$ in *C_ToSolve*, the corresponding cell is set to $\times$; if $c_i$ is removed from *C_ToSolve*,

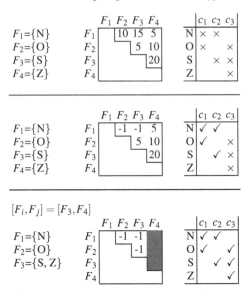

**Fig. 4.13**  An example of the execution of function **Fragment** in Fig. 4.12

the cell is set to $\checkmark$. At the beginning, all constraints are not solved and there is a fragment $F$ for each attribute in $\mathscr{A}_f$. First, $M$ is updated by setting to $-1$ the cells representing constraints involving only two attributes, that is, constraints $c_1$ and $c_2$, which are then removed from $C\_ToSolve$. Function **Fragment** chooses the cell in $M$ with the highest affinity, that is, $M[F_3,F_4] = 20$. Consequently, $F_4$ is merged with $F_3$ (the 4th column becomes dark grey to denote that fragment $F_4$ does not exist anymore). Then, values in the affinity matrix are updated: cell $M[F_1,F_3]$ is set to $-1$, since $M[F_1,F_3]$ were $-1$ before the merge operation; $M[F_2,F_3]$ should be set to $M[F_2,F_3]+M[F_2,F_4] = 5+10 = 15$, but it represents fragment $\{O,S,Z\}$ that violates constraint $c_3$, therefore the cell is set to $-1$ and $c_3$ is removed from $C\_ToSolve$. The final solution is $Max=\{\{\texttt{Name}\}, \{\texttt{Occupation}\}, \{\texttt{Sickness,ZIP}\}\}$, with affinity equal to 20. (Note that the solution computed by function **Fragment** in Fig. 4.8, and represented in Fig. 4.9, has 2 fragments only, but its affinity is 10.)

We note that function **Fragment** in Fig. 4.12 can be used to simulate function **Fragment** in Fig. 4.8 by sorting the attributes in the order with which they are considered by the function in Fig. 4.12 and considering an initial affinity matrix containing 0 as affinity value between each pair of attributes. The ordering of attributes can be simply computed by iteratively calculating the number of unsolved constraints $N\_con[a]$ involving each attribute $a$, and inserting, as next element of the ordered list, the attribute that maximizes $N\_con[a]$. Since the affinity matrix contains values 0 and $-1$ only, the order for choosing pair of fragments as the next maximum affinity pair is the same of function **Fragment** in Fig. 4.8.

## 4.8.2 Correctness and Complexity

Before proving the correctness and complexity of our heuristic, we introduce two lemmas proving the monotonicity property of fragmentation affinity with respect to the dominance relationship $\preceq$ and the correctness of the matrix computation, respectively.

**Lemma 4.2 (Monotonicity).** *Let R be a relation, M be an affinity matrix for R, $\mathscr{C}$ be a set of well defined constraints over R, and $\mathscr{F}$ and $\mathscr{F}'$ be two correct fragmentations for R. If $\mathscr{F} \preceq \mathscr{F}' \Longrightarrow$ affinity($\mathscr{F}$)$\leq$affinity($\mathscr{F}'$).*

*Proof.* By definition, given two fragmentations $\mathscr{F}=\{F_1,\ldots,F_n\}$ and $\mathscr{F}' = \{F_1',\ldots,F_m'\}$ such that $\mathscr{F} \prec \mathscr{F}'$, then $V_{\mathscr{F}}[a] \subseteq V_{\mathscr{F}'}[a], \forall a \in \mathscr{A}_f$. Therefore, for each $a$ such that $V_{\mathscr{F}}[a]=V_{\mathscr{F}'}[a]$, the affinity of the two fragments $F$ and $F'$ containing $a$ in $\mathscr{F}$ and $\mathscr{F}'$ respectively, is the same. On the contrary, for all attributes $a$ such that $V_{\mathscr{F}}[a] \subset V_{\mathscr{F}'}[a]$, the affinity of the two fragments $F$ and $F'$ containing $a$ in $\mathscr{F}$ and $\mathscr{F}'$ respectively, is such that $aff(F) \leq aff(F')$. In fact, $aff(F')=aff(F)+\sum M[a_i,a_j]$, $\forall a_i \in F', a_j \in (F'-F)$ with $i < j$. Since $M[a_i,a_j]$ is always a non negative value, it holds that if $\mathscr{F} \prec \mathscr{F}'$, then $affinity(\mathscr{F}) \leq affinity(\mathscr{F}')$.
If $\mathscr{F} = \mathscr{F}'$ it is straightforward to see that $affinity(\mathscr{F})=affinity(\mathscr{F}')$.

**Lemma 4.3.** *At the beginning of each iteration of the* **while** *loop in function* **Fragment** *in Fig. 4.12, $M[F_i,F_j] = -1 \Longleftrightarrow \exists c \in \mathscr{C}:c \subseteq (F_i \cup F_j)$.*

*Proof.* At initialization, function **Fragment** checks constrains involving exactly two attributes $\{a_x,a_y\}$ and sets to $-1$ the cell in $M$ corresponding to the pair of fragments $F_x=\{a_x\}$ and $F_y=\{a_y\}$. Also, these constraints are removed from *C_ToSolve*.

When function **Fragment** merges two fragments $F_i$ and $F_j$ $(i<j)$, $j$ is removed from *FragmentIndex*. For each $k$ in *FragmentIndex* but $i$, cell $M[F_{min(i,k)},F_{max(i,k)}]$ is set to $-1$ if either $M[F_{min(i,k)},F_{max(i,k)}]$ or $M[F_{min(j,k)},F_{max(j,k)}]$ were $-1$ before the update. Indeed, if either $F_i \cup F_k$ or $F_j \cup F_k$ violated a constraint before merging $F_i$ with $F_j$, also $F_i \cup F_k$ (i.e., $\exists c \in \mathscr{C}$ such that $c \subseteq F_i$ or $c \subseteq F_j$) since $F_i$ is set to $F_i \cup F_j$ after the update. Note that constraints removed from *C_ToSolve* are represented by $-1$ being always kept in $M$. Also, when $F_i \cup F_k$ is checked against constraints, the algorithm looks for constraints representing a subset of $F_i \cup F_k$ in *C_ToSolve*, and the corresponding constraints are removed from *C_ToSolve*, since there is a $-1$ in $M$ representing it.

**Theorem 4.9 (Correctness).** *Function* **Fragment** *in Fig. 4.12 terminates and finds a vector-minimal fragmentation (Definition 4.12).*

*Proof.* Function **Fragment** always terminates. In fact, the **while** loop terminates because at each iteration the number of indexes in *FragmentIndex* decreases by one, and the iterations are performed only if *FragmentIndex* contains at least two indexes.

We now prove that a solution $\mathscr{F}$ computed by this function over $\mathscr{A}_f$ and $\mathscr{C}_f$ is a vector-minimal fragmentation. According to Definition 4.12 of minimality, a fragmentation $\mathscr{F}$ is *vector-minimal* if and only if (1) it is correct, (2) it maximizes visibility, and (3) $\nexists \mathscr{F}':\mathscr{F} \prec \mathscr{F}'$ that satisfies the two conditions above. A fragmentation $\mathscr{F}$ computed by function **Fragment** in Fig. 4.12 satisfies these three properties.

1. Function **Fragment** starts with a simple correct fragmentation ($F_i := \{a_i\}$, for all $a_i \in \mathscr{A}_f$), and it iteratively merges only fragments that form a correct fragment, since the pair of fragments to be merged is extracted as the pair with maximum affinity and the fragments are merged only if their affinity is a positive value. By Lemma 4.3, only fragments whose union does not violate constraints are merged. We can therefore conclude that $\mathscr{F}$ correctly enforces $\mathscr{C}$.

2. Since each attribute in $\mathscr{A}_f$ is initially inserted exactly into one fragment, and when two fragments are merged only the result of their union is kept in $\mathscr{F}$, function **Fragment** produces a fragmentation $\mathscr{F}$ such that the condition of maximal visibility is satisfied.

3. By contradiction, let $\mathscr{F}'$ be a fragmentation satisfying the constraints in $\mathscr{C}_f$ and maximizing visibility, such that $\mathscr{F} \prec \mathscr{F}'$. Let $V_{\mathscr{F}}$ and $V_{\mathscr{F}'}$ be the fragment vectors associated with $\mathscr{F}$ and $\mathscr{F}'$, respectively.

   As already proved for Theorem 4.6, $\mathscr{F}'$ contains a fragment $V_{\mathscr{F}'}[a_i]$ that is the union of two different fragments, $V_{\mathscr{F}}[a_i]$ and $V_{\mathscr{F}}[a_j]$, of $\mathscr{F}$. We need then to prove that function **Fragment** cannot terminate with two different fragments whose union does not violate any constraint.

   Let $F_h$ and $F_k$ be the two fragments computed by function **Fragment**, corresponding to $V_{\mathscr{F}}[a_i]$ and $V_{\mathscr{F}}[a_j]$, respectively. Assume, without loss of generality, that $h < k$ (since the proof in the case $h > k$ immediately follows by symmetry). By Lemma 4.3, $M$ contains non-negative values only for pairs of fragments whose union generates a correct fragment, and therefore function **Fragment** cannot terminate with fragmentation $\mathscr{F}$ since $M$ still contains a non negative value to be considered ($M[F_h, F_k]$). This generates a contradiction.

Therefore the solution $\mathscr{F}$ computed by **Fragment** in Fig. 4.12 is a vector-minimal fragmentation.

**Theorem 4.10 (Complexity).** *Given a set of constraints $\mathscr{C} = \{c_1, \dots, c_m\}$ and a set of attributes $\mathscr{A} = \{a_1, \dots a_n\}$ the complexity of function* **Fragment**$(\mathscr{A}, \mathscr{C})$ *in Fig. 4.12 is $O(n^3 m)$ in time.*

*Proof.* The first **for** and **for each** loops of function **Fragment** cost $O(n + m)$. The **while** loop is performed $O(n)$ times, since at each iteration an element from *FragmentIndex* is extracted. The **for each** loop nested into the **while** loop updates the cells corresponding to fragments $F_i$ and $F_j$ in the affinity matrix. While $j$ is simply removed from *FragmentIndex*, and the column $F_j$ in the matrix is simply ignored, the update of the cells corresponding to $F_i$, which are $O(n)$ in number, costs $O(n^2 m)$ because all the constraints in *C_ToSolve* containing $F_i \cup F_j$ are considered. Each extraction of the pair of fragments with maximum affinity from $M$ simply scans (in the worst case) the affinity matrix, and its computational cost is $O(n^2)$ in time. The overall time complexity is therefore $O(n^3 m)$.

## 4.9 Query Cost Model

The standard approach to physical database design considers a representative set of queries as the starting point for the concrete identification of a satisfying solution. The same approach can also be applied for fragmenting data by taking into consideration the gain due to sets of attributes with more than two plaintext attributes appearing in the same fragment. To this purpose, we first introduce the following query cost function.

Given a fragmentation $\mathscr{F}$ for $R$, any query $Q$ can be evaluated on each of the fragments composing $\mathscr{F}$ because the corresponding physical fragment contains all the attributes of $R$, either in encrypted or in clear form. However, the execution cost of a query varies depending on the schema of the fragment used for query computation. Overall, with respect to a given query workload, some fragmentations can exhibit a lower cost than others. We are then interested in identifying a correct fragmentation with maximal visibility characterized by the minimum cost. To this purpose, we introduce a query cost model for query execution on a fragmented schema.

We describe a query workload $\mathscr{Q}$ as a set $\{Q_1,\ldots,Q_m\}$ of queries, where each query $Q_i$, $i = 1,\ldots,m$, is characterized by an execution frequency $freq(Q_i)$ and is of the form:

SELECT $a_{i_1},\ldots,a_{i_n}$
FROM $R$
WHERE $\bigwedge_{j=1}^{k} (a_j$ IN $V_j)$

where $V_j$ is a set of values in the domain of attribute $a_j$. Given a fragment $F_l \in \mathscr{F}$ and a query $Q_i \in \mathscr{Q}$, the cost of executing query $Q_i$ over $F_l$ depends on the set of attributes appearing in clear form in $F_l$ and on their selectivity; the availability of more attributes in clear form in a fragment permits a more efficient execution of queries on the fragment. We therefore estimate the *selectivity* of query $Q_i$ on $F_l$ in terms of the percentage of tuples in $F_l$ that are returned by the execution of query $Q_i$ on $F_l$. First, we evaluate the selectivity of each single condition in query $Q_i$ as follows. The selectivity of the $j$-th condition is computed as the ratio of the number of tuples in the fragment such that the value of attribute $a_j$ is a value in $V_j$, over the number of tuples in $F_l$, which corresponds to the number of tuples in the original relation $R$: $\frac{\Sigma_{v \in V_j} num\_tuples(a_j,v)}{|R|}$, where $num\_tuples(a_j,v)$ denotes the number of tuples whose value for attribute $a_j$ is $v$. Since we assume that the values of different attributes are distributed independently of each other, the selectivity of $\bigwedge_{j=1}^{k} (a_j$ IN $V_j)$ in query $Q_i$ on fragment $F_l$, denoted $S(Q_i,F_l)$, is the product of the selectivity of each single condition. In particular, the $j$-th condition contributes to the computation of the selectivity if and only if the corresponding attribute $a_j$ appears in clear form in $F_l$; otherwise the condition cannot be evaluated on the fragment and it is therefore not useful to select the tuples to be returned in response to the query (this restriction will be relaxed when we will consider in Sect. 4.12 the introduction of indexes on encrypted attributes).

The cost of evaluating query $Q_i$ on fragment $F_l$, denoted $Cost(Q_i,F_l)$, is then estimated by the size of the information returned, which is computed by multiplying $S(Q_i,F_l)$ (i.e., the selectivity of $Q_i$ on $F_l$) by the number of tuples in the considered fragment, and by the size in bytes, denoted $size(t_l)$, of the result tuples:

$$Cost(Q_i,F_l) = S(Q_i,F_l) \cdot |R| \cdot size(t_l)$$

This is a common assumption in cost models for query optimizers, particularly in systems where information has to be exchanged among different components, where the computational cost of queries is considered less important. We note that in the architecture only symmetric encryption is used, which current processors are typically able to apply even on high-rate transfers. It is reasonable then to build a cost model that does not consider this aspect.

Note that both the set of attributes in the SELECT clause and the set of attributes in the WHERE clause of query $Q_i$ determine the size in bytes of each result tuple. Indeed, $size(t_l)$ is obtained by summing the size in bytes of each attribute in the SE-LECT clause that appears in clear form in $F_l$ and the size in bytes of the *enc* attribute of the fragment, if there exists at least one attribute in the SELECT or WHERE clauses that does not appear in clear form in $F_l$. The rationale is that the encrypted portion of the fragment is needed to subsequently retrieve the desired attribute by decrypting it. The final cost of evaluating query $Q_i$ on $\mathscr{F}$ is therefore the minimum among the costs of evaluating the query on each of the fragments in $\mathscr{F}$. In other words, given $\mathscr{F} = \{F_1,\dots,F_r\}$, the cost of evaluating query $Q_i$ on $\mathscr{F}$ is:

$$Cost(Q_i,\mathscr{F}) = Min(Cost(Q_i,F_1),\dots,Cost(Q_i,F_r))$$

The cost of fragmentation $\mathscr{F}$ with respect to $\mathscr{Q}$ is the sum of the costs $Cost(Q_i,\mathscr{F})$ of each single query $Q_i$ weighted by its frequency, as formally stated in the following definition.

**Definition 4.14 (Fragmentation cost).** Let $R$ be a relation schema, $\mathscr{C}$ be a set of well defined constraints over $R$, $\mathscr{F}$ be a fragmentation of $R$ maximizing visibility, and $\mathscr{Q}=\{Q_1,\dots,Q_m\}$ be a query workload for $R$. The *fragmentation cost* of $\mathscr{F}$ with respect to $\mathscr{Q}$, denoted $Cost(\mathscr{Q},\mathscr{F})$, is computed as:

$$Cost(\mathscr{Q},\mathscr{F}) = \sum_{i=1}^{m}(freq(Q_i) \cdot Cost(Q_i,\mathscr{F}))$$

*Example 4.8.* Consider the fragmentation of the Patient relation in Fig. 4.2. Given query $Q$:

```
SELECT *
FROM    Patient
WHERE   Sickness='Latex al.' AND Occupation='Nurse'
```

the selectivity of the fragments is: $S(Q,F_1)=1$, since neither Sickness nor Occupation are plaintext represented in $F_1$; $S(Q,F_2)=2/6$, since Occupation belongs to $F_2$ and there are 2 nurses out of 6 patients; $S(Q,F_3)=3/6$, since Sickness belongs to $F_3$ and there are 3 patients suffering from Latex allergy. Supposing, for simplicity, that $size(t_1)=size(t_2)=size(t_3)=1$, we have that $Cost(Q,\mathscr{F})=Min(6,2,3)$. $Cost(Q,F_2)=2$.

The cost function here defined enjoys a nice property. Indeed, it is monotonic with respect to the dominance relationship $\preceq$, as proved by the following lemma.

**Lemma 4.4 (Monotonicity).** *Given a relation schema R, a set $\mathscr{C}$ of well defined constraints over R, the set $\mathscr{A}_f \subseteq R$ of attributes to be fragmented, and a query workload $\mathscr{Q}$ for R, $\forall \mathscr{F}_i, \mathscr{F}_j \in \mathfrak{F}$: $\mathscr{F}_i \preceq \mathscr{F}_j \implies Cost(\mathscr{Q},\mathscr{F}_j) \leq Cost(\mathscr{Q},\mathscr{F}_i)$.*

*Proof.* Consider two fragmentations $\mathscr{F}_i$ and $\mathscr{F}_j$ such that $\mathscr{F}_i \preceq \mathscr{F}_j$, $\mathscr{F}_i = \{F_1^i, \ldots, F_n^i\}$, and $\mathscr{F}_j = \{F_1^j, \ldots, F_{n-1}^j\}$. By Definition 4.8, $\mathscr{F}_j$ is obtained by merging two fragments in $\mathscr{F}_i$, say $F_a^i$ and $F_b^i$, into $F_c^j$. Therefore, $\forall F_x^j, x \neq c$ there exists a fragment $F_y^i = F_x^j$, and then $\forall Q_k \in \mathscr{Q}, S(Q_k, F_x^j) = S(Q_k, F_y^i)$. Considering now fragment $F_c^j$, we conclude that $\forall Q_k \in \mathscr{Q}, S(Q_k, F_c^j) \leq S(Q_k, F_a^i)$ and $S(Q_k, F_c^j) \leq S(Q_k, F_b^i)$, since $F_c^j = F_a^i \cup F_b^i$ and the selectivity of any condition ($a$ IN $V$) is between 0 and 1. Also, since $F_c^j$ has more attributes in clear from than $F_a^i$ (and $F_b^i$), the evaluation of any query $Q_k$ can be more precise in projecting attributes. Therefore, $size(t_a) \geq size(t_c)$ and $size(t_b) \geq size(t_c)$. As a consequence, $\forall Q_k \in \mathscr{Q}, Cost(Q, F_c^j) \leq Cost(Q_k, F_a^i)$ and $Cost(Q, F_c^j) \leq Cost(Q_k, F_b^i)$.

Since $\forall Q_k \in \mathscr{Q}, Cost(Q_k, \mathscr{F})$ is computed as the minimum among $Cost(Q_k, F)$, all the queries assigned to $F_a^i$ and $F_b^i$ by $\mathscr{F}_i$ are assigned to $F_c^j$ by $\mathscr{F}_j$, thus $Cost(Q_k, \mathscr{F}_j) \leq Cost(Q_k, \mathscr{F}_i)$ for these queries. Queries not assigned by $\mathscr{F}_i$ to $F_a^i$ and $F_b^i$ may be assigned by $\mathscr{F}_j$ to $F_c^j$. This happens only if $Cost(Q_k, F_c^j)$ is lower than $Cost(Q_k, F_x^i)$ for the previously chosen fragment $F_x^i$. Consequently, $\forall Q_k \in \mathscr{Q}, Cost(Q_k, \mathscr{F}_j) \leq Cost(Q_k, \mathscr{F}_i)$. Since the frequency of queries is the same for both $\mathscr{F}_i$ and $\mathscr{F}_j$, we conclude that $Cost(\mathscr{Q}, \mathscr{F}_j) \leq Cost(\mathscr{Q}, \mathscr{F}_i)$.

This property is easily extended to any pair of fragmentations $\mathscr{F}_i$ and $\mathscr{F}_j$, $\mathscr{F}_i \preceq \mathscr{F}_j$. Considering $(\mathfrak{F}, \preceq)$, there is a path from $\mathscr{F}_i$ to $\mathscr{F}_j$. Each solution $\mathscr{F}_a$ in the path dominates the solution $\mathscr{F}_b$ preceding it in the path. Therefore, $Cost(\mathscr{Q}, \mathscr{F}_a) \leq Cost(\mathscr{Q}, \mathscr{F}_b)$. By inductively applying this observation along all the path from $\mathscr{F}_i$ to $\mathscr{F}_j$, we obtain that $Cost(\mathscr{Q}, \mathscr{F}_j) \leq Cost(\mathscr{Q}, \mathscr{F}_i)$.

We are now interested in finding a correct fragmentation $\mathscr{F}$ with maximal visibility that minimizes the cost associated with a specific query workload, meaning that there does not exist another fragmentation satisfying constraints, maximizing visibility, and such that its cost is less than the cost associated with $\mathscr{F}$. This problem can be formalized as follows.

**Problem 4.3 (Minimum cost).** Given a relation schema $R$, a set $\mathscr{C}$ of well defined constraints over $R$, and a query workload $\mathscr{Q}=\{Q_1, \ldots, Q_m\}$ for $R$, find a fragmentation $\mathscr{F}$ of $R$ such that all the following conditions hold:

1. $\mathscr{F}$ correctly enforces $\mathscr{C}$ (Definition 4.5);
2. $\mathscr{F}$ maximizes visibility (Definition 4.6);
3. $\nexists \mathscr{F}'$ satisfying the conditions above and such that $Cost(\mathscr{Q}, \mathscr{F}') < Cost(\mathscr{Q}, \mathscr{F})$.

Like Problems 4.1 and 4.2, the minimum cost problem is *NP-hard*, as formally stated by the following theorem

**Theorem 4.11.** *The minimum cost problem is NP-hard.*

*Proof.* The proof is a reduction from the NP-hard minimum hitting set problem [50], which can be formulated as follows: *given a collection C of subsets of a set S, find the smallest subset S′ of S such that S′ contains at least one element from each subset in C.*

The reduction of the hitting set problem to the minimum cost problem can be defined as follows. Let $S′$ be the solution of the minimum hitting set problem, let $R = S$ be a relation composed of only binary attributes where 0 and 1 values are equally distributed, and let $\mathcal{Q}$ be the query workload of the system.

As for the proof of Theorem 4.8, we consider only the sets $s_i$ in $C$ with cardinality greater than 1 and such that there does not exists $s_j \in C$, $s_j \subset s_i$. Let $\mathscr{C}_f = \{s \in C: |s| > 1 \text{ and } \forall s′ \in C, s′ \not\subset s\}$ be the set of association constraints, and let $\mathscr{A}_f = \{a \in R: \{a\} \not\in C\}$ be the set of attributes to be fragmented. We note that the construction of the set of constraints $\mathscr{C}_f$ is polynomial in $C$. Also, by construction, $\mathscr{C}_f$ is well defined and does not contain singleton constraints.

Let us now suppose that $\mathcal{Q} = \{Q\}$, with $Q =$"SELECT * FROM $R$ WHERE $\bigwedge_{a_i \in \mathscr{A}_f}$ $(a_i=0)$" and $freq(Q) = 1$. Since the attribute values are equally distributed, the selectivity of all the conditions in $Q$ is the same. As a consequence, the cost of $Q$ with respect to an arbitrary fragment $F$ is proportional to the number of attributes in the fragment itself. The fragment $F$ in a fragmentation $\mathscr{F}$ that minimizes the cost with respect to the given query is therefore the one containing the maximum number of attributes. As described in the proof of Theorem 4.8, computing the fragment with the maximum cardinality corresponds to solve the minimum hitting set problem, since $S′ = R - F$.

## 4.10 A Heuristic Approach to Minimize Query Cost Execution

The two heuristic algorithms proposed in previous sections are not suited for solving Problem 4.3, since they do not take into account the advantage that arises in having sets of plaintext attributes appearing in the same fragment. Due to the monotonicity of the cost function introduced in the previous section with respect to the dominance relationship (see Lemma 4.4), the complete search algorithm proposed in Sect. 4.5 could also be used to compute a solution for Problem 4.3. In this case, function **Evaluate** should implement the $Cost(\mathcal{Q}, \mathscr{F})$ function. The complete search algorithm remains however exponential in the number of attributes. While this may not be an issue for small schemas, it may make the algorithm not applicable for complex schemas. We then propose a heuristic algorithm working in polynomial time.

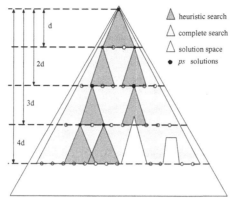

**Fig. 4.14** Depiction of the search spaces

## 4.10.1 Computing a Vector-minimal Fragmentation with the Cost Function

Our heuristic is based on a variant of the depth-first search algorithm proposed for the complete search, where a selected number of subtrees composing the fragmentation tree are visited following the same strategy proposed for the complete search algorithm. As shown in Fig. 4.14, the fragmentation lattice is logically divided into $\lceil \frac{n}{d} \rceil$ bands, where:

- $n$ is the cardinality of $\mathscr{A}_f$;
- $d$ is a parameter indicating the number of levels in the tree completely visited at each step;[3]
- $ps$ is a parameter indicating number of promising fragmentations explored at each step.

The first subtree of depth $d$ is built considering as a root vertex the top element $\mathscr{F}_\top$ of the lattice. At level $x \cdot d$, $ps$ subtrees are visited (where $ps$ is another parameter of the heuristic), taking as a root one of the fragmentations computed at level $x \cdot d$. These visits artificially stop at level $(x+1) \cdot d$, where the best $ps$ solutions are chosen as the root for the next in-depth visits of the solution space.

The function in Fig. 4.15 takes as input the set $\mathscr{A}_f$ of attributes to be fragmented, the set $\mathscr{C}_f$ of well defined non singleton constraints, and $d$ and $ps$ additional parameters. It computes a vector-minimal fragmentation $Min$ of $\mathscr{A}_f$, by visiting a subset of the fragmentations in $\mathfrak{F}$.

The algorithm uses variables: $marker[\mathscr{F}]$, representing the position of the marker within fragmentation $\mathscr{F}$; $Min$, representing the current minimal fragmentation; $MinCost$, representing the number of fragments composing $Min$; $currentqueue$, containing the best $ps$ fragmentations at level $x \cdot d$ that represent the roots of the subtrees

---

[3] If $d$ is equal to $|\mathscr{A}_f|$ the heuristic approach degenerates in a complete search.

**FRAGMENT**($\mathcal{A}_f, \mathcal{C}_f, d, ps$)
*nextqueue*:= NULL /* priority queue of promising solutions */
*currentqueue*:= NULL /* queue containing the best *ps* solutions */
**for each** $a_i \in \mathcal{A}_f$ **do** $F_i^\top := \{a_i\}$ /* root of the search tree $\mathcal{F}_\top$ */
*marker*$[\mathcal{F}_\top] := 1$ /* next fragment to be merged */
*Min* := $\mathcal{F}_\top$ /* current minimal fragmentation */
*MinCost* := *Cost*($\mathcal{Q}$,*Min*)
/* compute the best *ps* solution within *d* levels from $\mathcal{F}_\top$ */
**insert**(*nextqueue*,*Min*,*MinCost*)
**while** *nextqueue* $\neq$ NULL **do**
    $i := 1$
    **while** ($i \leq ps$) $\wedge$ (*nextqueue* $\neq$ NULL) **do**
        $i := i+1$
        **enqueue**(*currentqueue*,**extractmin**(*nextqueue*))
    *nextqueue* := NULL
    **while** *currentqueue* $\neq$ NULL **do**
        $\mathcal{F}$ := **dequeue**(*currentqueue*)
        *marker*$[\mathcal{F}] := 1$
        **BoundedSearchMin**($\mathcal{F}$,*d*)
**return**(*Min*)

**BOUNDEDSEARCHMIN**($\mathcal{F}_p$,*dist*)
*localmin* := *true* /* minimal correct fragmentation */
**for** $i=marker[\mathcal{F}_p] \ldots (|\mathcal{F}_p|-1)$ **do**
    **for** $j:=(i+1) \ldots |\mathcal{F}_p|$ **do**
        **if** $F_i^p.last <_A F_j^p.first$ **then** /* $F_i^p$ fully precedes $F_j^p$ */
            **for** $l=1 \ldots |\mathcal{F}_p|$ **do**
                **case**:
                    $(l<j \wedge l \neq i)$: $F_l^c := F_l^p$
                    $(l>j)$:         $F_{l-1}^c := F_l^p$
                    $(l=i)$:         $F_i^c := F_i^p F_j^p$
            *marker*$[\mathcal{F}_c] := i$
            **if** **SatCon**($F_i^c$) **then**
                *localmin* := *false*
                **if** *dist*= 1 **then**
                    **insert**(*nextqueue*,$\mathcal{F}_c$,*Cost*($\mathcal{Q}$,$\mathcal{F}_c$))
                **else**
                    **BoundedSearchMin**($\mathcal{F}_c$,*dist*$-1$) /* recursive call */
**if** *localmin* **then**
    *cost* := *Cost*($\mathcal{Q}$,$\mathcal{F}_p$)
    **if** *cost*<*MinCost* **then**
        *MinCost* := *cost*
        *Min* := $\mathcal{F}_p$

**Fig. 4.15** Function that finds a vector-minimal fragmentation with minimal cost

to be visited; and *nextqueue*, containing, in increasing cost order, the correct fragmentations at level $(x+1) \cdot d$ computed by the visits of the subtrees rooted at the solutions in *currentqueue*. At start, the algorithm initializes variable *Min* to $\mathcal{F}_\top$ and variable *MinCost* to the cost of $\mathcal{F}_\top$. Then, the algorithm calls function **BoundedSearchMin** on $\mathcal{F}_\top$ that iteratively builds the children of $\mathcal{F}_\top$ according to Definition 4.11. Function **BoundedSearchMin**($\mathcal{F}_p$) is then recursively called on each $\mathcal{F}_c$, child of $\mathcal{F}_p$, only if $\mathcal{F}_c$ satisfies all the constraints (i.e., if function **SatCon** returns *true*) and level *d* has not been reached. In this latter case, if $\mathcal{F}_c$ is correct, it is inserted in *nextqueue*. Note that the function exploits the monotonicity of the cost function adopted and compares the cost of $\mathcal{F}_p$ with *Min* only if $\mathcal{F}_p$ is locally minimal (i.e., it does not have correct children).

When the subtree rooted at $\mathcal{F}_\top$ has been visited, the first *ps* fragmentations in *nextqueue* become the content of *currentqueue* and *nextqueue* is re-initialized to

| Bounded($\mathcal{F}_p$,dist) | $F_i^p$ | $F_j^p$ | $\mathcal{F}_c$ | SatCon($F_i^c$) | Bounded($\mathcal{F}_c$,dist) | Cost($\mathcal{Q},\mathcal{F}_c$) | Min | nextqueue |
|---|---|---|---|---|---|---|---|---|
| N\|O\|S\|Z,1 | N | O | NO\|S\|Z | false | – | | | |
| | | S | NS\|O\|Z | false | – | | | |
| | | Z | NZ\|O\|S | true | – | 18 | | NZ\|O\|S,18 |
| | O | S | N\|OS\|Z | true | – | 12 | | N\|OS\|Z,12 |
| | | Z | N\|OZ\|S | true | – | 8 | | N\|OZ\|S,8 |
| | S | Z | N\|O\|SZ | true | – | 5 | | N\|O\|SZ,5 |
| N\|O\|SZ,1 | N | O | NO\|SZ | false | – | | | |
| | | SZ | NSZ\|O | false | – | | | |
| | O | SZ | N\|OSZ | false | – | 5 | N\|O\|SZ | |
| N\|OZ\|S,1 | N | OZ | NOZ\|S | false | – | | | |
| | | S | NS\|OZ | false | – | | | |
| | OZ | S | – | – | – | 8 | | |

(a)

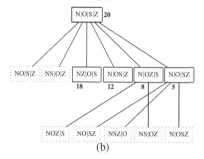

(b)

**Fig. 4.16** An example of the execution of function **Fragment** in Fig. 4.15

NULL. Function **BoundedSearchMin** is then called for each $\mathcal{F} \in currentqueue$, but moving back the marker of $\mathcal{F}$ to its first fragment. The re-initialization of the marker implies that, for the root fragmentation $\mathcal{F}$ of each subtree, all the fragmentations that represent a child of $\mathcal{F}$ in the lattice are re-evaluated, but possibly not in the order-based cover exploited by the complete search. We note that this strategy could visit more than once the same vertex in the lattice. However, the maximum number of times that a fragmentation can be generated is $ps$. When $currentqueue$ becomes empty, it is replaced with the first $ps$ fragmentations in $nextqueue$, until the last layer in the tree is reached.

*Example 4.9.* Figure 4.16 illustrates the execution, step by step, of function **BoundedSearchMin** (**Bounded** for short) applied to Example 4.1, assuming $d = 1$ and $ps = 2$. The table in Fig. 4.16(a) describes, for each (recursive) call to **Bounded-SearchMin**, the updates to the variables as well as to $nextqueue$. Therefore, the table in Fig. 4.16(a) has the same structure as the table in Fig. 4.7(a), except for the last column, which is dedicated to $nextqueue$, and for the column dedicated to the number of fragments in the solution, which is substituted here by the cost of the same. Fig. 4.16(b) illustrates the portion of the lattice visited by the algorithm. At the beginning variable $Min$ is initialized to [N|O|S|Z], which is the fragmentation representing the root of the tree, the cost $MinCost$ is initialized to 20, and $nextqueue$ is initially empty. First, function **BoundedSearchMin** is called on [N|O|S|Z], with

$dist = 1$. Since $dist-1$ is 0, the fragmentations generated from $[\underline{N}|O|S|Z]$ and satisfying constraints do not cause a recursive call to **BoundedSearchMin**, but they are inserted in *nextqueue* after the evaluation of their cost. Then, **BoundedSearchMin** is called on the first two fragmentations extracted from *nextqueue*, that is, $[N|O|\underline{SZ}]$ and $[N|\underline{OZ}|S]$. The final fragmentation computed by the heuristic algorithm is the same computed by **SearchMin**.

### 4.10.2 Correctness and Complexity

We now evaluate the correctness and the complexity of function **Fragment** in Fig. 4.15.

**Theorem 4.12 (Correctness).** *Function **Fragment** in Fig. 4.15 terminates and finds a vector-minimal fragmentation (Definition 4.12).*

*Proof.* Function **Fragment** terminates if all the **while** loops composing it terminate. The external **while** loop terminates when *nextqueue* is empty, provided the two internal loops terminate. The first internal loop terminates since variable $i$ is increased by one at each step. It terminates when $i > ps$. The second internal **while** loop terminates since, at each iteration, an element is extracted from *currentqueue* and function **BoundedSearchMin** terminates. Indeed, function **BoundedSearch-Min** at each recursive call, combines two of the fragments in the parent to compute its children and the recursion terminates, since at each call *dist* is decreased by one. Since **BoundedSearchMin** terminates, the number of items inserted in *nextqueue* is finite. Also, the number of layers in the fragmentation tree is finite. Therefore, *nextqueue* becomes empty and **Fragment** terminates.

We now prove that a solution $\mathscr{F}$ computed by this function over $\mathscr{A}_f$ and $\mathscr{C}_f$ is a vector-minimal fragmentation. According to Definition 4.12 of minimality, a fragmentation $\mathscr{F}$ is *vector-minimal* if and only if (1) it is correct, (2) it maximizes visibility, and (3) $\nexists \mathscr{F}' : \mathscr{F} \prec \mathscr{F}'$ that satisfies the two conditions above. The first two properties come directly from the proof of Theorem 4.4, since function **Bounded-SearchMin** works exactly as **SearchMin** when generating candidate solutions. We need only to prove the third property.

By contradiction, let $\mathscr{F}'$ be a fragmentation satisfying the constraints in $\mathscr{C}_f$ and maximizing visibility, such that $\mathscr{F} \prec \mathscr{F}'$. Let $V_{\mathscr{F}}$ and $V_{\mathscr{F}'}$ be the fragment vectors associated with $\mathscr{F}$ and $\mathscr{F}'$, respectively. As already proved in the proof of Theorem 4.6, $\mathscr{F}'$ contains a fragment $V_{\mathscr{F}'}[a_i]$ that is the union of two different fragments, $V_{\mathscr{F}}[a_i]$ and $V_{\mathscr{F}}[a_j]$, of $\mathscr{F}$. We need then to prove that function **Fragment** cannot terminate with two different fragments whose union does not violate any constraint.

There are two different situations when invoking **BoundedSearchMin**($\mathscr{F}$,*dist*), that is, *dist*> 1 or *dist*= 1. In the first case, $\mathscr{F}'$ is generated and **BoundedSearchMin**($\mathscr{F}'$,*dist* − 1) called. In the second case, $\mathscr{F}'$ is generated and inserted in *nextqueue*. Since *nextqueue* is an ordered queue, **BoundedSearchMin**($\mathscr{F}'$,*dist*) is called only if there are no more than *ps* solution with cost lower than *nextqueue*. But if $\mathscr{F}$ is returned as a solution of **Fragment**, no solution in *nextqueue* has lower cost than $\mathscr{F}$, since **BoundedSearchMin**($\mathscr{F}''$) is called for each $\mathscr{F}'' \in nextqueue$. This generates a contradiction since, from Lemma 4.4, $Cost(\mathscr{Q},\mathscr{F}') \leq Cost(\mathscr{Q},\mathscr{F})$.

Therefore the solution $\mathscr{F}$ computed by **Fragment** in Fig. 4.15 is a vector-minimal fragmentation.

**Theorem 4.13 (Complexity).** *Given a set of constraints* $\mathscr{C} = \{c_1,\ldots,c_m\}$, *a set of attributes* $\mathscr{A} = \{a_1,\ldots a_n\}$, *and the two parameters d and ps, the complexity of function* **Fragment**($\mathscr{A},\mathscr{C},d,ps$) *in Fig. 4.15 is* $O(\frac{ps}{d}n^{2d+2}m)$ *in time.*

*Proof.* The maximum number of iterations for the external **while** loop in function **Fragment** is $O(\frac{n}{d})$, since the fragmentation tree is composed of $n$ layers and, at each iteration, solutions inserted in *nextqueue* are $d$ layers under the solutions currently in *nextqueue*. Function **BoundedSearchMin**($\mathscr{F}_p,d$) is recursively called for each $\mathscr{F}_p \in currentqueue$, which contains at most $ps$ solutions, since it is filled in during the preceding **while** loop. Function **BoundedSearchMin**, which behavior is similar to function **SearchMin**, visits the solutions in the subtree rooted at $\mathscr{F}_p$ within $d$ layers. Therefore, the number of solutions built at each recursion of **BoundedSearchMin**($\mathscr{F}_p,d$) is $O(n^{2d})$ and each generated solution is compared with constraints in $\mathscr{C}$. The overall time complexity is therefore $O(\frac{ps}{d}n^{2d+2}m)$.

## 4.11 Query Execution

Fragmentation of a relation $R$ implies that only fragments, which are stored in place of the original relation to satisfy confidentiality constraints, are used for query execution. The fragments can be stored on a single server or on multiple servers. The server (or servers) storing the fragments while needs not to be trusted with respect to the confidentiality, since accessing single fragments or encrypted information does not expose to any privacy breach, it is trusted for correctly evaluating queries on fragments (honest-but-curious).

Users who are not authorized to access the content of the original relation $R$ have only a *partial view* on the data, meaning that they can only access the fragments. A query submitted by a user with a partial view can be presented directly to the server(s) storing the desired fragment. Users who are authorized to access the content of the original relation have a *full view* on the data and can present queries referring to the schema of the original relation. The queries issued by users with full view are then translated into equivalent queries operating on the encrypted and fragmented data stored on the server(s). The translation process is executed by a trusted component, called *query mapping component*, invoked every time there is the need to access sensitive information (see Fig. 4.17). In particular, the query mapping component receives a query $Q$ submitted by a user with full view along with the key $k$ possibly needed for decrypting the query result computed by the server, and returns the result of query $Q$ to the user. Since every physical fragment of $R$

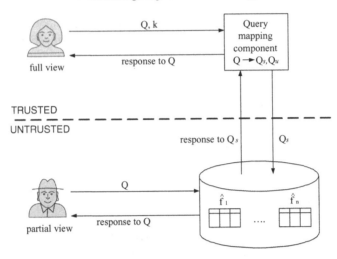

**Fig. 4.17** Interactions among users and server storing the fragments

contains all the attributes of $R$, either in encrypted or in clear form, no more than one fragment needs to be accessed to respond to $Q$. The query mapping component therefore maps the user's query $Q$ onto an equivalent query $Q_s$, working on a specific fragment. The server executes the received query $Q_s$ on the required fragment and returns the result to the query mapping component. Note that, whenever query $Q$ may involve attributes that do not appear in the clear form in the selected fragment, the query mapping component may need to execute an additional query $Q_u$ on the decrypted results of $Q_s$, which is in charge of enforcing all conditions that cannot be evaluated on the physical fragment or of projecting the attributes reported in the SELECT clause of query $Q$. In this case, the query mapping component decrypts the result received, executes query $Q_u$ on it, and returns the result of $Q_u$ to the user. We now describe the query translation process in more details.

We consider *select-from-where* SQL queries of the form $Q =$"SELECT $A_Q$ FROM $R$ WHERE $C$", where $A_Q$ is a subset of the attributes of $R$, and $C$ is a conjunction of basic conditions $c_1 \ldots c_n$ of the form $(a \ op \ v)$ or $(a_j \ op \ a_k)$, with $a$, $a_j$, and $a_k$ attributes of $R$, $v$ constant value, and $op$ comparison operator in $\{=, \neq, >, <, \leq, \geq\}$. Let us then consider the evaluation of query $Q$ on physical fragment $\hat{F}_i(\underline{salt}, enc, a_{i_1}, \ldots, a_{i_n})$, where *salt* is the primary key, *enc* contains the encrypted attributes, and $a_{i_1}, \ldots, a_{i_n}$ are the plaintext attributes (see Sect. 4.3). Suppose, for generality, that $C$ contains some conditions that involve attributes stored in the clear form in $\hat{F}_i$ and some others that cannot instead be evaluated on $\hat{F}_i$. The query mapping component translates the original query $Q$ into a query $Q_s$ operating on the physical fragment and defined as:

SELECT $A_Q \cap \{a_{i_1}, \ldots, a_{i_n}\}$, *salt*, *enc*
FROM $\quad \hat{F}_i$
WHERE $\bigwedge_{c_j \in C_i^e} c_j$

| Original query on $R$ | Translation over encrypted fragments |
|---|---|

| | |
|---|---|
| $Q :=$    SELECT   SSN, Name<br>      FROM     Patient<br>      WHERE    Sickness='Latex al.'<br>              AND<br>              ZIP='94140' | $Q_{s.3} :=$    SELECT   salt, enc<br>           FROM     $\hat{F}_3$<br>           WHERE    Sickness='Latex al.' AND<br>                        ZIP='94140'<br><br>$Q_u :=$    SELECT   SSN, Name<br>        FROM     $Decrypt(Q_{s.3}, Key)$ |
| $Q' :=$    SELECT   SSN, Name<br>       FROM     Patient<br>       WHERE    Sickness='Latex al.'<br>              AND<br>              ZIP='94140'<br>              AND<br>              Occupation='Nurse' | $Q'_{s.3} :=$    SELECT   salt, enc<br>           FROM     $\hat{F}_3$<br>           WHERE    Sickness='Latex al.' AND<br>                        ZIP='94140'<br><br>$Q'_u :=$    SELECT   SSN, Name<br>        FROM     $Decrypt(Q'_{s.3}, Key)$<br>        WHERE    Occupation='Nurse' |

**Fig. 4.18** An example of query translation over a fragment

where $C_i^e$ is the set of basic conditions in $C$ that can be evaluated on physical fragment $\hat{F}_i$, that is, $C_i^e = \{c_j : c_j \in C \wedge attributes(c_j) \in \hat{F}_i\}$, with $attributes(c_j)$ representing the attributes appearing in $c_j$. Note that the *salt* and *enc* attributes in the SELECT clause of $Q_s$ are specified only if the SELECT or WHERE clauses of the original query $Q$ involve attributes not appearing in clear form in the fragment. The query mapping component then decrypts the tuples received and executes on them a query $Q_u$ defined as:

SELECT $A_Q$
FROM    $Decrypt(Q_s, k)$
WHERE $\bigwedge_{c_j \in \{C - C_i^e\}} c_j$

where $Decrypt(Q_s, k)$ denotes a temporary relation including the tuples returned by $Q_s$ and where attribute *enc* has been decrypted through key $k$. The WHERE clause of $Q_u$ includes all conditions defined on attributes that do not appear in clear form in the physical fragment and that can be only evaluated on the decrypted result. The final result of query $Q_u$ is then returned to the user.

Note that since we are interested in minimizing the query evaluation cost, a query optimizer can be used to select the fragment that allows the execution of more selective queries by the server, thus decreasing the workload of the application and maximizing the efficiency of the execution [25]. For instance, the physical fragment $\hat{F}_i$ exploited by $Q_s$ can be conveniently chosen as the fragment minimizing $Cost(Q, F_i)$ as defined in Sect. 4.9.

*Example 4.10.* Consider the relation in Fig. 4.1(a) and its fragments in Fig. 4.2.

- Consider a query Q retrieving the Social Security Number and the name of the patients whose Sickness is *Latex al.* and whose ZIP is 94140. Since fragment $\hat{F}_3$ contains both Sickness and ZIP, it can evaluate both the conditions in the WHERE clause and is chosen for query evaluation. Figure 4.18 illustrates the translation of Q to queries $Q_{s.3}$ executed by the server on the fragment (notation $Q_{s.x}$ indicates a query executed by the server on fragment $x$), and $Q_u$ executed by the application. Query $Q_{s.3}$ returns to the application only the tuples belonging to the final result. The application just needs to decrypt them for projecting attributes SSN and Name.

• Consider a query $Q'$ retrieving the Social Security Number and the name of the patients whose Sickness is *Latex al.*, whose ZIP is 94140, and whose occupation is *Nurse*. Fragment $\hat{F}_3$ contains both Sickness and ZIP and $S(Q',F_3)=1/6$. Fragment $F_2$ contains only Occupation and $S(Q',F_3)=1/3$. The query mapping component therefore translates query $Q'$ into queries $Q'_{s.3}$ executed by the server on the fragment, and $Q'_u$ executed by the application (see Fig. 4.18). Since ZIP does not appear in clear form in fragment $\hat{F}_3$, the condition on it needs to be evaluated by the application, which also performs the projection of the SSN and Name attributes after decrypting the result computed by $Q_{s.3}$.

Note that queries whose WHERE clause contains negated conditions can be easily managed by the query mapping component since whenever a basic condition $c$ can be evaluated on a physical fragment, also its negation (i.e., NOT($c$)) can be evaluated on the same fragment. Queries whose WHERE clause contains disjunctions need special consideration. As a matter of fact, according to the semantics of the OR operator, any condition that cannot be evaluated over a fragment but that is in disjunction with other conditions that can be evaluated on the fragment cannot be simply evaluated on the result returned by the server (like done in the case of conjunction). Three scenarios are then possible. *1)* The query conditional part can be reduced to a conjunctive normal form; then the query mapping and evaluation can proceed as illustrated in the conjunctive case above. *2)* The query conditional part can be reduced to a disjunctive normal form where all components can be evaluated over different fragments; in this case the query mapping component will ask the server for the execution of as many queries as the components of the disjunction and will then merge (union) their results. *3)* The query conditional part contains a basic condition (to be evaluated in disjunction with others) that cannot be evaluated on any fragment (as it involves a sensitive attribute or attributes that appear in two different fragments); in this case the query mapping component will need to retrieve the entire fragment (any fragment will do) and evaluate the query condition at its site.

## 4.12 Indexes

As discussed in Sect. 4.3, each physical fragment reports in the clear only some of the attributes (as dictated by the fragmentation) while reporting the remaining attributes as a single encrypted tuple. This clearly has an impact on the performance of queries that need to evaluate selection predicates on both data appearing in clear and on data appearing in encrypted form (see Sect. 4.11). In the encrypted database proposals, queries on encrypted data are typically evaluated by means of indexes built on encrypted attributes: each cleartext query is translated into a query on the indexes and the result (complete but maybe including spurious tuples) is then decrypted and filtered by a trusted client (see Fig. 4.17). As discussed in Chap. 2, different kinds of indexes have been proposed, each providing a different balance between efficiency and confidentiality. We distinguish here these methods in three main classes.

- **Direct index.** The index is obtained by applying an encryption (unsalted) function on the cleartext values of the attribute [58].
- **Hash index.** The index is obtained by applying a keyed hash function to the cleartext values and restricting the result to produce collisions [24].
- **Flattened hash index.** The index is obtained by applying a keyed hash function with collision as in the case of hash index while applying a post processing that flattens the distribution of index values (so to avoid exposures of outliers) [45, 96].

In the encrypted database scenario, direct indexes are the most efficient, as conditions on cleartext values have a one to one correspondence with conditions on indexed values; at the same time they exhibit a major vulnerability making them applicable only in restricted situations. Hash indexes may create exposure problems only in the presence of outliers or in the case of use of multiple indexes in the same table, but otherwise guarantee confidentiality. Flattened hash indexes provide better protection. While one may think that the same properties could hold for fragmentations, unfortunately the application of indexes to fragments (which, unlike encrypted databases, report some cleartext values) introduces new vulnerabilities. In this section we briefly discuss the vulnerabilities to the aim of identifying a safe use of indexes, which we apply to our scenario. For simplicity, in the discussion we refer to a simple fragmentation problem characterized by a relation $R(a_1, a_2)$ and by a single confidentiality constraint $\{a_1, a_2\}$. We then examine the exposure risk of a fragment where $a_1$ appears in the clear jointly with an index of $a_2$, for each of the above classes of indexes. An instance of such a configuration, to which we refer for concreteness in the examples, is table Patient in Fig. 4.1(a) restricted to attributes Name and Sickness, together with the confidentiality constraint on them ($c_2$). We then evaluate the protection of the fragment reporting Name (Fig. 4.2(a)) in the clear when indexes on attribute Sickness are added. Fig. 4.19(c–e) reports the indexed fragments under the different indexing assumptions.

To examine the vulnerability of the indexed fragments, we first need to identify the knowledge available to the adversary, whose aim is to reconstruct the protected association (Name, Sickness). We can identity two kinds of knowledge: *vertical knowledge* and *horizontal knowledge*, characterized as follows.

- **Vertical knowledge.** Vertical knowledge is due to the fact that the values not appearing in the clear in one fragment (for a confidentiality constraint forbidding their association with other values) may appear in the clear in other fragments. Vertical knowledge does not require any additional external information for the adversary since, apart from the case where the attribute appears in a singleton constraint, it refers to information immediately present in other accessible

| Knowledge | | | Indexed fragment $\hat{f}_1$ | | | | | | | | | | | | | | | |
|---|---|---|---|---|---|---|---|---|---|---|---|---|---|---|---|---|---|---|

| Sickness | Name | Sickness | salt | enc | Name | $i_{s_1}$ | salt | enc | Name | $i_{s_2}$ | salt | enc | Name | $i_{s_3}$ |
|---|---|---|---|---|---|---|---|---|---|---|---|---|---|---|
| Latex al. | A. Smith | Latex al. | $s_1$ | $\alpha$ | A. Smith | $\lambda$ | $s_1$ | $\alpha$ | A. Smith | $\sigma$ | $s_1$ | $\alpha$ | A. Smith | $\eta$ |
| Latex al. | | | $s_2$ | $\beta$ | B. Jones | $\lambda$ | $s_2$ | $\beta$ | B. Jones | $\sigma$ | $s_2$ | $\beta$ | B. Jones | $\eta$ |
| Latex al. | | | $s_3$ | $\gamma$ | C. Taylor | $\lambda$ | $s_3$ | $\gamma$ | C. Taylor | $\sigma$ | $s_3$ | $\gamma$ | C. Taylor | $\eta$ |
| Celiac | | | $s_4$ | $\delta$ | D. Brown | $\phi$ | $s_4$ | $\delta$ | D. Brown | $\rho$ | $s_4$ | $\delta$ | D. Brown | $\mu$ |
| Pollen al. | | | $s_5$ | $\varepsilon$ | E. Cooper | $\pi$ | $s_5$ | $\varepsilon$ | E. Cooper | $\sigma$ | $s_5$ | $\varepsilon$ | E. Cooper | $\mu$ |
| Nickel al. | | | $s_6$ | $\zeta$ | F. White | $\psi$ | $s_6$ | $\zeta$ | F. White | $\rho$ | $s_6$ | $\zeta$ | F. White | $\mu$ |
| (a) vk | (b) hk | | (c) di | | | | (d) hi | | | | (e) fhi | | | |

**Fig. 4.19** Adversary knowledge (a,b) and choices for indexed fragments (c,d,e)

fragments (Fig. 4.2(c)). Figure 4.19(a) reports the vertical knowledge for our example, illustrating the projection of the `Sickness` attribute of Fig. 4.1(a). An adversary observing the fragments can then have complete knowledge of the distribution (cleartext values and their number of occurrences) of the indexed attributes. In the example, the observer knows that there are three patients with latex allergy.

- **Horizontal knowledge.** Horizontal knowledge is due to possible external knowledge that the adversary has with respect to the presence of specific tuples (corresponding to sensitive associations) in the table. In its simplest form, horizontal knowledge is then represented by knowledge of a single tuple $(v_1, v_2)$. In the example, the adversary may know that A. Smith suffers from latex allergy, that is, (A. Smith, latex al.) belongs to the original table $R$. Figure 4.19(b) reports this example of horizontal knowledge.

Let us now examine the exposure risk of indexed fragments under the assumption of horizontal and vertical knowledge.[4]

**Direct index, vertical knowledge (di-vk).** Sensitive associations are exposed depending on their distinguishability with respect to the number of occurrences of the indexed values. In our example, the index corresponding to latex allergy is completely recognizable being the only one with three occurrences. Consequently, the adversary infers that A. Smith, B. Jones, and C. Taylor suffer from latex allergy. As for the other three patients, the adversary can estimate they suffer from one of the three other sicknesses, each with equal probability.

**Direct index, horizontal knowledge (di-hk).** By joining this knowledge on the attribute appearing in the clear in the indexed fragment (`Name`), the adversary can retrieve the index value $\lambda$ corresponding to the specific cleartext value of the indexed attribute (`Sickness`). This exposes the associations having the same index value as the one the adversary knows. In our example, knowledge of the association (A. Smith, latex al.) allows the adversary to know that $\lambda$ is the index for latex allergy and therefore to infer that also B. Jones, and C. Taylor suffer from latex allergy.

---

[4] We note that the treatment of vertical knowledge strictly resembles threat models, proposed for encrypted databases, that assume that the adversary had complete knowledge of the cleartext database and aimed at reconstructing the correspondence between cleartext and index values (scenario **Freq+DB$^{\mathbf{K}}$** in [24]).

**Hash index, vertical knowledge (hi-vk).** The use of the hash index diminishes the exposure of association since different cleartext values may be represented by the same index value. However, values with a high number of occurrences (outliers), typically remain recognizable. In the example, the adversary can infer that index $\sigma$ refers to latex allergy, since it is the only one with at least 3 occurrences. She can then infer that 3 out of the 4 patients have latex allergy (i.e., each one has latex allergy with 0.75 probability).

**Hash index, horizontal knowledge (hi-hk).** Like in the direct index case, the adversary can recognize the index value representing the known cleartext value, with the only difference that the index value can correspond also to other cleartext values. The adversary can then infer that some associations are not present in the database (tuples with a different index value will certainly not have the known cleartext value). Together with vertical knowledge, it allows the adversary to infer the probability that some sensitive associations (with the known cleartext value) belong to the database. In the example, knowledge of the association (A. Smith, latex al.) allows the adversary to know that $\sigma$ is the index for latex allergy. Since there are 3 occurrences of latex allergy and 4 occurrences of $\sigma$, by removing the known one, the adversary can infer that B. Jones, C. Taylor, and E. Cooper have a 0.66 probability of suffering from latex allergy.

**Flattened hash index, vertical knowledge (fhi-vk).** Flattening the occurrences of the index values makes impossible to establish correspondences between cleartext values and index values on the basis of the number of occurrences. Flattened hash indexes are not vulnerable to vertical knowledge.

**Flattened hash index, horizontal knowledge (fhi-hk).** Like in the hashed case, the adversary can recognize the index value representing the known cleartext value. Together with vertical knowledge, it allows the adversary to identify the subset of tuples that may be associated with the cleartext value for which the index is known, with an estimate of the probability of their association. In the example, knowledge of the association (A. Smith, latex al.) allows the adversary to know that $\eta$ is the index for latex allergy and therefore to infer that B. Jones and C. Taylor have a 1.0 probability of suffering from latex allergy (since there are only three occurrences of latex allergy).

In summary, vertical and horizontal knowledge create inference risks on the basis of the number of occurrences of cleartext (and corresponding index) values. Even when values are equally distributed, all indexes above remain vulnerable to horizontal knowledge, allowing the adversary to infer associations with the known cleartext value. It is easy to see that such vulnerabilities are blocked when values are equally distributed and horizontal knowledge refers to association with indexed values that have only one occurrence. Both conditions are certainly satisfied when indexes refer to key attributes. Without compromising confidentiality of fragments, we can therefore apply indexes on attributes corresponding to candidate keys of the original relations.

Indexes can be easily integrated in our cost model, by simply refining $Cost(\mathcal{Q},\mathcal{F})$ function. This can easily be done by considering the selectivity of indexes for con-

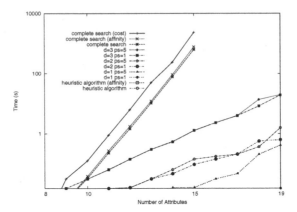

**Fig. 4.20** Computational time of the algorithms

ditions on indexed values. Indexes do not have any impact on the monotonicity property of the cost function on fragments (Lemma 4.4) and therefore on the applicability of our solutions. With reference to our example we can then consider direct indexes on SSN and Name (assuming Name is a candidate key) in any fragment where they appear encrypted (all fragments for SSN and those in Fig. 4.2(b) and Fig. 4.2(c) for Name).

## 4.13 Experimental Results

The heuristic algorithms presented in Sects. 4.6, 4.8, and 4.10 have been implemented as C programs to obtain experimental data and assess their behavior in terms of execution time and quality of the returned solution. Aiming to a comparison of the results computed by our heuristic algorithms to the optimal solutions, we also implemented three versions of the algorithm presented in Sect. 4.5, analyzing the complete solution space computing the fragmentation with the minimal number of fragments, the one with maximum affinity, and the one with minimum cost, since all these three functions are monotonic with respect to $\preceq$. The relation schema we considered in the experiments is composed of 19 attributes and is inspired by a database of medical information. Taking into account possible confidentiality requirements we expressed up to 18 confidentiality constraints. These constraints are well defined (see Definition 4.2) and composed of a number of attributes varying from 2 to 4 (we did not consider singleton constraints as they cannot be solved via fragmentation). The content of the affinity matrix has been produced using a pseudo-random generation function. We considered 14 queries, each characterized by a frequency value. The experiments have considered configurations with an increasing number of attributes, from 3 to 19, taking into account, for every configuration, only the constraints completely fitting in the selected attributes. The number of constraints

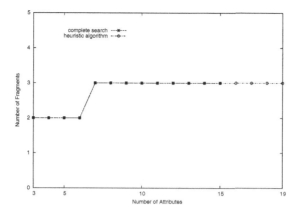

**Fig. 4.21** Number of fragments of the solution produced by the algorithms

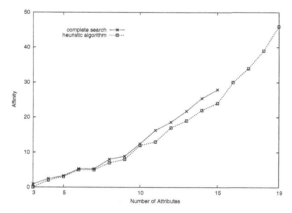

**Fig. 4.22** Affinity of the solution produced by the algorithms

for a configuration with $n$ attributes ranges between $n-3$ to $n+1$. The system implemented presents as an option the use of indexes, according to the analysis of Sect. 4.12.

Figure 4.20 compares the time required for the execution of the complete search algorithms with the heuristic algorithms presented in this chapter. Consistently with the fact that the problem of minimizing the number of fragments, the problem of maximizing affinity, and the problem of minimizing cost while satisfying confidentiality constraints are NP-hard, the three complete search strategies require exponential time in the number of attributes. The complete search then becomes unfeasible even for a relatively small number of attributes; with the availability of large computational resources it would still not be possible to consider large configurations (in our experiments we were able only to run the complete search for schemas with less than 15 attributes). By contrast, the time required for the execution of the heuristic analysis always remains low. The heuristic functions computing the vector minimal

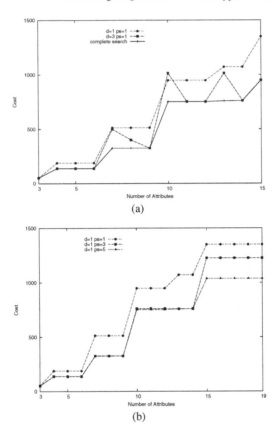

**Fig. 4.23** Cost of the solution produced by the algorithms

fragmentation and the vector minimal fragmentation maximizing affinity have computational time near 0. On the other hand, the time required by the heuristic for the minimum cost fragmentation problem increases exponentially with the increase in the look-ahead depth and linearly with the increase in the number of parallel steps, always showing a limited time for the simplest search ($d=1, ps=1$). It is therefore important to have available a family of heuristics, so to apply in real systems a dynamic approach where initially a search is executed with the most efficient heuristic, increasing the depth according to the amount of available resources. The number of parallel steps is a parameter that should become particularly interesting for the implementation of the heuristics on a multi-core architecture, where each core can manage the exploration of one of the alternatives.

Obviously, a successful heuristics presents a good behavior if it combines time efficiency with a demonstrated ability to produce good solutions. We therefore compared the solutions computed by the execution of each of the heuristic algorithms with those returned by the corresponding complete search algorithms.

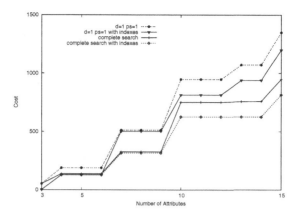

**Fig. 4.24** Cost of the solution with indexes

Figure 4.21 presents the number of fragments obtained by the execution of the heuristic algorithm computing a vector-minimal fragmentation (Sect. 4.6) compared with in a solution computed by the complete search function. As the graph shows, in all the cases that allow the comparison, our heuristic has always identified an optimal solution.

Figure 4.22 instead compares the affinity of the fragmentation computed through our heuristic (Sect. 4.8) with the optimal affinity produced by the complete search strategy. As the graph shows, for all the cases that allow the comparison, the affinity of the solution computed by the heuristic algorithm is close to the optimal value: the average of the difference is 4.2% and the maximum percentage difference is around 14.1%.

Figure 4.23(a) compares the cost of the solution obtained by our heuristic algorithm (Sect. 4.10) in two configurations: ($d = 1, ps = 1$) and ($d = 3, ps = 1$) with the optimal cost produced by the complete search strategy. The graph shows that even the simplest configuration ($d = 1, ps = 1$) guarantees good-quality fragmentations. Figure 4.23(b) shows the cost of the solutions produced by the heuristic with different values for parameter $ps$ (i.e., 1, 3, and 5) and with the fixed value $d = 1$. It is sufficient to use $ps = 5$ to obtain near-optimum fragmentations.

Finally, experiments have been run to evaluate the benefit of indexes and they have proved (see Fig. 4.24) that the use of indexes on encrypted attributes can produce a significant benefit. The amount of the benefit is highly dependent on specific features of the relation schema and query profile.

## 4.14 Chapter Summary

We presented an approach combining fragmentation and encryption to efficiently enforce privacy constraints over data collections, with particular attention to query execution efficiency. The algorithms proposed for fragmentation take into account the information available about the system, to the aim of efficiently executing queries on the fragmented data.

Besides the technical contribution, the ideas illustrated in this chapter can represent a step towards the effective enforcement, as well as the establishment, of privacy regulations. Technical limitations are in fact claimed as one of the main reasons why privacy cannot be achieved and, consequently, regulations not be put into enforcement. Research along the line presented here can then help in providing the building blocks for a more precise specification of privacy needs and regulations, as well as their actual enforcement, together with the benefit of a clearer and more direct integration of privacy requirements within existing ICT infrastructures.

# Chapter 5
# Distributed Query Processing under Safely Composed Permissions[1]

The integration of information sources detained by distinct parties, either for security or efficiency reasons, is becoming of great interest. A crucial issue in this scenario is the definition of mechanisms for the integration that correctly satisfy the commercial and business policies of the organization owning the data. In this chapter, we propose a new model based on the characterization of access privileges for a set of servers on the components of a relational schema. The proposed approach is based on three concepts: *i)* flexible permissions identify portions of the data being authorized, *ii)* relations are checked for release not with respect to individual authorizations but rather evaluating whether the information release they (directly or indirectly) entail is allowed by the permissions, and *iii)* each basic operation necessary for query evaluation entails different data exchanges among the servers. Access control is effectively modeled and efficiently executed in terms of graph coloring and composition. The query execution plan is checked against privileges to evaluate if it can or cannot be exploited for query evaluation.

## 5.1 Introduction

More and more emerging scenarios require different parties, each withholding large amounts of independently managed information, to cooperate with other parties in a larger distributed system to the aim of sharing information and perform distributed computations. Such scenarios range from: traditional distributed database systems,

---

[1] Part of this chapter appeared under S. De Capitani di Vimercati, S. Foresti, S. Jajodia, S. Paraboschi, and P. Samarati, "Assessing Query Privileges via Safe and Efficient Permission Composition," in Proc. of the 15th ACM Conference Conference on Computer and Communications Security (CCS 2008), Alexandria, VA, October 2008 [42] ©2008 ACM, Inc. Reprinted by permission http://doi.acm.org/10.1145/1455770.1455810; and under ©2008 IEEE, reprinted, with permission, from S. De Capitani di Vimercati, S. Foresti, S. Jajodia, S. Paraboschi, P. Samarati,"Controlled Information Sharing in Collaborative Distributed Query Processing," in Proc. of the 28th International Conference on Distributed Computing Systems (ICDCS 2008), Beijing, China, June 2008 [43].

where a centrally planned database design is distributed to different locations; to federated systems, where independently developed databases are merged together; to dynamic coalitions and virtual communities, where independent parties may need to selectively share part of their knowledge towards the completion of common goals. Regardless of the specific scenario, a common point of such a merging and sharing process is that it is selective: if on the one hand there is a need to share some data and cooperate, there is on the other hand an equally strong need to protect those data that, for various reasons, should not be disclosed.

The correct definition and management of protection requirements is therefore a crucial point for an effective collaboration and integration of heterogeneous large-scale distributed systems. The problem calls for a solution that must be expressive to capture the different data protection needs of the cooperating parties as well as simple and coherent with current mechanisms for the management of distributed computations, to be seamlessly integrated in current systems and fully exploit the availability of technical solutions that are the fruit of a large amount of research and development. To this aim and for the sake of concreteness, in this chapter we address the problem with specific consideration to distributed database systems, while noting that our approach can be extended to other data models.

Current approaches for the specification and enforcement of authorizations in relational databases claim flexibility and expressiveness because of the possibility of referring to views. Users can be given access to a specific portion of the data by the definition of the corresponding view (in the database schema) and the consequent granting of the authorization on the view to the user. It is then responsibility of the user to query the view itself. Queries on a table (base relation or view) are controlled with respect to authorizations specified on the table and granted only if authorized. When the diversity of users and possible views is considerable and dynamic such an approach clearly results limiting as it: *i)* requests to explicitly define a view for each possible access needed and *ii)* imposes on the user/application the burden of knowing and directly querying the view. The evaluation of query compliance in terms of existing authorization views has been considered in [71, 80, 81, 82].

We propose an expressive, flexible, and powerful, yet simple approach for the specification and enforcement of permissions that overcomes such limitations. Our permissions express privileges not on specific existing views but on stable components of the database schema, exploiting both relations and joins between them, effectively identifying the specific portion of the data whose access is being authorized. Another important aspect of our approach is that we do not limit ourselves to a simple relation-authorization control but allow data release whenever the information carried by the relation (either directly or indirectly due to the dependence of the attributes with other data not explicitly released) is legitimate according to the specified permissions. This is an important paradigm shift with respect to current solutions, departing from the need of specifying views to identify the portion of the data to be authorized but explicitly supporting such a specification in the permissions themselves.

A further novel aspect of the model is the definition of distinct access profiles for the users in the system, with explicit support for a cooperative management of queries. This is an important feature in distributed settings, where the minimization of data exchanges and the execution of steps of the queries in locations where it can be less costly is a crucial factor in the identification of an execution strategy characterized by good performance.

### 5.1.1 Chapter Outline

The remainder of the chapter is organized as follows. Section 5.2 introduces the preliminary concepts of distributed query evaluation, which are referred in our approach. Section 5.3 illustrates our security model. Section 5.4 illustrates a graph-based representation of the components of the proposed authorization model (database schema, relation profiles, and permissions). Section 5.5 describes a safe and efficient permission composition method, exploited for evaluating if a given release is to be authorized or denied. Section 5.6 discusses query planning and how protection requirements stated by permissions should impact its execution to ensure data are properly protected by the distributed computation. Section 5.7 proposes an algorithm for determining whether a query plan can be executed in the respect of the authorizations and determine, if it exists, a safe assignment of tasks to the distributed cooperating parties for the execution of the query plan. Finally, Sect. 5.8 concludes the chapter.

## 5.2 Preliminary Concepts

We consider a distributed system composed of different subjects, denoted $\mathscr{S}$, some of which act as servers storing different relations, denoted $\mathscr{R}$. In this section, we briefly introduce the basic concepts and assumptions on the data model and the distributed query execution.

### 5.2.1 Data Model

We refer in this chapter to the relational database model discussed in Sect. 3.2, which is basically composed of a set $\mathscr{R}$ of relations, each with a primary key, and of a set of referential integrity constraints.

*Example 5.1.* Consider a distributed system managing medical data, whose schema is represented in Fig. 5.1. The system is composed of four servers with one relation each: Employee stored at server $S_E$; Patient stored at server $S_P$; Treatment stored at server $S_T$, and Doctor, stored at server $S_D$. Underlined attributes denote primary keys. There are two referential integrity constraints: ⟨Treatment.SSN,Patient.SSN⟩, implying that treatments can only be given

| $\mathscr{R}$ | EMPLOYEE(<u>SSN</u>,Job,Salary) |
| | PATIENT(<u>SSN</u>,DoB,Race) |
| | TREATMENT(<u>SSN</u>,<u>IdDoc</u>,Type,Cost,Duration) |
| | DOCTOR(<u>IdDoc</u>,Name,Specialty) |
| $\mathscr{I}$ | ⟨Treatment.SSN,Patient.SSN⟩ |
| | ⟨Treatment.IdDoc,Doctor.IdDoc⟩ |
| $\mathscr{J}$ | ⟨Employee.SSN,Patient.SSN⟩ |

**Fig. 5.1** An example of relations, referential integrity constraints, and joins

to patients (values appearing for SSN in Treatment can be only values appearing for SSN in Patient), and ⟨Treatment.IdDoc,Doctor.IdDoc⟩, implying that treatments can only be prescribed by doctors (values appearing for IdDoc in Treatment can be only values appearing for IdDoc in Doctor).

Information in different relations can be combined by using the join operation, which allows the combination of tuples belonging to different relations imposing conditions on how tuples can be combined. For simplicity of exposition, we assume that attributes that can be joined appear with the same name in the different relations, and consider then all joins to be *natural joins*, that is, joins whose conditions are conjunctions of equality conditions that compare the value of two attributes with the same name. We denote a conjunction of equality conditions with a pair $\langle A_l, A_r \rangle$, where $A_l$ ($A_r$, resp.) is the list of attributes of the left (right, resp.) operand of the join. Note that while possible joins obviously include all referential integrity constraints, other joins are possible; in the following we denote with $\mathscr{J}$ the set of pairs representing the equality conditions of such additional joins. As an example, with respect to the relations in Fig. 5.1, Employee and Patient can be joined over attribute SSN (retrieving all people that are both employees and patients). Like the set of relations and the referential integrity constraints, possible joins are also specified at the time of database design [49].

We assume all attributes in the different relations to have distinct names, apart from attributes that can be joined, which appear instead with the same name. The intuitive rationale behind such a homonymity is that attributes that can be joined actually represent the same concept of the real world. For instance, SSN denotes social security numbers of people, who can then appear, for example, as patients or employees. We adopt the usual dot notation when necessary to distinguish the attribute in a specific relation (to refer to the occurrence of its specific values). For instance, Employee.SSN denotes the social security numbers of employees and Patient.SSN denotes the social security numbers of patients.

Different join operations can also be used to combine tuples belonging to more than two relations. The following definition introduces a *join path* as a sequence of natural join conditions.

**Definition 5.1 (Join path).** A *join path* over a sequence of relation schemas $R_1, \ldots, R_n$ is a sequence of $n-1$ joins $J_1, \ldots, J_{n-1}$ such that $\forall i = 1, \ldots, n-1$,

$J_i = \langle J_{li}, J_{ri} \rangle \in (\mathscr{I} \cup \mathscr{J})$ and $J_{li}$ are attributes of a relation appearing in a join $J_k$, with $k < i$.

*Example 5.2.* With reference to the relations in Fig. 5.1, an example of join path (combining more than two relations) is, $\{\langle \texttt{Patient.SSN,Treatment.SSN}\rangle,$ $\langle \texttt{Treatment.IdDoc,Doctor.IdDoc}\rangle\}$, allowing combination of tuples of the relations `Patient`, `Treatment`, and `Doctor` to retrieve, for example, the specialty of the caring doctor of patients of a given race.

While noting that the permission model we propose in the next section can be applied to any schema, in this chapter we assume that the schema is *acyclic* and *lossless* [1, 5, 9]. Acyclicity implies that the join path over any subset of the relations $\{R_1,\ldots,R_n\}$ in the schema, denoted *joinpath*$(\{R_1,\ldots,R_n\})$, is unique. Acyclicity rules out schemas that present recursion or multiple independent join conditions among the same relations. Acyclicity can be immediately evaluated on the schema graph (see Sect. 5.4), considering arcs without orientation. Losslessness of the schema guarantees that joins among relations produce only correct information (according to the real world). Intuitively, two relations produce a *lossless join* if the join among them does not produce spurious tuples. Losslessness can be evaluated by means of attribute intersections and functional dependencies (see Sect. 5.4). Acyclicity and losslessness assumptions are often used in relational databases, because they permit the realization of simple and efficient procedures on the data, at the same time capturing the requirements of most real-word situations [9].

## 5.2.2 Distributed Query Execution

Since relations are distributed at different servers, query execution may require communication and data exchanges among the different servers involved in the query (i.e., on which the relations to be accessed are stored). We assume that each server implements a relational engine able to compute queries and that it can require the execution of queries to other servers. We assume communication relies on trusted channels and that servers use robust authentication mechanism (e.g., SSL/TLS with 2-way authentication using certificates).

We consider simple *select-from-where* queries of the form: "SELECT $A$ FROM *Joined relations* WHERE $C$", corresponding to algebra expression $\pi_A(\sigma_C(R_1 \bowtie \ldots \bowtie R_n))$, where $A$ is a set of attributes, $C$ is the selection conditions, and $R_1 \bowtie \ldots \bowtie R_n$ are the joins in the FROM clause. Each query execution can be represented as a binary tree (called query tree plan) where leaves correspond to the physical relations accessed by the query (appearing in the FROM clause), each non-leaf node is a relational operator receiving in input the result produced by its children and producing a relation as output, and the root corresponds to the last operation and returns the result of the query evaluation. To simplify and without loss of generality, we assume the query plan to satisfy the usual minimization criteria, and, in particular, we assume that projections are "pushed down" the tree, to eliminate unnecessary

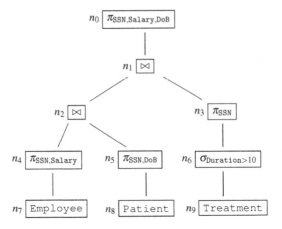

**Fig. 5.2** An example of query tree plan

attributes as soon as possible. While usually adopted for efficiency, this assumption is also important for security purposes, as it restricts the attributes being potentially disclosed to those strictly needed for the computation.

*Example 5.3.* Consider the relations in Fig. 5.1, and consider the following query.

```
SELECT E.SSN, Salary, DoB
FROM   Employee AS E JOIN Patient AS P ON E.SSN=P.SSN
                     JOIN Treatment AS T ON P.SSN=T.SSN
WHERE Duration> 10
```

The corresponding relational algebra expression is $\pi_{SSN,Salary,DoB}$ ($\sigma_{Duration>10}$ (Employee $\bowtie$ Patient $\bowtie$ Treatment)). An example of tree representing the execution of this query is represented in Fig. 5.2, where the selection on Duration> 10 on relation Treatment has been pushed down the tree (i.e., it is executed before the join operation). Also, projections on necessary attributes are added before join operations.

Queries may involve joins among relations stored at different servers, which therefore need to cooperate, and possibly exchange data, for performing the computation. We therefore propose an authorization model to regulate the view that each server (subject in general) can have on the data and ensure that query computation exposes to each server only data that the server can view.

We assume that each server is responsible for the definition of the access policy on its resources and permissions involving data stored at different servers are jointly specified and administered. A centralized query optimizer is responsible for the construction of the query plan, taking into account the schema and the permissions from each server. This is compatible with all the proposals for distributed databases aiming at a realization on concrete systems, which assume the use of a centralized optimizer; a purely distributed approach based on some form of negotiation protocol among the servers is considered impractical.

In the following, given an operation involving a relation stored at a server, we will use the term *operand* to refer independently to the relation or to the server storing it, when the semantics is clear from the context.

## 5.3 Security Model

We first present our simple, while expressive, permissions regulating how data can be released to each server. We then introduce the concept of relation profile that characterizes the information content of a relation.

### 5.3.1 Permissions

Consistently with standard practice in the security world, we assume a "closed" policy, where data can be made visible only to parties explicitly authorized for that.

Different subjects in the system may be authorized to view portions of the whole database content. We consider permissions in a simple, yet powerful form, specifying visibility *permissions* for subjects to view certain schema components. Formally, permissions are defined as follow.

**Definition 5.2 (Permission).** A *permission* $p$ is a rule of the form $[Att, Rels] \rightarrow S$ where:

- *Att* is a set of attributes, belonging to one or more relations, whose release is being authorized;
- *Rels* is a set of relations such that for every attribute in *Att* there is a relation including it;
- $S$ is a subject in $\mathscr{S}$.

Permission $[Att, Rels] \rightarrow S$ states that subject $S$ can view the sub-tuples over the set of attributes *Att* belonging to the join among relations *Rels* (on conditions *joinpath(Rels)*).

Note that, according to the definition, only attribute names (without indication of the relation) appear in the first component of the permission, whereas the relation (or relations) to which the attribute belongs is specified in the second component. This occurs even when the attribute appears in more than one relation (specified in *Rels*), consistently with the semantics that all the occurrences represent the same entity in the real world.

*Example 5.4.* Figure 5.3 illustrates some permissions on the relations in Fig. 5.1 that give Alice the visibility of:

- SSN, Date of Birth, and Race of all patients ($p_1$);

| |
|---|
| $p_1$: [(SSN,DoB,Race),(Patient)] →Alice |
| $p_2$: [(SSN,Type,Cost,Duration),(Treatment)] →Alice |
| $p_3$: [(Race,Specialty),(Treatment,Patient,Doctor)] →Alice |
| $p_4$: [(SSN,Job,Salary),(Employee)] →Alice |
| $p_5$: [(Name),(Treatment,Doctor)] →Alice |

**Fig. 5.3** Examples of permissions

- SSN of treated patients, together with Type, Cost, and Duration of their treatments ($p_2$);
- Race of patients and Specialty of their caring doctors ($p_3$);
- SSN, Job, and Salary of all employees ($p_4$);
- Name of doctors who have prescribed some treatment ($p_5$).

Note that the *presence of a relation* (and therefore the enforcement of the corresponding join condition) in a permission may *decrease the set of tuples* that are made visible (to only those tuples that participate in the join). However, such an elimination of tuples does not correspond to less information, rather it *adds information* on the fact that the visible tuples actually join with (i.e., have values appearing in) other tuples of the joined relations. For instance, permission $p_5$ while restricting the set of doctor's names visible to Alice to only the names of the doctors who have prescribed treatments, it allows Alice to see that such doctors have prescribed treatments (i.e., they appear in relation Treatment).

The only case where including an additional relation in the permission does not influence the result, and therefore does not imply an indirect information disclosure, occurs when the additional relations are reachable via referential integrity constraints (from the foreign to the primary key it references) from a relation in *Rels*. For instance, permissions $p_2$ in Fig. 5.3 and a permission with the same first component as $p_2$ and having (Treatment,Patient,Doctor) as a second component, are completely equivalent as they permit (direct or indirect) release of exactly the same information. Indeed, given the existing referential integrity constraints (see $\mathscr{I}$ in Fig. 5.1), all SSN and all IdDoc appearing in Treatment also appear in Patient and Doctor respectively. The added joins are therefore ineffective.

Note how the simple form of permissions above, with the specification of the relations as a separate element, proves quite expressive. In particular, the *Rels* component may also include relations whose attributes do not appear in the set *Att* of attributes. This may be due to either:

- *connectivity constraints*, where these relations are needed to build the association among attributes of other relations (i.e., the relations are in the join path). For instance, in permission $p_3$ in Fig. 5.3, Treatment relation appears in the join path to establish the association between each patient and her caring doctors, but none of its attributes is released. Note how the permission allows Alice to view the speciality of patients' doctors without need of knowing their treatment.
- *instance-based restrictions*, where the relations are needed to restrict the attributes to be released to only those values appearing in tuples that can be asso-

ciated with such relations. For instance, permission $p_5$ in Fig. 5.3 allows `Alice` to view the names of all the doctors who prescribed at least a treatment (i.e., tuples in the `Doctor` relation satisfying `Doctor.IdDoc=Treatment.IdDoc` condition) but not of those doctors who never prescribed a treatment. Note how instance-based restrictions can also be used to support situations where some information can be released only if explicit input is requested (the input is viewed in this case as a relation to be joined). For instance, we can define a permission such that providing the employees' SSN, the company can retrieve their treatments.

### 5.3.2 Relation Profiles

Permissions restrict the data (view) that can be released to each subject. To determine whether a release should be authorized or not, we first need to capture the information content of the released relation, which can be either base or computed by a query. To this purpose, we introduce the concept of *relation profile* as follows.

**Definition 5.3 (Relation profile).** Given a relation $R$, the *relation profile* of $R$ is a triple $[R^\pi, R^{\bowtie}, R^\sigma]$, where:

- $R^\pi$ is the set of attributes in $R$ (i.e., $R$'s schema);
- $R^{\bowtie}$ is the, possibly empty, set of base relations joined for the definition/construction of $R$;
- $R^\sigma$ is the, possibly empty, set of attributes involved in selection conditions in the definition/construction of $R$.

According to the definition above, the relation profile of a base relation $R(a_1, \ldots, a_n)$ is $[\{a_1, \ldots, a_n\}, R, \emptyset]$.

The reason why both *i)* the attributes being returned as result (i.e., the attributes in the SELECT clause) and *ii)* the attributes on which the query imposes conditions (i.e., the attributes in the WHERE clause) appear in the profile reflects the fact that the query result returns indeed information on both (or, equivalently, the subject needs permissions to view both for accessing the relation to be released).

Note also that, like for permissions, only attribute names (without indication of the relation) appear in the first component of the query profile, while the relation (or relations) to which the attributes belong is specified in the second component. Indeed, if an attribute belongs to more than one relation (and therefore participates in the join), the common values of such an attribute in all relations are released by the query, regardless of the specific relation mentioned in the SELECT clause, which is needed for disambiguating attribute names. The consideration of the attribute names allows us to conveniently capture this aspect regardless of the specific way in which the query has been written. For instance, with respect to the query in Example 5.3, the set of social security numbers released by the query is the intersection of the set of SSN values of patients, employees, and treatments as captured in the profile:

| Operation | Profile | | |
|---|---|---|---|
| | $R^\pi$ | $R^\bowtie$ | $R^\sigma$ |
| $R := \pi_A(R_l)$ | $A$ | $R_l^\bowtie$ | $R_l^\sigma$ |
| $R := \sigma_A(R_l)$ | $R_l^\pi$ | $R_l^\bowtie$ | $R_l^\sigma \cup A$ |
| $R := R_l \bowtie_j R_r$ | $R_l^\pi \cup R_r^\pi$ | $R_l^\bowtie \cup R_r^\bowtie$ | $R_l^\sigma \cup R_r^\sigma$ |

**Fig. 5.4** Profiles resulting from operations

[(SSN,Salary,DoB), (Employee,Patient,Treatment), (Duration)]. As a matter of fact, a query equal to the query in Example 5.3 but releasing P.SSN or T.SSN instead of E.SSN, while slightly different in the syntax, would carry exactly the same information content and, consequently, would have the same profile.

According to the semantics of the relational operators, the profile resulting from a relational operation, summarized in Fig. 5.4,[2] is as follows.

- *Projection* ($\pi$). A projection operation returns a *subset of the attributes* of the operand. Hence, $R^\bowtie$ and $R^\sigma$ of the resulting relation $R$ are the same as the ones of the operand, while $R^\pi$ contains only those attributes being projected.
- *Selection* ($\sigma$). A selection operation returns a *subset of the tuples* of the operand. Hence, $R^\bowtie$ and $R^\pi$ of the resulting relation $R$ are the same as the ones of the operand, while $R^\sigma$ needs to include also the attributes appearing in the selection condition.
- *Join* ($\bowtie$). A join operation returns a relation that contains the *association of the tuples of the operands*, thus capturing the information in both operands as well as the information on their association (conditions in the join). Hence, $R^\sigma$, $R^\pi$, and $R^\bowtie$ of the resulting relation $R$ are the union of those of the operands, implicitly capturing the join path *joinpath*($R^\bowtie$) among the relations composing $R^\bowtie$ and consequently the set of conditions that each tuple in $R$ satisfies.

## 5.4 Graph-based Model

We model database schema, permissions, and queries via mixed graphs, that is, graphs with both undirected and directed arcs.

The *schema graph* of a set $\mathscr{R}$ of relations is a mixed graph whose nodes correspond to the different attributes of the relations, whose non-oriented arcs correspond to the possible joins ($\mathscr{J}$), and whose oriented arcs correspond to the referential integrity constraints ($\mathscr{I}$) and the functional dependencies between the primary key of a relation and its non-key attributes. Attributes appearing with the same name in more than one relation appear as different nodes. To disambiguate, nodes are identi-

---

[2] For the sake of simplicity, with a slight abuse of notation, in the table we write $\sigma_A(R)$ as a short hand for any expression $\sigma_{condition}(R)$, where $A$ is the set of attributes of $R$ involved in *condition*.

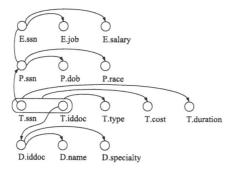

**Fig. 5.5**  Schema graph for the relations in Fig. 5.1

fied with the usual dot notation by the pair *relation.attribute*. This is formalized by the following definition.

**Definition 5.4 (Schema graph).** Given a set $\mathscr{R}$ of relations, a set $\mathscr{I}$ of referential integrity constraints over $\mathscr{R}$, and a set $\mathscr{J}$ of join conditions over $\mathscr{R}$, a *schema graph* is a graph $G(\mathscr{N},\mathscr{E})$ where:

- $\mathscr{N} = \{R_i.* : R_i \in \mathscr{R}\}$
- $\mathscr{E} = \mathscr{J} \cup \mathscr{I} \cup \{(R_i.K, R_i.a) : R_i \in \mathscr{R} \wedge a \notin K\}$

Figure 5.5 represents the schema graph corresponding to the set of relations, referential integrity constraints, and join conditions in Fig. 5.1 (for simplicity, we only report the initials of the relations).

Permissions and relation profiles correspond to *views* over the set $\mathscr{R}$ of relations and are characterized by a pair $[A,\mathbb{R}]$, corresponding to $[Att,Rels]$ appearing in the permissions, and to $[R^{\pi} \cup R^{\sigma}, R^{\bowtie}]$ in the relation profile of relation $R$, respectively.

**Definition 5.5 (Entailed view).** Given a set $\mathscr{R}$ of relations and a permission $p=[Att,Rels]$ over it, the view $V=[A,\mathbb{R}]$ entailed by $p$ is defined as: $A=Att$ and $\mathbb{R}=Rels$. Given a set $\mathscr{R}$ of relations and a relation profile $[R^{\pi}, R^{\bowtie}, R^{\sigma}]$, the view $V=[A,\mathbb{R}]$ entailed by the profile is defined as: $A=R^{\pi} \cup R^{\sigma}$ and $\mathbb{R}=R^{\bowtie}$.

In the characterization of the view, we take into consideration the fact that referential integrity constraints can be used to extend the relations in $\mathbb{R}$ to include all relations reachable from the ones appearing in $\mathbb{R}$ by following referential integrity connections from a foreign key to the referenced primary key. We can then include such relations in the set $\mathbb{R}$. Given a set $\mathbb{R}$ of relations, $\mathbb{R}^*$ denotes the relations obtained by closing $\mathbb{R}$ with respect to referential integrity constraints. For instance, with respect to the schema graph in Fig. 5.5, the closure of $\mathbb{R}=\{\texttt{Treatment}\}$ is $\mathbb{R}^*=\{\texttt{Treatment}, \texttt{Patient}, \texttt{Doctor}\}$.

Given a relation profile/permission, we graphically represent the view entailed through it as a *view graph* obtained by coloring the original schema graph with three colors: *black* for information that the view carries (i.e., it explicitly contains or indirectly conveys); *white* for all the non-black attributes belonging to relations in $\mathbb{R}^*$ and the arcs connecting them to the primary key; and *clear* for any other attribute or arc. Intuitively, clear nodes/arcs are attributes/arcs belonging to the original graph that are ineffective with respect to the evaluation and composition of permissions. The reason for maintaining them in the view graphs is so that every query/permission is a coloring (in contrast to a subgraph) of the schema graph. View graph is formally defined as follows.

**Definition 5.6 (View graph).** Given a set $\mathscr{R}$ of relations characterized by schema graph $G(\mathscr{N},\mathscr{E})$ and a view $V = [A,\mathbb{R}]$ entailed by a permission/relation profile on it, the *view graph* of $V$ over $G$ is a graph $G_V(\mathscr{N},\mathscr{E},\lambda_V)$, where $\lambda_V : \{\mathscr{N} \cup \mathscr{E}\} \rightarrow \{black,white,clear\}$ is a coloring function defined as follows.

$$
\lambda_V(n) = 
\begin{cases}
black, & n{=}R.a, R \in \mathbb{R}^* \wedge a \in A \\[1em]
white, & n{=}R.a, R \in \mathbb{R}^* \wedge a \notin A \\[1em]
clear, & \text{otherwise}
\end{cases}
$$

$$
\lambda_V(n_i,n_j) = 
\begin{cases}
black, & (n_i,n_j) \in \text{joinpath}(\mathbb{R}^*) \vee \\
 & \quad (n_i{=}R.K, n_j{=}R.a, R \in \mathbb{R}^*,(a \in A \vee R.a \text{ appears in joinpath}(\mathbb{R}^*))) \\[1em]
white, & n_i{=}R.K, n_j{=}R.a, R \in \mathbb{R}^*, \\
 & \quad \neg(a \in A \vee R.a \text{ appears in joinpath}(\mathbb{R}^*)) \\[1em]
clear, & \text{otherwise}
\end{cases}
$$

According to this definition, a node is colored as: *black* if it appears in $A$, *white* if it is not black and it belongs to a relation appearing in $\mathbb{R}^*$, and *clear* otherwise. An arc is colored: *black* if either it belongs to *joinpath*$(\mathbb{R}^*)$ or it is an arc going from the key of a relation in $\mathbb{R}^*$ to an attribute which either belongs to $A$ or appears in *joinpath*$(\mathbb{R}^*)$; *white* if it is an arc from the key of a relation in $\mathbb{R}^*$ to one of its attributes which neither belongs to $A$ nor appears in *joinpath*$(\mathbb{R}^*)$; *clear* otherwise.

Figure 5.6 illustrates the **ColorGraph** function that given the schema graph $G$ and a pair $[A,\mathbb{R}]$ denoting either the view entailed by a permission or by a relation profile, implements Definition 5.6 and returns the corresponding view graph. **ColorGraph**, whose interpretation is immediate, starts by assigning a clear color to all nodes and arcs and proceeds by coloring black and white arcs and nodes as prescribed by the definition.

Figure 5.7 reports the view graphs corresponding to the permissions in Fig. 5.3. Figure 5.8 reports some examples of relations obtained through queries over the schema in Fig. 5.5. The figure reports the queries originating the relations, the relation profiles, and the corresponding view graphs.

Before closing this section we introduce two dominance relationships between view graphs that will be used in the remainder of the chapter.

```
COLORGRAPH(G,[A,ℝ])
𝒩_V := 𝒩
ℰ_V := ℰ
for each n∈𝒩_V do λ_V (n) := clear
for each (n_i,n_j)∈ℰ_V do λ_V (n_i,n_j) := clear
for each R∈ℝ* do
    for each a∈R.* do /* color nodes */
        if a∈A then
            λ_V (R.a) := black
        else
            λ_V (R.a) := white
    for each (n_i,n_j)∈joinpath(ℝ*) do /* color the join path */
        λ_V (n_i,n_j) := black
    for each (n_i,n_j)∈{(n_i,n_j): ∃R∈ℝ*, n_i=R.K ∧n_j⊆R.*} do
        if λ_V (n_j)=black ∨ n_j appears in joinpath(ℝ*) then
            λ_V (n_i,n_j) := black
        else
            λ_V (n_i,n_j) := white
G_V := (𝒩_V,ℰ_V,λ_V)
return(G_V)
```

**Fig. 5.6**  Function for coloring a view graph

**Definition 5.7** ($\preceq_N$, $\preceq_{NE}$). Given a schema graph $G(\mathcal{N},\mathcal{E})$, and two view graphs $G_{V_i}(\mathcal{N},\mathcal{E},\lambda_{V_i})$ and $G_{V_j}(\mathcal{N},\mathcal{E},\lambda_{V_j})$ over $G$, the following dominance relationships are defined:

- $G_{V_i}\preceq_N G_{V_j}$, when $\forall n\in \mathcal{N}$ and $\forall(n_h,n_k) \in (\mathcal{J}\cup\mathcal{I})$:

    - $\lambda_{V_i}(n)$ = black $\Longrightarrow$ $\lambda_{V_j}(n)$=black, and
    - $\lambda_{G_i}(n_h,n_k)$ = black $\Longleftrightarrow$ $\lambda_{G_j}(n_h,n_k)$ = black.

- $G_{V_i}\preceq_{NE} G_{V_j}$, when $\forall n\in \mathcal{N}$ and $\forall(n_h,n_k) \in \mathcal{E}$:

    - $\lambda_{V_i}(n)$ = black $\Longrightarrow$ $\lambda_{V_j}(n)$=black, and
    - $\lambda_{G_i}(n_h,n_k)$ = black $\Longrightarrow$ $\lambda_{G_j}(n_h,n_k)$ = black.

According to this definition, given two graphs $G_{V_i}$ and $G_{V_j}$ on the same database schema, $G_{V_i} \preceq_N G_{V_j}$ if they have exactly the same black referential integrity and join arcs and the black nodes of $G_{V_i}$ are a subset of the black nodes of $G_{V_j}$. $G_{V_i} \preceq_{NE} G_{V_j}$ if the black arcs and nodes of $G_{V_i}$ are a subset of the black arcs and nodes of $G_{V_j}$. For instance, with reference to the view graphs in Figs. 5.7 and 5.8, it is easy to see that: $G_{p_3}\preceq_N G_{Q_3}$ and that $G_{p_1}\preceq_{NE} G_{Q_2}$.

## 5.5  Authorized Views

To evaluate a query requested by a subject against her permissions and to determine if the query can be executed, we implement the following intuitive concept.

**Principle 5.1** *A relation (either base or resulting from a query evaluation) can be released to a subject if she has permissions to view the information content carried by the relation.*

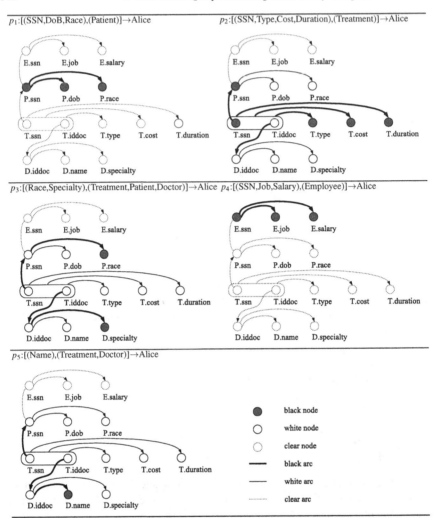

**Fig. 5.7**  Examples of permissions and their view graphs

We first discuss when a permission authorizes the release of a relation. We will then address permission composition and cooperation in query evaluation.

In the reminder of this section we refer our discussion to permissions and relation profiles of a *specific subject* and omit, for simplicity, the subject component of permissions in the formalization.

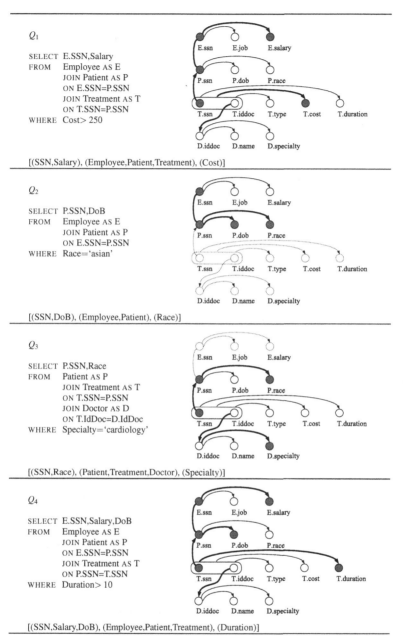

$Q_1$

SELECT E.SSN,Salary
FROM Employee AS E
     JOIN Patient AS P
     ON E.SSN=P.SSN
     JOIN Treatment AS T
     ON T.SSN=P.SSN
WHERE Cost> 250

[(SSN,Salary), (Employee,Patient,Treatment), (Cost)]

$Q_2$

SELECT P.SSN,DoB
FROM Employee AS E
     JOIN Patient AS P
     ON E.SSN=P.SSN
WHERE Race='asian'

[(SSN,DoB), (Employee,Patient), (Race)]

$Q_3$

SELECT P.SSN,Race
FROM Patient AS P
     JOIN Treatment AS T
     ON T.SSN=P.SSN
     JOIN Doctor AS D
     ON T.IdDoc=D.IdDoc
WHERE Specialty='cardiology'

[(SSN,Race), (Patient,Treatment,Doctor), (Specialty)]

$Q_4$

SELECT E.SSN,Salary,DoB
FROM Employee AS E
     JOIN Patient AS P
     ON E.SSN=P.SSN
     JOIN Treatment AS T
     ON P.SSN=T.SSN
WHERE Duration> 10

[(SSN,Salary,DoB), (Employee,Patient,Treatment), (Duration)]

**Fig. 5.8** Examples of queries, their relation profiles, and their view graphs

## 5.5.1 Authorizing Permissions

Intuitively, a permission authorizes a release if and only if the information (directly or indirectly) entailed by the relation profile is a subset of the information that the permission authorizes to view. Note that this is different from saying that the relation should contain only data that are a subset of the data authorized by the permission, as this denotes only the information directly released. A correct enforcement should also ensure that no indirect release occurs. There are two main sources of indirect release:

- the presence, in the query generating the relation, of conditions on attributes that are not returned (i.e., attributes that appear in the WHERE clause but do not appear in the SELECT clause);
- the presence of join conditions restricting the tuples returned by the query.

The first aspect is easily taken into consideration as it is already captured by the inclusion, in the relation profile (Definition 5.3), of $R^\sigma$ component, which is included in $A$ for the entailed view definition (Definition 5.5). To illustrate the problem of the second aspect, consider permission $p_1$ in Fig. 5.7, which allows Alice to view the complete information in Patient, and therefore the whole tuples representing all patients. Permission $p_1$ by itself is then sufficient to grant Alice the ability to view the data of all patients (i.e., relation obtained through query "SELECT P.SSN,DoB FROM Patient AS P WHERE Race='asian' "). Suppose instead that Alice is interested in the relation resulting from $Q_2$ in Fig. 5.8. This latter query returns a subset of all the tuples of patients, and therefore only tuples that Alice, according to $p_1$, is authorized to see. However, permission $p_1$ is not sufficient for granting Alice such visibility on data, since the query result conveys the additional information that the returned tuples refer to patients who are also employees of the considered company (information which permission $p_1$ does not authorize).

As already commented in Sect. 5.4, the only case when joins do not add information is when there is a referential integrity constraint among the involved relations. Consider, for example, permission $p_2$ authorizing the release of different attributes in Treatment. For instance, query "SELECT T.SSN FROM Treatment AS T" is clearly authorized by $p_2$. Consider then the same query containing, in the FROM clause, also relations Patient and Doctor with the corresponding joins. Despite the presence of the additional joins, such a query does not bear additional information (indirect release) and should therefore be authorized by $p_2$. As a matter of fact, because of the referential integrity constraints between the involved relations, all SSN's and IdDoc's appearing in Treatment also appear in Patient and Doctor, respectively, and therefore the joins do not impose restrictions. The consideration of the peculiar characteristics of joins due to referential integrity constraints is easily taken into account, since it is already captured by the coloring, in the view graph, of all the relations reachable from the ones appearing in the query, by following referential integrity constraints (Definition 5.6).

Let us then proceed to formally define when a permission authorizes the release of a relation. We start by identifying permissions applicable to a relation profile. Intuitively, a permission applies to a relation when it refers to the complete set of tuples composing the relation. Since tuple restriction is due to joins not following the direction from a foreign key to the referenced key in a referential integrity constraint (as commented above), this is equivalent to saying that the permission applies to a relation profile if it does not contain additional joins (apart from those corresponding to referential integrity constraints). This is formalized by the following definition.

**Definition 5.8 (Applicable).** A permission $[Att, Rels]$ is applicable to a relation profile $[R^\pi, R^\bowtie, R^\sigma]$ iff $Rels^* \subseteq R^{\bowtie*}$.

In terms of view graphs, this definition is equivalent to say that the black and white nodes of the view graph $G_p$ of permission $p$ should be a subset of the black and white nodes of the view graph $G_R$ of the relation profile of $R$.

According to the discussion above, a permission authorizes the release of a relation if and only if the permission applies to the relation profile and authorizes the release, either direct of indirect, of the information in the profile. This means that the permission should include (at least) all attributes composing the relation or accessed for its definition/computation as well as all the join conditions. In terms of the view graphs, this is equivalent to say that the view graph $G_R$ of the relation profile and the view graph $G_p$ of the permission have exactly the same black referential integrity and join arcs and that all nodes that are black in the view graph of the relation profile are also black in the view graph of the permission, that is, $G_R \preceq_N G_p$. This is formally captured by the following definition.

**Definition 5.9 (Authorizing permission).** Given a permission $p=[Att, Rels]$ applicable to a relation profile $R=[R^\pi, R^\bowtie, R^\sigma]$, $p$ *authorizes* the release of $R$ iff $G_R \preceq_N G_p$.

As an example, with reference to the permissions in Fig. 5.7 and the relation computed through query $Q_2$ in Fig. 5.8, the set of permissions applicable includes $p_1$ and $p_4$. However, neither $p_1$ nor $p_4$ authorize the release of the query result. By contrast, considering query "SELECT P.SSN,DoB FROM Patient AS P WHERE Race='asian' ", with profile [(SSN,DoB), (Patient), (Race)] permission $p_1$ is the only applicable permission that also authorizes the query.

## 5.5.2 Composition of Permissions

Checking relation profiles against individual permissions is not sufficient for a true enforcement of Principle 5.1. Indeed, it might be that for a relation profile there is no permission that singularly taken authorizes the release of the relation, however information released (directly or indirectly) by the relation profile is authorized. As an example, consider permissions $p_1$ and $p_4$ in Fig. 5.3 and suppose that Alice requests the relation resulting from query $Q_2$ in Fig. 5.8, returning the tuples associated with patients whose SSN appears also in the Employee relation. While neither $p_1$ nor $p_4$ authorize the relation profile (as, for each of them, the relation profile has the additional join condition that the permission does not authorize), it is clear that the relation does not contain any information that Alice is not authorized to see. As a matter of fact, Alice could indeed separately query both relations and then join the two results. In the spirit of Principle 5.1, the release of the result of

---

**COMPOSE**$(G,p_i,p_j)$
$p := [Att_i \cup Att_j, Rels_i \cup Rels_j]$
$\mathcal{N}_p := \mathcal{N}$
$\mathcal{E}_p := \mathcal{E}$
**for each** $n \in \mathcal{N}_p$ **do** $\lambda_V(n) :=$ clear
**for each** $(n_i,n_j) \in \mathcal{E}_p$ **do** $\lambda_V(n_i,n_j) :=$ clear
**for each** $n \in \mathcal{N}_p$ **do**
    **if** $\lambda_{p_i}(n)=$black$\vee\lambda_{p_j}(n)=$black **then**
      $\lambda_p(n)=$black
    **else**
    **if** $\lambda_{p_i}(n)=$white$\vee\lambda_{p_j}(n)=$white **then**
      $\lambda_p(n)=$white
**for each** $(n_h,n_k) \in \mathcal{E}_p$ **do**
    **if** $\lambda_{p_i}(n_h,n_k)=$black$\vee\lambda_{p_j}(n_h,n_k)=$black$\vee$ $(\lambda_p(n_h)=$black$\wedge\lambda_p(n_k)=$black$)$ **then**
      $\lambda_p(n_h,n_k)=$black
    **else**
    **if** $\lambda_{p_i}(n_h,n_k)=$white$\vee\lambda_{p_j}(n_h,n_k)=$white **then**
      $\lambda_p(n_h,n_k)=$white
**return**$(p)$

---

**Fig. 5.9** Function composing two permissions

query $Q_2$ to `Alice` should therefore be authorized. To enforce this principle, we compose permissions and consider a release of a relation authorized if there exists a composition of permissions that authorizes it.

Composition of permissions must however be performed carefully to ensure that composition does not authorize additional queries that were authorized by neither of the original permissions. To illustrate, consider again the permissions in Fig. 5.7 and suppose that `Alice` is interested in the relation resulting from query $Q_3$. One could think that such a release can be authorized by composing $p_1$ in Fig. 5.7 (authorizing the release of `SSN`'s and `Race`'s) and $p_3$ (authorizing the release of the race of patients together with the specialty of their caring doctor). However, such a composition does not authorize the relation release. Indeed, the relation profile conveys the associations between a patient and her caring doctor, which neither of the individual permissions authorize and which `Alice` would not be able to reconstruct by separately exploiting the privileges granted by the two permissions. The problem, in this case, is that the composition of the two permissions returns more information than that entailed by the two permissions individually taken. If this is the case, the two permissions should not be composed.

To determine when two permissions can be composed, we exploit one of the foundational results of the theory of joins for relational databases, expressed by the theorem presented in [5], which states that two relations produce a *lossless join* if and only if at least one of the two relations *functionally depends* from the intersection of their attributes. The relations that are considered in the theorem correspond to generic projections on the set of attributes that characterizes the "universal relation" obtained joining all the relations of our lossless acyclic schema; this means that each permission corresponds to a relation and that the composition of permissions is correct only if the above requirement is satisfied. For instance, consider the previous examples and the permissions in Fig. 5.7. Permissions $p_1$ and $p_4$ can be combined because their intersection is represented by attribute `SSN`, which is a key for all the attributes in $p_1$ (and $p_4$). Permissions $p_1$ and $p_3$ cannot be combined because their intersection is represented by attribute Race, and neither $p_1$ nor $p_3$ functionally depend on it.

The application of this basic result of the theory of joins in our scenario is slightly complicated by the fact that the views corresponding to given permissions may include attributes from different relations. (We note here that intersection of permissions is computed based only on the attribute names, without considering the relation they belong to, since attributes with the same name represent the same real world concept and natural joins impose them to be equal in all the resulting tuples.) Given two permissions $p_i=[Att_i, Rels_i]$ and $p_j=[Att_j, Rels_j]$ their composability depends on the intersection of their visible attributes (i.e., $Att_i \cap Att_j$) but the functional dependency of the visible attributes of one of the two permissions from the common attributes needs to be evaluated by taking into account also the referential integrity constraints. This concept can be easily captured by analyzing the view graphs $G_{p_i}$ and $G_{p_j}$ corresponding to the two permissions. The basic idea is that there is a dependence between $p_i$ and $p_j$ when there is a black path from nodes corresponding to the attributes that are listed both in $Att_i$ and in $Att_j$ to all the black nodes in $G_{p_i}$ or in $G_{p_j}$. This intuitive concept of dependency is formalized as follows.

**Definition 5.10 (Dependence).** Given two permissions $p_i=[Att_i, Rels_i]$ and $p_j=[Att_j, Rels_j]$ with view graphs $G_{p_i}(\mathcal{N}, \mathcal{E}, \lambda_{p_i})$ and $G_{p_j}(\mathcal{N}, \mathcal{E}, \lambda_{p_j})$, respectively, let $B_j$ be the set of nodes corresponding to $\{Att_i \cap Att_j\}$ in $G_{p_j}$. We say that $p_j$ *depends* on $p_i$, denoted $p_i \rightarrow p_j$, iff $\forall n_j \in \mathcal{N}$ such that $\lambda_{p_j}(n_j)=$black, $\exists n \in B_j$ such that there is a path of only directed black arcs from $n$ to $n_j$ in $G_{p_j}$.

In the following, notation $p_i \leftrightarrow p_j$ denotes that both $p_i \rightarrow p_j$ and $p_j \rightarrow p_i$ hold. Similarly, $p_i \nleftrightarrow p_j$ denotes that neither $p_i \rightarrow p_j$ nor $p_j \rightarrow p_i$ hold.

For instance, with reference to the permissions in Fig. 5.7, as already noted, $p_2 \rightarrow p_1$, since common attribute SSN is key for the Patient relation authorized by $p_1$, and $p_1 \nrightarrow p_2$, since the attributes released by $p_2$ depend on the pair of attributes SSN and IdDoc. We also note that $p_1 \leftrightarrow p_4$, since the SSN attribute, common to the two permissions, is the key of both the Patient and Employee relations. On the contrary, as already pointed out, $p_1 \nleftrightarrow p_3$.

If $p_i \rightarrow p_j$ (or $p_j \rightarrow p_i$, respectively), then the two permissions can be *safely composed*, as formally stated by the following definition.

**Definition 5.11 (Safe composition).** Given two permissions $p_i=[Att_i, Rels_i]$ and $p_j=[Att_j, Rels_j]$, $p_i$ and $p_j$ can be *safely composed* when $p_i \rightarrow p_j$, or $p_j \rightarrow p_i$, or both.

For instance, $p_1$ can be safely composed with $p_2$, since $p_2 \rightarrow p_1$. Also, since $p_1 \leftrightarrow p_4$, $p_1$ can be safely composed with $p_4$.

Similarly to the composition of relations presented in the theory of normal forms for relational databases, the composition of $p_i$ with $p_j$ generates a new permission that combines the viewing privileges of the two, as stated by the following definition.

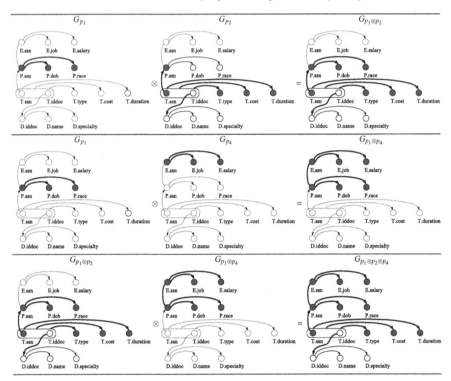

**Fig. 5.10** Examples of permission compositions

**Definition 5.12 (Composed permission).** Given two permissions $p_i=[Att_i,Rels_i]$ and $p_j=[Att_j,Rels_j]$, their composition is the permission $p_i \otimes p_j=[Att_i \cup Att_j,Rels_i \cup Rels_j]$.

It is easy to see that the view graph of the resulting composed permission is obtained from the view graphs of the components as follows. A node in $G_{p_i \otimes p_j}$ is: *black* if it is black in either $G_{p_i}$ or $G_{p_j}$; *white* if it is not black and it is white in either $G_{p_i}$ or $G_{p_j}$; it is *clear* otherwise. An arc in $G_{p_i \otimes p_j}$ is: *black* if it is black in either $G_{p_i}$ or $G_{p_j}$ or if it is incident on only black nodes in $G_{p_i \otimes p_j}$; *white* if it is not black and is white in either $G_{p_i}$ or $G_{p_j}$; it is *clear* otherwise. Figure 5.10 represents the view graphs resulting from a subset of the safe compositions of the privileges in Fig. 5.7, that is, $p_1 \otimes p_2$, $p_1 \otimes p_4$, and $p_1 \otimes p_2 \otimes p_4$.

A permission obtained by composing permissions $p_i$ and $p_j$ ($p_i \otimes p_j$) can be composed with a permission $p_k$ that did not satisfy the composition requirements with $p_i$ nor with $p_j$. In general, each new permission produces new opportunities for composition that have to be considered. The consideration of all the potential compositions is modeled by the following concept.

**Definition 5.13 (Composition closure).** Given a set of permissions $\mathscr{P}$, the *closure on composition* of $\mathscr{P}$, denoted $\mathscr{P}^{\otimes}$, is the set of permissions obtained as a fixpoint by the procedure which repeatedly extends $\mathscr{P}$ with all permissions obtained by the safe composition of the permissions in $\mathscr{P}$.

For instance, with reference to the set of permissions in Fig. 5.7, their closure is $\mathscr{P}^{\otimes}=\{p_1,p_2,p_3,p_4,p_5,p_1\otimes p_2,p_1\otimes p_4,p_2\otimes p_4,p_1\otimes p_2\otimes p_4\}$.

The closure represents the greatest representation of the permissions available to a subject. This concept permits to identify in a complete way if a specific relation profile is authorized for a subject.

**Definition 5.14 (Authorized release).** Given a set $\mathscr{P}$ of permissions applicable to a relation profile $[R^\pi,R^\bowtie,R^\sigma]$, $\mathscr{P}$ authorizes $R$ iff $\exists p \in \mathscr{P}^{\otimes}$ such that $p$ authorizes $R$ (according to Definition 5.9).

The computation of the closure on composition of permissions is potentially an expensive procedure. In the following, we present an efficient algorithm that avoids computing the whole set of permissions in the composition closure while ensuring completeness of the control, needed to evaluate if a release is authorized.

### 5.5.3 Algorithm

Given a set $\mathscr{P}$ of $n$ permissions of a subject $S$ applicable to a relation profile $[R^\pi,R^\bowtie,R^\sigma]$, the control for the authorized release does not require to compute all the possible $2^n - 1$ permission compositions, since given two permissions $p_i$ and $p_j$, if $p_j \to p_i$ then $p_j$ is subsumed by $p_i \otimes p_j$, and whenever a permission $p_k$ can be composed with $p_j$, $p_k$ can also be composed with $p_i \otimes p_j$, as stated by the following theorem.

**Theorem 5.1 (Permission implication).** *Given two permissions $p_i=[\mathrm{Att}_i,\mathrm{Rels}_i]$, $p_j=[\mathrm{Att}_j,\mathrm{Rels}_j] \in \mathscr{P}$ such that $p_j \to p_i$, $\forall p_k=[\mathrm{Att}_k,\mathrm{Rels}_k] \in \mathscr{P}$:*

*1. $p_j \to p_k \Rightarrow (p_i \otimes p_j) \to p_k$;*
*2. $p_k \to p_j \Rightarrow p_k \to (p_i \otimes p_j)$.*

*Proof.* Let us consider the two cases above.

1. Let $p_i \otimes p_j=[\mathrm{Att}_{i,j},\mathrm{Rels}_{i,j}]$. Attributes in $\mathrm{Att}_i \cap \mathrm{Att}_k$ also appear in the intersection between $\mathrm{Att}_{i,j}$ and $\mathrm{Att}_k$. Therefore, there exists a path of only directed black arcs from a node corresponding to some attributes in $\mathrm{Att}_j \cap \mathrm{Att}_k$ to each black node in $G_{p_k}$.
2. From the hypothesis, we know that there is a path of only directed black arcs from a node corresponding to some attributes in $\mathrm{Att}_j \cap \mathrm{Att}_k$ to each black node in $G_{p_j}$. Also, we know that there is a path of only directed black arcs from a node corresponding to some attributes in $\mathrm{Att}_i \cap \mathrm{Att}_j$ to each black node in $G_{p_i}$. By combining these paths, it follows that also $p_k \to p_i$ and, therefore, that $p_k \to (p_i \otimes p_j)$.

---

**AUTHORIZED**($G_R,S$)

Let *Applicable* be the set of permissions [Att, Rels]$\rightarrow S_i$ such that:
$\{n\in\mathcal{N}_p:\lambda_p(n)=\text{black}\vee\text{white}\}\subseteq\{n\in\mathcal{N}_R:\lambda_R(n)=\text{black}\vee\text{white}\}\wedge S_i=S$
/* check individual permissions */
**for each** $p\in Applicable$ **do**
    **if** $G_R\preceq_N G_p$ **then return**(*true*)
/* compose permissions */
*maxid* := |*Applicable*|
*counter* := 1
**for each** $p\in Applicable$ **do**
    *p.id* := *counter*
    *p.maxcfr* := *counter*
    *counter* := *counter* + 1
*idmin$_i$* := 1
**repeat**
    Let $p_i$ be the permission with $p_i.id=idmin_i$
    *idmin$_j$* := **Min**($\{p.id:p\in Applicable\wedge p_i.maxcfr<p.id\}$)
    Let $p_j$ be the permission with $p_j.id=idmin_j$
    *dominated* := NULL
    **if** $(G_{p_i}\npreceq_{NE}G_{p_j})\wedge(G_{p_j}\npreceq_{NE}G_{p_i})$ **then**
        **if** $p_j\rightarrow p_i$ **then** *dominated* := *dominated* $\cup\{p_j\}$
        **if** $p_i\rightarrow p_j$ **then** *dominated* := *dominated* $\cup\{p_i\}$
        $p_i.maxcfr$ := $p_j.id$
        **if** *dominated* $\neq$ NULL **then**
            *maxid* := *maxid* + 1
            $p_{maxid}$ := **Compose**($G,p_i,p_j$)
            $p_{maxid}.id$ := *maxid*
            $p_{maxid}.maxcfr$ := *maxid*
            *Applicable* := *Applicable* − *dominated* $\cup\{p_{maxid}\}$
            *idmin$_i$* := **Min**($\{p.id:p\in Applicable\wedge p.maxcfr<maxid\}$)
**until** *idmin$_i$*=NULL
/* check resulting permissions */
**for each** $p\in Applicable$ **do**
    **if** $G_R\preceq_N G_p$ **then return**(*true*)
**return**(*false*)

---

**Fig. 5.11** Function that checks if a release is authorized

This theorem implies that permission $p_j$ can be removed from the set $\mathscr{P}$ without compromising the composition process. It is also easy to see that since the composed permission is again applicable to the relation profile $[R^\pi,R^\bowtie,R^\sigma]$, the set of permissions to be composed always contains at most $n$ permissions (i.e., the composed permission substitutes one, or both, of the composing permissions). Function **Authorized** in Fig. 5.11 applies this observation to check whether a relation profile release is authorized. The function takes as input the view graph $G_R$ representing the relation profile and the subjects requesting the release; on the basis of the set of applicable permissions, it returns *true* or *false*, depending on whether or not the query is authorized.

Initially, **Authorized** determines the set *Applicable* of applicable permissions and checks if one of these permissions dominates ($\preceq_N$) $G_R$. If this is the case, function **Authorized** returns *true*. Otherwise, the function starts the composition process that exploits Theorem 5.1 according to which permission $p_i$ can be removed from set *Applicable* if $p_j\rightarrow p_i$. The applicable permissions are first ordered according to a numeric identifier *id*, ranging from 1 to |*Applicable*|, which is associated with each permission. In the **repeat until** loop, each permission $p_i$ is compared with a permission $p_j$ such that $p_i.id < p_j.id$. If the set of black nodes and arcs of $G_{p_i}$ is not a subset of the set of black nodes and arcs of $G_{p_j}$ (i.e., $G_{p_i} \npreceq_{NE} G_{p_j}$, meaning that $p_j$ has not been computed in a previous iteration by composing $p_i$ with another authorization) and viceversa, function **Authorized** checks whether $p_i$ and $p_j$ can be composed (i.e., $p_j \rightarrow p_i$ or $p_i \rightarrow p_j$). If this is the case, the identifier of the resulting composed permission (if any) becomes equal to the current maximum identifier (*maxid*) incremented by one. Each permission $p$ is also associated with a variable *p.maxcfr* that keeps track of the highest identifier of the permissions compared to $p$. This variable avoids to check the same pair of permissions more than once. The composition process terminates when *maxcfr* of all permissions is equal to the highest identifier *maxid*. The function then checks if any of the permissions in *Applicable* dominates ($\preceq_N$) $G_R$. If this is the case, function **Authorized** returns *true*; otherwise it returns *false*.

*Example 5.5.* Consider the schema graph in Fig. 5.5, the set of permissions in Fig. 5.7, and the relation $R_1$ computed by query $Q_1$ in Fig. 5.8. As it is visible from the view graphs, all the five permissions are applicable to the profile of the relation resulting from $Q_1$. The table in Fig. 5.12 represents the execution, step by step, of function **Authorized** on $G_{Q_1}$ by reporting the evolution of variable *p.maxcfr* for both original and composed permissions. Each column in the table corresponds to a permission, whose identifier is the label of the column itself. Note that when a permission is removed from *Applicable*, its *maxcfr* is not reported anymore. Each row in the table represents an iteration of the **repeat until** loop, reporting both the dependence relationship between the composing permissions and the *maxcfr* for all permissions. Also, in each row the *maxcfr* of the permissions checked for a possible composition are reported in italic. When a permission is removed from *Applicable* (because subsumed by an added composed permission), its *maxcfr* is not reported anymore. Figure 5.10 represents the view graph of the permissions obtained by the composition. We then conclude that the relation resulting from the evaluation of query $Q_1$ can be released to `Alice`, since $p_1 \otimes p_2 \otimes p_4$ authorizes it.

The following theorems state the correctness and complexity of function **Authorized**.

**Theorem 5.2 (Correctness).** *Given a relation profile $R = [R^\pi, R^\bowtie, R^\sigma]$ and a set Applicable of applicable permissions, function **Authorized** terminates and returns true iff the release of $R$ is authorized by $Applicable^\otimes$.*

*Proof. Termination.* All the **for** loops terminate, since *Applicable* (by Theorem 5.1) is composed of at most $n$ permissions. At each iteration of the **repeat until** loop, function **Authorized** evaluates a pair of permissions $\langle p_i, p_j \rangle$ such that $p_i.maxcfr < p_j.id$. Two cases can occur: $p_i$ and $p_j$ cannot be composed, or $p_i$ and $p_j$ can be composed (and we suppose, without loss of generality, that $p_j \rightarrow p_i$). In the first case, in the subsequent iterations $p_i$ and $p_j$ are no more checked, since $p_i.id$ and $p_j.id$ do not change and $p_i.maxcfr$ is set to $p_j.id$. In the second case, $p_i$ is removed from *Applicable*, while the composed permission $p = p_i \otimes p_j$ is added to *Applicable*.

| id | 1 | 2 | 3 | 4 | 5 | 6 | 7 | 8 |
|---|---|---|---|---|---|---|---|---|
| | $p_1$ | $p_2$ | $p_3$ | $p_4$ | $p_5$ | | | |
| initialization | 1 | 2 | 3 | 4 | 5 | | | |
| $p_2 \rightarrow p_1$ | 1 | 2 | 3 | 4 | 5 | $p_1 \otimes p_2$ | | |
| $p_1 \nrightarrow p_3$ | 2 | | 3 | 4 | 5 | 6 | | |
| $p_1 \leftrightarrow p_4$ | 3 | | 3 | 4 | 5 | 6 | $p_1 \otimes p_4$ | |
| $p_3 \nrightarrow p_5$ | | | 3 | | 5 | 6 | 7 | |
| $p_3 \nrightarrow (p_1 \otimes p_2)$ | | | 5 | | 5 | 6 | 7 | |
| $p_5 \nrightarrow (p_1 \otimes p_2)$ | | | 6 | | 5 | 6 | 7 | |
| $p_3 \nrightarrow (p_1 \otimes p_4)$ | | | 6 | | 6 | 6 | 7 | |
| $p_5 \nrightarrow (p_1 \otimes p_4)$ | | | 7 | | 6 | 6 | 7 | |
| $(p_1 \otimes p_2) \rightarrow (p_1 \otimes p_4)$ | | | 7 | | 7 | 6 | 7 | $p_1 \otimes p_2 \otimes p_4$ |
| $p_3 \nrightarrow (p_1 \otimes p_2 \otimes p_4)$ | | | 7 | | 7 | 7 | 8 | |
| $p_5 \nrightarrow (p_1 \otimes p_2 \otimes p_4)$ | | | 8 | | 7 | 7 | 8 | |
| $G_{p_1 \otimes p_4} \preceq_{NE} G_{p_1 \otimes p_2 \otimes p_4}$ | | | 8 | | 8 | 7 | 8 | |
| | | | 8 | | 8 | 8 | 8 | |

**Fig. 5.12** An example of the execution of function **Authorized**

Since $p_j \preceq_{NE} p$, in the following iterations, when they are compared they do not generate new permissions. Since each possible combination is checked only once and the number of possible combination is finite, the **repeat until** loop terminates.

*Correctness.* If there exists a permission $p \in Applicable^{\otimes}$ that authorizes the release of $R$, two cases can occur: $p \in Applicable$, or $p$ is a composed permission. In the first case, **Authorized** returns *true* since the first **for** loop iterates on all permissions in *Applicable*. In the second case, the **repeat until** loop removes from *Applicable* only non-necessary permissions (see Theorem 5.1) and checks all non-redundant pairs of permissions in *Applicable*. The **repeat until** loop terminates when, for all $p$ in *Applicable*, $p.maxcfr=maxid$. Since $p.maxcfr$ is initialized to $p.id$ and updated to the minimum $p_i.id$ such that $p.maxcfr<p_i.id$, each permission is compared to all the other permissions following it in the order established by $id$. Also, for each new permission $p_i$, $maxid$ increases by 1 and $p_j.id$ is set to the new value of $maxid$. Since, for each permission $p$ but $p_i$ in *Applicable*, $p.maxcfr$ is less than $p_j.id$, the subsequent iterations of the **repeat until** loop check the new permission with all the other permissions in *Applicable*. This means that the **repeat until** loop checks all possible pairs of permissions and therefore it finds the permission authorizing the release of $R$.

Note also that, if a permission $p_i$ removed from *Applicable* (because $p_j \rightarrow p_i$) authorizes $R$, the composed permission $p_j \otimes p_i = [Att_{ij}, Rels_{ij}]$ belongs to *Applicable* and authorizes the release of $R$. In fact, $Att_{ij} = (Att_i \cup Att_j) \supseteq (R^\pi \cup R^\sigma)$. Also, $Rels_{ij}{}^* = Rels_i{}^* = R^{\bowtie *}$.

**Theorem 5.3 (Complexity).** *Given a relation profile $R = [R^\pi, R^\bowtie, R^\sigma]$ and a set Applicable of $n$ applicable permissions, the complexity of function **Authorized** is $O(n^3)$ in time.*

*Proof.* The function matches every permission with every other permission in the *Applicable* set, to verify if they can be composed. Any time $p_i \rightarrow p_j$, $p_i$ is removed from *Applicable*, while $p_i \otimes p_j$ is added to the same. Since, thanks to the ordering among permissions, no match between pairs of permissions is repeated, each per-

| Oper. | [m,s] | Operation/Flow | Views($S_l$) | Views($S_r$) | View profiles |
|---|---|---|---|---|---|
| $\pi_X(R_l)$ | $[S_l,\text{NULL}]$ | $S_l$: $\pi_X(R_l)$ | | | |
| $\sigma_X(R_l)$ | $[S_l,\text{NULL}]$ | $S_l$: $\sigma_X(R_l)$ | | | |
| $R_l\bowtie_{J_{l_r}}R_r$ | $[S_l,\text{NULL}]$ | $S_r$: $R_r\to S_l$ <br> $S_l$: $R_l\bowtie R_r$ | $R_r$ | | $[R_r^\pi,R_r^\bowtie,R_r^\sigma]$ |
| | $[S_r,\text{NULL}]$ | $S_l$: $R_l\to S_r$ <br> $S_r$: $R_l\bowtie R_r$ | | $R_l$ | $[R_l^\pi,R_l^\bowtie,R_l^\sigma]$ |
| | $[S_l,S_r]$ | $S_l$: $R_{J_l} := \pi_J(R_l)$ <br> $S_l$: $R_{J_l}\to S_r$ <br> $S_r$: $R_{J_{l_r}}:=R_{J_l}\bowtie R_r$ <br> $S_r$: $R_{J_{l_r}}\to S_l$ <br> $S_l$: $R_{J_{l_r}}\bowtie R_l$ | $\pi_J(R_l)\bowtie R_r$ | $\pi_J(R_l)$ | $[J,R_l^\bowtie,R_l^\sigma]$ <br> $[R_r^\pi,R_l^\bowtie\cup R_r^\bowtie,R_l^\sigma\cup R_r^\sigma]$ |
| | $[S_r,S_l]$ | $S_r$: $R_{J_r} := \pi_J(R_r)$ <br> $S_r$: $R_{J_r}\to S_l$ <br> $S_l$: $R_{lJ_r}:=R_l\bowtie R_{J_r}$ <br> $S_l$: $R_{lJ_r}\to S_r$ <br> $S_r$: $R_{lJ_r}\bowtie R_r$ | $\pi_J(R_r)$ | $R_l\bowtie(\pi_J(R_r))$ | $[J,R_r^\bowtie,R_r^\sigma]$ <br> $[R_l^\pi,R_l^\bowtie\cup R_r^\bowtie,R_l^\sigma\cup R_r^\sigma]$ |

**Fig. 5.13** Execution of operations and required views with corresponding profiles

mission is compared to at most $n-1$ permissions generating, at most $n$ versions of the same. Therefore the function makes at most $n^3$ comparisons.

## 5.6 Safe Query Planning

To determine whether and how a query can be executed over the distributed system, we need first to determine the data releases that the execution entails, so that only executions implying authorized releases are performed. Since we can assume each server to be authorized to view the relation it holds, each unary operation (projection and selection) can be executed by the server itself, while a join operation can be executed if all the data communications correspond to authorized releases.

The table in Fig. 5.13 summarizes the operations and data exchanges needed to perform a relational operation reporting, for every data communication, the profile of the relation being communicated (and hence the information exposure implied by it); data access by a server on its own relation is implicit. For each operation/communication we also show, before the "∶", the server executing it. For join operations, we first note that a (natural) join operation $R_l\bowtie R_r$, where $R_l$ and $R_r$ represent the left and right input relations, respectively, can be executed either as a regular join or a semi-join. We call *master* the server in charge of the join computation and *slave* the server that cooperates with the master during the computation. We then distinguish four different cases resulting from whether the join is executed as a *regular* join or as a *semi-join* and from which operand serves as master (slave, respectively). The assignment is specified as a pair, where the first element specifies the operand that serves as master and the second the operand that serves as slave. We briefly discuss the cases where the left operand serves as master (denoted $[S_l, \text{NULL}]$ for the regular join and $[S_l, S_r]$ for the semi-join), with the note that the cases where the right operand serves as master ($[S_r, \text{NULL}]$ and $[S_r, S_l]$) are symmetric.

- $[S_l, \text{NULL}]$: in the *regular join* processed by $S_l$, server $S_r$ sends (i.e., needs to release) its relation to $S_l$, and $S_l$ computes the join. For execution, $S_l$ needs to hold a permission (either base or composed) authorizing it to view $R_r$, which has profile $[R_r^\pi, R_r^\bowtie, R_r^\sigma]$.
- $[S_l, S_r]$: the *semi-join* requires a longer sequence of steps. First, $S_l$ computes the projection $R_{J_l}$ of the attributes $J$ in its relation $R_l$ participating in the join. Second, $S_l$ sends $R_{J_l}$ to $S_r$; this operation entails a data release characterized by the profile of $R_{J_l}$, which (according to Definition 5.3) is $[J, R_l^\bowtie, R_l^\sigma]$. Third, $S_r$ locally computes $R_{J_l r}$ as the join between $R_{J_l}$ and its relation $R_r$. Fourth, $S_r$ sends $R_{J_l r}$ to $S_l$; this operation entails a data release characterized by the profile of $R_{J_l r}$, namely $[R_r^\pi, R_l^\bowtie \cup R_r^\bowtie, R_l^\sigma \cup R_r^\sigma]$ (note that the first component contains only $R_r^\pi$, since $J$ must be a subset of $R_r^\pi$). Fifth, $S_l$ computes the join between $R_{J_l r}$ and its own relation $R_l$.

Semi-joins are usually more efficient than regular joins as they minimize communication (which also benefits security): the slave server needs only to send those tuples that participate in the join, instead of its complete relation.

For instance, consider the query in Example 5.3. If the join at node $n_2$ in the tree is executed as a regular join, $S_E$ sends the all the tuples in Employee relation, restricted to attributes SSN and Salary, to $S_P$ (or vice versa). If the join is executed as a semi-join where $S_E$ acts as a master, $S_E$ sends to $S_P$ the projection of the Employee relation on SSN. $S_P$ then sends back to $S_E$ the SSN and DoB values in Patient relation joined with the list of values of SSN received from $S_E$.

A function $\varepsilon_T$ assigns to each node $n$ of a query tree plan $T(N_T, E_T)$ a server or a pair of servers, called *executor*, responsible for the execution of the algebraic operation represented by $n$. To formally capture this intuitive idea, the definition of the *executor assignment* function $\varepsilon_T$ is introduced as follows.

**Definition 5.15 (Executor assignment).** Given a query tree plan $T(N_T, E_T)$, an *executor assignment function* $\varepsilon_T : N_T \to \mathscr{S} \times \{\mathscr{S} \cup \text{NULL}\}$ is an assignment of pairs of servers to nodes such that:

1. each *leaf* node (corresponding to a relation $R$) is assigned the pair $[S, \text{NULL}]$, where $S$ is the server where $R$ is stored;
2. each non-leaf node $n$, corresponding to *unary* operation *op* on operands $R_l$ (left child) at server $S_l$, is assigned a pair $[S_l, \text{NULL}]$.
3. each non-leaf node $n$, corresponding to a *join* operation on operand $R_l$ (left child) at server $S_l$ and $R_r$ (right child) at server $S_r$, is assigned a pair $[master, slave]$ such that $master \in \{S_l, S_r\}$, $slave \in \{S_l, S_r, \text{NULL}\}$, and $master \neq slave$.

Given a query plan, our algorithm determines an assignment of the computation steps to different servers, in such a way that the execution given by the assignment entails only releases allowed by the permissions.

| [m,s] | Operation/Flow | Views($S_l$) | Views($S_r$) | Views($S_t$) | View profiles |
|---|---|---|---|---|---|
| [$S_t$,NULL] | $S_l$: $R_l \to S_t$ | | | $R_l$ | $[R_l^\pi, R_l^{\bowtie}, R_l^\sigma]$ |
| | $S_r$: $R_r \to S_t$ | | | $R_r$ | $[R_r^\pi, R_r^{\bowtie}, R_r^\sigma]$ |
| | $S_t$: $R_l \bowtie R_r$ | | | | |
| [$S_t$,$S_r$] | $S_l$: $R_l \to S_t$ | | | $R_l$ | $[R_l^\pi, R_l^{\bowtie}, R_l^\sigma]$ |
| | $S_l$: $R_{J_l} := \pi_J(R_l)$ | | | | |
| | $S_l$: $R_{J_l} \to S_r$ | | $\pi_J(R_l)$ | | $[J, R_l^{\bowtie}, R_l^\sigma]$ |
| | $S_r$: $R_{J_l r} := R_{J_l} \bowtie R_r$ | | | | |
| | $S_r$: $R_{J_l r} \to S_t$ | | | $\pi_J(R_l) \bowtie R_r$ | $[R_r^\pi, R_l^{\bowtie}\cup R_r^{\bowtie}, R_l^\sigma\cup R_r^\sigma]$ |
| | $S_t$: $R_{J_l r} \bowtie R_l$ | | | | |
| [$S_t$,$S_l$] | $S_r$: $R_r \to S_t$ | | | $R_r$ | $[R_r^\pi, R_r^{\bowtie}, R_r^\sigma]$ |
| | $S_t$: $R_{J_r} := \pi_J(R_r)$ | | | | |
| | $S_t$: $R_{J_r} \to S_l$ | $\pi_J(R_r)$ | | | $[J, R_r^{\bowtie}, R_r^\sigma]$ |
| | $S_l$: $R_{J_r l} := R_l \bowtie R_{J_r}$ | | | | |
| | $S_l$: $R_{J_r l} \to S_t$ | | | $R_l \bowtie (\pi_J(R_r))$ | $[R_l^\pi, R_l^{\bowtie}\cup R_r^{\bowtie}, R_l^\sigma\cup R_r^\sigma]$ |
| | $S_t$: $R_{J_r l} \bowtie R_r$ | | | | |
| [$S_l$,$S_t$] | $S_l$: $R_{J_l} := \pi_J(R_l)$ | | | | |
| | $S_l$: $R_{J_l} \to S_t$ | | | $\pi_J(R_l)$ | $[J, R_l^{\bowtie}, R_l^\sigma]$ |
| | $S_r$: $R_r \to S_t$ | | | $R_r$ | $[R_r^\pi, R_r^{\bowtie}, R_r^\sigma]$ |
| | $S_t$: $R_{J_l r} := R_{J_l} \bowtie R_r$ | | | | |
| | $S_t$: $R_{J_l r} \to S_l$ | $\pi_J(R_l) \bowtie R_r$ | | | $[R_r^\pi, R_l^{\bowtie}\cup R_r^{\bowtie}, R_l^\sigma\cup R_r^\sigma]$ |
| | $S_t$: $R_{J_l r} \bowtie R_l$ | | | | |
| [$S_r$,$S_t$] | $S_r$: $R_{J_r} := \pi_J(R_r)$ | | | | |
| | $S_r$: $R_{J_r} \to S_t$ | | | $\pi_J(R_r)$ | $[J, R_r^{\bowtie}, R_r^\sigma]$ |
| | $S_l$: $R_l \to S_t$ | | | $R_l$ | $[R_l^\pi, R_l^{\bowtie}, R_l^\sigma]$ |
| | $S_t$: $R_{J_r l} := R_l \bowtie R_{J_r}$ | | | | |
| | $S_t$: $R_{J_r l} \to S_r$ | | $R_l \bowtie (\pi_J(R_r))$ | | $[R_l^\pi, R_l^{\bowtie}\cup R_r^{\bowtie}, R_l^\sigma\cup R_r^\sigma]$ |
| | $S_r$: $R_{J_r l} \bowtie R_r$ | | | | |
| [$S_t$,$S_l$,$S_r$] | $S_l$: $R_{J_l} := \pi_J(R_l)$ | | | | |
| | $S_r$: $R_{J_r} := \pi_J(R_r)$ | | | | |
| | $S_l$: $R_{J_l} \to S_t$ | | | $\pi_J(R_l)$ | $[J, R_l^{\bowtie}, R_l^\sigma]$ |
| | $S_r$: $R_{J_r} \to S_t$ | | | $\pi_J(R_r)$ | $[J, R_r^{\bowtie}, R_r^\sigma]$ |
| | $S_t$: $R_{J_l J_r} := R_{J_l} \bowtie R_{J_r}$ | | | | |
| | $S_t$: $R_{J_l J_r} \to S_l$ | $(\pi_J(R_l)) \bowtie (\pi_J(R_r))$ | | | $[J, R_l^{\bowtie}\cup R_r^{\bowtie}, R_l^\sigma\cup R_r^\sigma]$ |
| | $S_t$: $R_{J_l J_r} \to S_r$ | | $(\pi_J(R_l)) \bowtie (\pi_J(R_r))$ | | $[J, R_l^{\bowtie}\cup R_r^{\bowtie}, R_l^\sigma\cup R_r^\sigma]$ |
| | $S_l$: $R_{J_l r l} := R_l \bowtie R_{J_l J_r}$ | | | | |
| | $S_r$: $R_{J_l r r} := R_{J_l J_r} \bowtie R_r$ | | | | |
| | $S_l$: $R_{J_l r l} \to S_t$ | | | $R_l \bowtie ((\pi_J(R_l)) \bowtie (\pi_J(R_r)))$ | $[R_l^\pi, R_l^{\bowtie}\cup R_r^{\bowtie}, R_l^\sigma\cup R_r^\sigma]$ |
| | $S_r$: $R_{J_l r r} \to S_t$ | | | $((\pi_J(R_l)) \bowtie (\pi_J(R_r))) \bowtie R_r$ | $[R_r^\pi, R_l^{\bowtie}\cup R_r^{\bowtie}, R_l^\sigma\cup R_r^\sigma]$ |
| | $S_t$: $R_{J_l r l} \bowtie R_{J_l r r}$ | | | | |

**Fig. 5.14** Different strategies for executing join operation, with the intervention of a third party

**Definition 5.16 (Safe assignment).** Given a query tree plan $T(N_T, E_T)$ and an executor assignment function $\varepsilon_T$, $\varepsilon_T(n)$ is said to be *safe* when one of the following conditions hold:

1. $n$ is a leaf node;
2. $n$ corresponds to a unary operation;
3. $n$ corresponds to a join and all the releases derived by the assignment are authorized.

$\varepsilon_T$ is said to be *safe* iff $\forall n \in N_T$, $\varepsilon_T(n)$ is safe.

A query plan is then feasible iff there is a safe assignment for it.

**Definition 5.17 (Feasible query plan).** A query plan $T(N_T, E_T)$ is said to be *feasible* iff there exists an executor assignment function $\varepsilon_T$ on $T$ such that $\varepsilon_T$ is safe.

## 5.6.1 Third Party Involvement

As already discussed, the execution of joins necessarily requires some communication of information among the operands, which we check against permissions (base or composed) and allow only if authorized. It may happen that, for a given join, none of the four possible modes of execution corresponds to a safe assignment. In such a case, we envision a third party can participate in the operation acting either as a proxy for one of the two operands or as a coordinator for them. Table in Fig. 5.14 summarizes the different ways in which a third party can be involved. We briefly comment them here.

- $[S_t,\text{NULL}]$: the third party receives the relations from the operands and independently computes the (regular) join.
- $[S_t,S_l]$ and $[S_t,S_r]$: the third party replaces $S_r$ ($S_l$, respectively) in the computation with the role of master with $S_l$ ($S_r$, respectively) in the role of slave.
- $[S_l,S_t]$ and $[S_r,S_t]$: the third party replaces $S_r$ ($S_l$, respectively) in the computation with the role of slave with $S_l$ ($S_r$, respectively) in the role of master.
- $[S_t,S_lS_r]$: the third party takes the role of master in charge of computing the join with $S_l$ and $S_r$ both working as slaves. In this case, each of the operands computes the projection of its attributes that participate in the join and sends it to the third party. The third party computes the join between the two inputs and sends back the result to each of the operands, each of which joins the input with its relation and returns the result to the third party. The third party can now join the relations received from the operands and compute the result.

Note that the first five scenarios are a simple adaptation of those already seen in the previous section, with the third party only acting as proxy, which therefore needs to have the permissions necessary to view the relation of the party for which it acts as a proxy, as well as the view required by its role (master/slave). The latter scenario $[S_t,S_lS_r]$ is instead a little more complex and, as it can be easily seen from the table, entails different data views. In this scenario the third party is required to only view the tuples of the operands that participate in the join (it does not need to have the complete view on a relation as in the case it acts as a proxy). Also, each of the slaves is required only to view the attributes of the other relation that joins with itself (instead of the complete list).

The consideration of a third party requires to slightly change the executor assignment definition (Definition 5.15) which becomes as follows.

**Definition 5.18 (Executor assignment - with third party).** Given a query plan $T(N_T,E_T)$, an *executor assignment function* $\varepsilon_T : N_T \to \mathscr{S} \times \{\mathscr{S} \cup [\mathscr{S} \times \mathscr{S}] \cup \text{NULL}\}$ is an assignment of pairs of servers to nodes such that:

1. each *leaf* node (corresponding to a relation $R$) is assigned the pair $[S,\text{NULL}]$, where $S$ is the server where $R$ is stored;
2. each non-leaf node $n$, corresponding to *unary* operation $op$ on operands $R_l$ (left child) at server $S_l$, is assigned a pair $[S_l,\text{NULL}]$.

| $p_6$: [(SSN,Job,Salary),(Employee)] → $S_E$ |
| $p_7$: [(SSN),(Patient)] → $S_E$ |
| $p_8$: [(SSN,DoB,Race),(Patient)] → $S_P$ |
| $p_9$: [(SSN,Job,Salary),(Employee,Patient)] → $S_P$ |
| $p_{10}$: [(SSN,IdDoc,Type,Cost,Duration),(Patient,Treatment)] → $S_P$ |
| $p_{11}$: [(SSN,IdDoc,Type,Cost,Duration),(Treatment)] → $S_T$ |
| $p_{12}$: [(IdDoc,Name,Specialty),(Doctor)] → $S_D$ |
| $p_{13}$: [(SSN,Type,Duration),(Treatment)] → $S_D$ |
| $p_{14}$: [(SSN,DoB,Race),(Employee,Patient)] → $S_D$ |

**Fig. 5.15** An example of servers' permissions

3. each non-leaf node $n$, corresponding to a *join* operation on operand $R_l$ (left child) at server $S_l$ and $R_r$ (right child) at server $S_r$, is assigned a pair [*master,slaves*] such that *master* $\in \mathscr{S}$, *slaves* $\in \{\mathscr{S} \cup [S_l, S_r] \cup \text{NULL}\}$, *master*$\neq$*slave*, and at least one of the elements is in $\{S_l, S_r, [S_l, S_r], \text{NULL}\}$.

The definitions of safe assignment and feasible query plan remain unchanged.

*Example 5.6.* Consider the scenario of Example 5.3 and the permissions held by servers storing data in Fig. 5.15. The outer join between (Employee⋈Patient) and Treatment can be safely assigned neither to $S_E$ and $S_P$ nor to $S_T$. It is then necessary to resort to the intervention of a third party. Specifically, a safe assignment for the given operation is [$S_P, S_D$]. As a matter of fact, $S_D$ is authorized to access attributes SSN, Type, and Duration of relation Treatment and attributes SSN, DoB, and Race from the join of Employee with Patient. $S_P$ is authorized to view the whole Treatment relation, provided join condition P.SSN=T.SSN holds.

We can now state the problem as follows.

**Problem 5.1.** Given a query plan $T(N_T, E_T)$ and a set of permissions $\mathscr{P}$: *1)* determine if $T$ is feasible and *2)* retrieve a safe assignment $\varepsilon_T$ for it.

In the next section we illustrate an algorithm for the solution of such a problem, which exploits permissions composition technique already introduced, and given a query plan and a set of base permissions determines if the plan is feasible and, if so, returns a safe assignment for it.

## 5.7 Build a Safe Query Plan

The determination of the safe assignment follows two basic principles, in order to minimize the cost of computation: *i)* we favor semi-joins (in contrast to regular joins); *ii)* if more servers are candidate to safely execute a join operation (at a given level in the tree), we prefer the server that is involved in a higher number of join

**INPUT**
$\mathscr{P}$
$G(\mathscr{N},e)$
$T(N_T,E_T)$

**OUTPUT**
$\mathcal{E}_T(n)$ /* as $n.executor$ */

/* $n.left$, $n.right$: left and right children */
/* $n.operator$, $n.parameter$: operation and its parameters */
/* $[n.\pi,n.\bowtie,n.\sigma]$: profile */
/* $n.leftslave$, $n.rightslave$: left and right slaves */
/* $n.leftthirdslave$: third party acting as left slave */
/* $n.rightthirdslave$: third party acting as right slave */
/* $n.candidates$: list of records of the form [$server,fromchild,counter$] stating candidate servers, the child
   (left, right) it comes or proxies for, and the number of joins for which the server is candidate in the subtree */
/* $n.executor.master$, $n.executor.slaves$: executor assignment */

**MAIN**
**FindCandidates(root($T$))**
**AssignExecutor(root($T$)**, NULL)
**return($T$)**

Fig. 5.16  Algorithm computing a safe assignment for a query plan

operations. To this aim, we associate with each candidate server a counter that keeps track of the number of join operations for which the server is a candidate.

The algorithm receives in input the set of permissions, the schema graph, and the query plan $T(N_T,E_T)$, where each leaf node (base relation $R$) is already assigned to executor [$server$,NULL], where $server$ is the server storing the relation. It returns, if it exists, a safe assignment for $T$.

The algorithm works by performing two traversals of the query tree plan. The first traversal (procedure **Find_candidates**) visits the tree in *post-order*. At each node, the profile of the node is computed (as in Fig. 5.4) based on the profile of the children and of the operation associated with the node. Also, the set of possible candidate assignments for the node is determined based on the set of possible candidates for its children as follows. If the node is a unary operation, the candidates for the node are all the candidates for its unique child. If the node is a join operation, procedure **Find_candidates** calls function **Authorized** in Fig. 5.11 whenever it is necessary to verify if a particular server can act as master, slave, or can calculate a regular join. **Authorized** is called on the view graph representing the profile of the views that should be made visible in the execution of an operation. The algorithm considers candidates of the left child in decreasing order of join counter (**GetFirst**) and stops at the first candidate found that can serve as left slave (inserting it into local variable *leftslave*). The algorithm proceeds examining all the candidates of the right child to determine if they can work as master for a semi-join (if a left slave was found) or as a regular join (if no left slave was found). Note that while we need to determine all servers that can act as master, as we need to consider all possible candidates for propagating them upwards in the tree, it is sufficient to determine one slave (a slave is not propagated upward in the tree). For each of such *server* candidates a triple [$server$,right,*counter*] is added to the *candidates* list, where counter is the counter that was associated with the server in the right child of the node incre-

**FINDCANDIDATES**(*n*)
*l* := *n.left*
*r* := *n.right*
**if** *l* ≠NULL **then FindCandidates**(*l*)
**if** *r* ≠NULL **then FindCandidates**(*r*)
**case** *n.operator* **of**

   π:  *n.π* := *n.parameter*; *n.⋈* := *l.⋈*; *n.σ* := *l.σ*
      **for** *c* **in** *l.candidates* **do** Add [*c.server*, left, *c.count*] to *n.candidates*

   σ:  *n.π* := *l.π*; *n.⋈* := *l.⋈*; *n.σ* := *l.σ* ∪ *n.parameter*
      **for** *c* **in** *l.candidates* **do** Add [*c.server*, left, *c.count*] to *n.candidates*

   ⋈:  *n.π* := *l.π* ∪ *r.π*; *n.⋈* := *l.⋈* ∪ *r.⋈* ∪ *n.parameter*; *n.σ* := *l.σ* ∪ *r.σ*
      *right_slave_view* := [*J_l*, *l.⋈*, *l.σ*]
      *left_slave_view* := [*J_r*, *r.⋈*, *r.σ*]
      *right_master_view* := [*l.π* ∪ *J_r*, *l.⋈* ∪ *r.⋈* ∪ *n.parameter*, *l.σ* ∪ *r.σ*]
      *left_master_view* := [*J_l* ∪ *r.π*, *l.⋈* ∪ *r.⋈* ∪ *n.parameter*, *l.σ* ∪ *r.σ*]
      *right_full_view* := [*l.π*, *l.⋈*, *l.σ*]
      *left_full_view* := [*r.π*, *r.⋈*, *r.σ*]
      /* check case [*S_r*,NULL] and [*S_r*,*S_l*] */
      *n.leftslave* := NULL
      *c* := **GetFirst**(*l.candidates*)
      **while** (*n.leftslave*=NULL)∧(*c*≠NULL) **do**
         **if Authorized**(*G_{left_slave_view}*, *c.server*) **then** *n.leftslave* := *c*
         *c* := *c.next*
      *regular* := NULL
      *rightmasters* = NULL
      **for** *c* **in** *r.candidates* **do**
         **if Authorized**(*G_{right_full_view}*, *c.server*) **then** Add [*c.server*, right, *c.count*+1] to *regular*
         **if Authorized**(*G_{right_master_view}*, *c.server*) **then** Add [*c.server*, right, *c.count*+1] to *rightmasters*
      **if** *n.leftslave*≠NULL **then**
        Add *rightmasters* to *n.candidates*
      **else**
        Add *regular* to *n.candidates*
      /* check case [*S_l*,NULL] and [*S_l*,*S_r*] */
      *n.rightslave* := NULL
      *c* := **GetFirst**(*r.candidates*)
      **while** (*n.rightslave*=NULL)∧(*c*≠NULL) **do**
         **if Authorized**(*G_{right_slave_view}*, *c.server*) **then** *n.rightslave* := *c*
         *c* := *c.next*
      *regular* := NULL
      *leftmasters* = NULL
      **for** *c* **in** *l.candidates* **do**
         **if Authorized**(*G_{left_full_view}*, *c.server*) **then** Add [*c.server*, left, *c.count*+1] to *regular*
         **if Authorized**(*G_{left_master_view}*, *c.server*) **then** Add [*c.server*, left, *c.count*+1] to *leftmasters*
      **if** *n.rightslave*≠NULL **then**
        Add *leftmasters* to *n.candidates*
      **else**
        Add *regular* to *n.candidates*
      /* check third party */
      **if** *n.candidates*=NULL **then** *n.candidates* := **FindThirdParty**(*n*,*leftmasters*,*rightmasters*)
      /* node cannot be executed */
      **if** *n.candidates*=NULL **then exit**(*n*)

**Fig. 5.17** Function that determines the set of safe candidates for nodes in *T*

mented by one (as candidate also for the join of the father, the server would execute one additional join compared to the number it would have executed at the child level). Then, the algorithm proceeds symmetrically to determine whether there is a candidate from the right child (considering the candidates in decreasing order of counter) that can work as slave, and then determining all the left candidates that can work as master, adding them to the set of candidates. At the end of this process,

ASSIGNEXECUTOR(*n*, *from_parent*)
if *from_parent*≠NULL then
    *chosen* := **Search**(*from_parent*, *n.candidates*)
else
    *chosen* := **GetFirst**(*n.candidates*)
*n.executor.master* := *chosen.server*
case *chosen.fromchild* of
    left: /* case [$S_l$,NULL], [$S_l$,$S_r$], [$S_l$,$S_t$] */
        if *n.left*≠NULL then **AssignExecutor**(*n.left*, *n.executor.master*)
        if *n.right*≠NULL then
            if  *n.rightslave*≠NULL then
                *n.executor.slaves* := {*n.rightslave*}
                **AssignExecutor**(*n.right*, *n.rightslave*)
            else *n.executor.slaves* := {*n.rightthirdslave*}
                **AssignExecutor**(*n.right*, NULL)

    right: /* case [$S_r$,NULL], [$S_r$,$S_l$], [$S_r$,$S_t$] */
        if *n.left*≠NULL then
            if  *n.leftslave*≠NULL then
                *n.executor.slaves* := {*n.leftslave*}
                **AssignExecutor**(*n.right*, *n.leftslave*)
            else *n.executor.slaves* := {*n.leftthirdslave*}
                **AssignExecutor**(*n.right*, NULL)
        if *n.right*≠NULL then **AssignExecutor**(*n.right*, *n.executor.master*)

    third_left: /* case [$S_t$,$S_r$] */
        *n.executor.slaves* := {*n.rightslave*}
        if *n.left*≠NULL then **AssignExecutor**(*n.left*, NULL)
        if *n.right*≠NULL then **AssignExecutor**(*n.right*, *n.rightslave*)

    third_right: /* case [$S_t$,$S_l$] */
        *n.executor.slaves* := {*n.leftslave*}
        if *n.left*≠NULL then **AssignExecutor**(*n.left*, *n.leftslave*)
        if *n.right*≠NULL then **AssignExecutor**(*n.right*, NULL)
    third: /* case [$S_t$,NULL], [$S_t$,$S_lS_r$] */
        *n.executor.slaves* := {*n.leftslave*, *n.rightslave*}
        if *n.left*≠NULL then **AssignExecutor**(*n.left*, *n.leftslave*)
        if *n.right*≠NULL then **AssignExecutor**(*n.right*, *n.rightslave*)

**Fig. 5.18** Function that chooses one candidate for each node in *T*

list *candidates* contains all the candidates coming from either the left or right child that can execute the join in any of the execution modes of Fig. 5.13. If no candidate was found, the algorithm determines whether the operation can be computed with the intervention of a third party by calling function **FindThirdParty** in Fig. 5.19 that similarly for the cases above, simply implements the controls according to the views that would be required for the execution (Sect. 5.6.1). If even such a call does not return any candidate, the algorithm exits returning the node at which the process was interrupted (i.e., for which no safe assignment exists) signaling that the tree is not feasible.

If **Find_candidates** completes successfully, the algorithm proceeds with the second traversal of the query tree plan. The second traversal (procedure **AssignExecutor**) recursively visits the tree in *pre-order*. At the root node, if more assignments are possible, the candidate server with the highest join count is chosen. Hence, the chosen candidate is pushed down to the child from which it was determined during the preceding post-order traversal. The other child (if existing) is pushed down the recorded candidate slave. If no slave was recorded as possible (i.e., *right-*

---

**FINDTHIRDPARTY**(*n,leftmasters,rightmasters*)
$l := n.left$; $r := n.right$; $list := $ NULL
$right\_slave\_view := [J_l, l.\bowtie, l.\sigma]$
$left\_slave\_view := [J_r, r.\bowtie, r.\sigma]$
$right\_master\_view := [l.\pi \cup J_r, l.\bowtie \cup r.\bowtie \cup n.parameter, l.\sigma \cup r.\sigma]$
$left\_master\_view := [J_l \cup r.\pi, l.\bowtie \cup r.\bowtie \cup n.parameter, l.\sigma \cup r.\sigma]$
$right\_full\_view := [l.\pi, l.\bowtie, l.\sigma]$
$left\_full\_view := [r.\pi, r.\bowtie, r.\sigma]$
$two\_slave\_view := [J_l \cup J_r, l.\bowtie \cup r.\bowtie \cup n.parameter, l.\sigma \cup r.\sigma]$
/* check if a third party can act as a *slave* */
**if** *leftmasters*≠NULL **then** /* case [$S_l,S_l$] */
  $n.rightthirdslave := $ NULL
  $i := 1$
  **while** ($n.rightthirdslave$=NULL)∧($i < |\mathcal{S}|$) **do**
    **if Authorized**($G_{right\_slave\_view}, S_i$) ∧ **Authorized**($G_{left\_full\_view}, S_i$) **then** $n.rightthirdslave := S_i$
    $i := i+1$
**if** $n.rightthirdslave$≠NULL **then**
  **for each** $c \in leftmasters$ **do** Add [$c.server$, left, $c.count$] to *list*
**if** *rightmasters*≠NULL **then** /* case [$S_r,S_l$] */
  $n.leftthirdslave := $ NULL
  $i := 1$
  **while** ($n.leftthirdslave$=NULL)∧($i < |\mathcal{S}|$) **do**
    **if Authorized**($G_{left\_slave\_view}, S_i$) ∧ **Authorized**($G_{right\_full\_view}, S_i$) **then** $n.leftthirdslave := S_i$
    $i := i+1$
**if** $n.leftthirdslave$≠NULL **then**
  **for each** $c \in rightmasters$ **do** Add [$c.server$, right, $c.count$] to *list*
**if** *list*≠NULL **then** **return**(*list*)
/* check if a third party can act as a *master* */
**for** $i := 1 \ldots |\mathcal{S}|$ **do**
  **if** $n.leftslave$≠NULL **then** /* case [$S_l,S_l$] */
    **if Authorized**($G_{right\_master\_view}, S_i$) ∧ **Authorized**($G_{left\_full\_view}, S_i$) **then** Add [$S_i$, third_right, 1] to *list*
  **else**
    **if** $n.rightslave$≠NULL **then** /* case [$S_l,S_r$] */
      **if Authorized**($G_{left\_master\_view}, S_i$) ∧ **Authorized**($G_{right\_full\_view}, S_i$) **then** Add [$S_i$, third_left, 1] to *list*
**if** *list*≠NULL **then** **return**(*list*)
/* check if a third party can execute the *regular* join: case [$S_l$,NULL] */
**for** $i := 1 \ldots |\mathcal{S}|$ **do**
  **if Authorized**($G_{left\_full\_view}, S_i$) ∧ **Authorized**($G_{right\_full\_view}, S_i$) **then** Add [$S_i$, third, 1] to *list*
**if** *list*≠NULL **then** **return**(*list*)
/* check if a third party can act as a *coordinator*: case [$S_t,S_l S_r$] */
$c := $ **GetFirst**(*l.candidates*)
**while** ($n.leftslave$=NULL)∧($c$≠NULL) **do**
  **if Authorized**($G_{two\_slave\_view}, c.server$) **then** $n.leftslave := c.server$
  $c := c.next$
**if** $n.leftslave$≠NULL **then**
  $c := $ **GetFirst**(*r.candidates*)
  **while** ($n.rightslave$=NULL)∧($c$≠NULL) **do**
    **if Authorized**($G_{two\_slave\_view}, c.server$) **then** $n.rightslave := c.server$
    $c := c.next$
**if** $n.rightslave$≠NULL **then**
  **for** $i := 1 \ldots |\mathcal{S}|$ **do**
    **if Authorized**($G_{left\_slave\_view}, S_i$) ∧ **Authorized**($G_{right\_slave\_view}, S_i$)
    ∧ **Authorized**($G_{left\_master\_view}, S_i$) ∧ **Authorized**($G_{right\_master\_view}, S_i$)
    **then** Add $S_i$ to *masterlist*
**if** *masterlist*≠NULL **then** **for each** $m \in masterlist$ **do** Add [$m$, third, 1] to *list*
**if** *list*≠NULL **then** **return**(*list*)

---

**Fig. 5.19** Function that evaluates the intervention of a third party for join operations

*slave/leftslave*=NULL or the slave is a third party) a NULL value is pushed down. At each children, the master executor is determined as the server pushed down by the

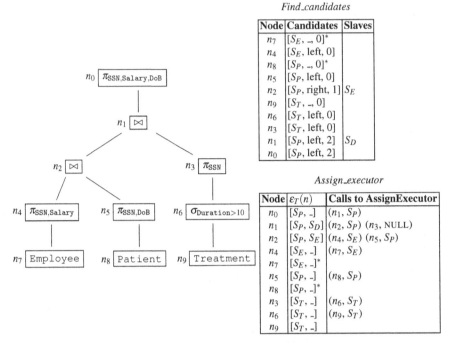

**Fig. 5.20** An example of execution of the algorithm in Fig. 5.16

parent (if it is not NULL) or the candidate server with the highest join count and the process is recursively repeated, until a leaf node is reached.

*Example 5.7.* Consider the query plan in Fig. 5.2 of query $Q_4$, reported in Fig. 5.20 for convenience, requested by `Alice`, who is authorized to view the query result (see composed permission $p_1 \otimes p_2 \otimes p_4$ in Fig. 5.10). Consider also the set of servers' permissions in Fig. 5.15. Figure 5.20 illustrates the working of procedures **Find_candidates** and **Assign_executor** reporting the nodes in the order they are considered by them and the candidates/executors determined. Candidates/executors with a "*" are those of the leaf nodes (already given in input). To illustrate the working, let us look at some sample calls. Consider, for example, the call **Find_candidates**($n_2$). Among the candidates of the children ($S_E$ from left child $n_4$ and $S_P$ from right child $n_5$) only the right child candidate $S_P$ survives as candidate for the join, which is executed as a semi-join since $S_E$ can act as a slave. When **Assign_executor** is called, the set of candidates at each node is as shown in the table summarizing the results of **Find_candidates**. Starting at the root node, the only possible choice assigns to $n_0$ executor $[S_P,\_]$, where $S_P$ was recorded as coming from the left (and only) child $n_1$, to which $S_P$ is then pushed with a recursive call. At $n_1$ the master is set as $S_P$ and, combining this with the slave field, the executor is set to $[S_P,S_D]$. Hence, $S_P$ is further pushed down to the left child (from where it was taken by **Find_candidates**) $n_3$, while $S_D$ is not pushed down to the left child $n_2$, since it was a third party helping in finding a correct assignment.

We conclude this section with a note regarding the integration of our approach with existing query optimizers. Optimization of distributed queries operates in *two-steps* [64]. First, the query optimizer identifies a good plan, analogous to the one it would produce for a centralized system; second, it assigns operations to the distinct servers in the system. Our algorithm nicely fits in such a two phase structure. In particular, while in the illustration of the algorithm we have assumed the complete query plan to be provided as input, we note that our algorithm could be nicely merged with the optimizers and perform its pre-order visit in conjunction with the construction of the tree by the query optimizer, computing candidates while the optimizers builds the plan, and its post-order visit for computing executors for the optimizers in the second phase.

## 5.8 Chapter Summary

We presented a simple, yet powerful, approach for the specification and enforcement of permissions regulating data release among data holders collaborating in a distributed computation, to ensure that query processing discloses only data whose release has been explicitly authorized. Data disclosure has been captured by means of profiles associated with each data computation that describe the information carried by the released relation. Allowed data releases have instead been captured by means of simple permissions, which can be efficiently composed without privacy breaches. In this chapter we presented a simple graphical representation of both permissions and profiles, allowing to easily enforce our secure chasing process. We also presented an algorithm that, given a query plan, determines whether it can be safely executed and produces a safe query planning for it. The main advantage of our approach is its simplicity that, without impacting expressiveness, makes it nicely interoperable with current solutions for collaborative computations in distributed database systems.

# Chapter 6
# Conclusions

In this book, we have addressed the problem of protecting information when outsourced to an external server. After a brief introduction and a discussion of related work, we focused on three specific aspects: access control enforcement, privacy protection, and safe data integration. In this chapter, we shortly summarize the contributions of this book and we outline some future work.

## 6.1 Summary of the Contributions

The contributions of this book are threefold.

**Access control enforcement.** We present an access control model based on the combination of access control with cryptography. This idea is in itself not new, but the problem of applying it in an outsourced architecture introduces several challenges. To the purpose of granting efficiency in accessing data, we proposed to exploit a key derivation approach and presented a strategy for defining an adequate hierarchy for key derivation. This basic model has then been extended to conveniently support policy updates at the server side while reducing the burden of the data owner. The proposed solution is based on two different encryption layers. The lower layer is managed directly by the data owner and is used to enforce the initial access control policy. The higher layer is managed by the remote server and enforces updates to the original policy without the data owner's direct intervention on data. This solution has been carefully analyzed to the aim of modeling the risk of collusion to which data are exposed.

**Privacy protection.** We design a technique supporting the management of privacy protection requirements over a relational database. The proposed approach is based on the representation of these requirements through *confidentiality constraints* and on their enforcement through encryption and fragmentation. A confidentiality constraint is defined as a set of attributes which joint visibility must be prevented to non authorized users. Privacy protection can therefore be granted by solving con-

S. Foresti, *Preserving Privacy in Data Outsourcing*, Advances in Information Security 51,
DOI 10.1007/978-1-4419-7659-8_6, © Springer Science+Business Media, LLC 2011

fidentiality constraints, imposing that no constraint is a subset of the schema of a fragment and preventing join among fragments by encrypting common attributes. To this aim, we proposed different fragmentation algorithms, which can be used to produce a good fragmentation, depending on the information about the system workload known at design time.

**Safe data integration.** We propose an approach for regulating data flows among parties collaborating for the integration of their information sources. The integration mechanism is based on the characterization of access privileges for the collaborating servers on the components of a relational schema and on their enforcement in distributed query evaluation. An access privilege is defined as a view on the data, which can flow to a given server. However, the complete enumeration of access privileges in a relational schema may be expensive. We therefore presented an algorithm for composing access privileges, without information leakage. The enforcement of access privileges is then obtained by controlling data exchanges during the query evaluation process. To this aim, we proposed an algorithm that can be used to produce a query execution plan satisfying (base or composed) access privileges.

## 6.2 Future Work

The research described in this book can be extended along several directions.

### 6.2.1 Access Control Enforcement

**Management of write operations.** Our access control system, based on selective encryption, manages access control enforcement and dynamic policy updates. However, it assumes access operations to be read only (see Chap. 3). This assumption, even if adequate in a data dissemination scenario, is not sufficient for the management of data subject to dynamic updates by different parties, which may not coincide with the original data owner. In the *multi-owner* scenario, each owner is authorized to modify the portion of data she owns, while she can only read a larger subset of the outsourced resources, possibly owned by another party. We plan then to extend the model proposed in this book, relaxing the assumption that accesses are read-only, and proposing a system able to efficiently manage also the multi-owner scenario. Current works on integrity in the data outsourcing scenario, while guarantee that write operations are performed by authorized users only, are not suited to the multi-owner scenario, since they do not allow administrators to grant selective write privileges to different users.

**Secrecy of the access control policy.** The mechanism proposed for access control enforcement exploits key derivation through an adequate hierarchy. The use of a key derivation hierarchy and its tokens, while greatly simplifying key management, introduces a new vulnerability related to policy confidentiality. As a matter of fact, the public availability of tokens and therefore the corresponding key derivation hierarchy, makes visible the relationship between users and resources they are authorized to access, and therefore the authorization policy the owner wishes to enforce. In several contexts, however, the policy itself should be considered confidential as owners do not wish to publicly declare to whom they give (or not give) access to their resources. Also, an analysis of the policy may allow observers to reconstruct the structure of the social network of users accessing the system, potentially obtaining information disclosing the identity of users and their relationships. Since the overall aim of these novel solutions is to allow an efficient confidentiality-preserving mechanism for resource dissemination, the protection of the access control policy appears a natural requirement that systems will be interested in supporting, as long as its protection does not introduce a significant impact on system performance. A straightforward solution to this problem consists in encrypting the token catalog. However, this solution has the disadvantage of making key derivation inefficient [40]. It is therefore necessary to define a solution that both protects the privacy of the access control policy and that ensures an efficient key derivation process.

## 6.2.2 Privacy Protection

**Management of data updates.** The privacy protection system based on the combined use of fragmentation and encryption presented in Chap. 4 makes the implicit assumptions that the original dataset is never updated. In particular, the proposed model assumes that no tuples are added to the original table. However, if a new tuple can be inserted and subsequently fragments on the available fragmentation, it becomes easy to reconstruct the original tuples: it is sufficient to concatenate the new tuple of each of the fragments. Obviously, this situation would violate the confidentiality constraints imposed for the system. It is therefore necessary to define an adequate strategy to safely manage data updates. A straightforward solution to this problem may consist in postponing data insertion, until a given number of new tuples is reached. This solution, however, does not always provide the desired privacy level, and data freshness cannot be guaranteed. A future line of research will focus on the definition of a model able to efficiently manage insertions and updates, while granting privacy protection and up to date information in a fragmentation.

**Avoiding encryption exploiting a trusted party.** As already noted, handling encrypted data is inefficient from the user's point of view, since she needs to cooperate with the remote server in query evaluation. A line of future work will consist in analyzing the possibility for the data owner to directly store a portion of her data. In this scenario, privacy constraints can be solved by fragmenting the original table in two fragments only: one fragment will be outsourced and therefore has to fulfill confidentiality constraints; and the other fragment will be directly managed by the data owner. The problem that needs to be solved in this scenario is related to the size of the fragment directly managed by the data owner. In fact, it is necessary to minimize the size of such a fragment, since otherwise the owner would not be interested in exploiting data outsourcing. Another aspect to consider is the workload for the data owner in query evaluation.

### 6.2.3 Safe Data Integration

**Instance-based authorization.** The authorization model defined for controlling flows of information in distributed systems has been designed on the schema of the distributed database. Therefore, the definition of the portion of the data visible to a server is based on a list of attributes and tables. Also, joins are exploited as a way for reducing the set of visible data to those satisfying a specific join condition. An interesting new line of research consists in allowing the specification of instance-based permissions. This extension of the security model will require the arrangement of both the algorithm for safely composing permissions and the algorithm that evaluates if a query execution plan is safe.

**Building a safe query execution tree.** In Chap. 5, we proposed an algorithm able to define if a given query execution plan is safe with respect to a given set of permissions. However, from the user's point of view, given a query it is interesting to have an algorithm that returns a safe query execution plan, if such a plan exists for the set of permissions characterizing the system. A naive solution to this problem consists, as briefly discussed in Chap. 5, in checking each possible query execution plan with respect to the profiles of the permissions. However, the number of possible plans for a query may be high, growing with the number of relations and servers involved in the evaluation. It is then necessary to find an alternative solution that may exploit permissions for directly building a safe query execution plan.

# References

1. Abiteboul, S., Hull, R., Vianu, V.: Foundations of Databases. Addison-Wesley (1995)
2. Aggarwal, G., Bawa, M., Ganesan, P., Garcia-Molina, H., Kenthapadi, K., Motwani, R., Srivastava, U., Thomas, D., Xu, Y.: Two can keep a secret: a distributed architecture for secure database services. In: Proc. of the 2nd Biennal Conference Innovative Data Systems Research (CIDR 2005). Asilomar, CA (2005)
3. Agrawal, R., Asonov, D., Kantarcioglu, M., Li, Y.: Sovereign joins. In: Proc. of the 22nd International Conference on Data Engineering (ICDE 2006). Atlanta, GA (2006)
4. Agrawal, R., Kierman, J., Srikant, R., Xu, Y.: Order preserving encryption for numeric data. In: Proc. of the 23rd SIGMOD International Conference on Management of Data (SIGMOD 2004). Paris, France (2004)
5. Aho, A., Beeri, C., Ullman, J.: The theory of joins in relational databases. ACM Transaction on Database Systems (TODS) **4**(3), 297–314 (1979)
6. Akl, S., Taylor, P.: Cryptographic solution to a problem of access control in a hierarchy. ACM Transactions on Computer System **1**(3), 239 (1983)
7. Anderson, J.: Computer security planning study. Tech. Rep. 73-51, Air Force Electronic System Division (1972)
8. Atallah, M., Frikken, K., Blanton, M.: Dynamic and efficient key management for access hierarchies. In: Proc. of the 12th ACM Conference on Computer and Communications Security (CCS 2005). Alexandria, VA (2005)
9. Atzeni, P., Ceri, S., Paraboschi, S., Torlone, R.: Database Systems - Concepts, Languages and Architectures. McGraw-Hill Book Company (1999)
10. Baralis, E., Paraboschi, S., Teniente, E.: Materialized views selection in a multidimensional database. In: Proc. of 23rd International Conference on Very Large Data Bases (VLDB 1997). Athens, Greece (1997)
11. Bernstein, P., Goodman, N., Wong, E., Reeve, C., J.B. Rothnie, J.: Query processing in a system for distributed databases (SDD-1). ACM Transaction on Database Systems (TODS) **6**(4), 602–625 (1981)
12. Birget, J., Zou, X., Noubir, G., Ramamurthy, B.: Hierarchy-based access control in distributed environments. In: Proc. of IEEE International Conference on Communications (ICC 2002). Helsinki, Finland (2002)
13. Biskup, J., Embley, D., Lochner, J.: Reducing inference control to access control for normalized database schemas. Information Processing Letters **106**(1), 8–12 (2008)
14. Biskup, J., Lochner, J.: Enforcing confidentiality in relational databases by reducing inference control to access control. In: Proc. of the 10th International Conference on Information Security (ISC 2007). Valparaíso, Chile (2007)
15. Blundo, C., Cimato, S., De Capitani di Vimercati, S., De Santis, A., Foresti, S., Paraboschi, S., Samarati, P.: Managing key hierarchies for access control enforcement: Heuristic approaches. Computers and Security **29**(5), 533–547 (2010)

16. Boneh, D., Crescenzo, G., Ostrovsky, R., Persiano, G.: Public-key encryption with keyword search. In: Proc. of the 23rd Annual Eurocrypt Conference (Eurocrypt 2004). Interlaken, Switzerland (2004)
17. Boneh, D., Franklin, M.: Identity-based encryption from the weil pairing. SIAM Journal on Computing **32**(3), 586–615 (2003)
18. Boneh, D., Gentry, C., Lynn, B., Shacham, H.: Aggregate and verifiably encrypted signatures from bilinear maps. In: Proc. of the 22rd Annual Eurocrypt Conference (Eurocrypt 2003). Warsaw, Poland (2003)
19. Boyens, C., Gunter, O.: Using online services in untrusted environments - a privacy-preserving architecture. In: Proc. of the 11th European Conference on Information Systems (ECIS 2003). Naples, Italy (2003)
20. Brinkman, R., Doumen, J., Jonker, W.: Using secret sharing for searching in encrypted data. In: Proc. of the 1st Secure Data Management Workshop (SDM 2004). Toronto, Canada (2004)
21. Calì, A., Martinenghi, D.: Querying data under access limitations. In: Proc. of the 24th International Conference on Data Engineering (ICDE 2008). Cancun, Mexico (2008)
22. California senate bill sb 1386 (2002)
23. Ceri, S., Pelagatti, G.: Distributed Databases: Principles and Systems. McGraw-Hill Book Company (1984)
24. Ceselli, A., Damiani, E., De Capitani di Vimercati, S., Jajodia, S., Paraboschi, S., Samarati, P.: Modeling and assessing inference exposure in encrypted databases. ACM Transactions on Information and System Security **8**(1), 119–152 (2005)
25. Chaudhuri, S.: An overview of query optimization in relational systems. In: Proc. of the 17th ACM SIGACT-SIGMOD-SIGART Symposium on Principles of Database Systems (PODS 1998). Seattle, WA (1998)
26. Chiu, D., Ho, Y.: A methodology for interpreting tree queries into optimal semi-join expressions. In: Proc. of the SIGMOD International Conference on Management of Data (SIGMOD 1980). Santa Monica, CA (1980)
27. Ciriani, V., De Capitani di Vimercati, S., Foresti, S., Jajodia, S., Paraboschi, S., Samarati, P.: Fragmentation and encryption to enforce privacy in data storage. In: Proc. of the 12th European Symposium On Research In Computer Security (ESORICS 2007). Dresden, Germany (2007)
28. Ciriani, V., De Capitani di Vimercati, S., Foresti, S., Jajodia, S., Paraboschi, S., Samarati, P.: Fragmentation design for efficient query execution over sensitive distributed databases. In: Proc. of the 29th International Conference on Distributed Computing Systems (ICDCS 2009). Montreal, Canada (2009)
29. Ciriani, V., De Capitani di Vimercati, S., Foresti, S., Jajodia, S., Paraboschi, S., Samarati, P.: Fragmentation and encryption to enforce privacy in data storage. ACM Transactions on Information and System Security (TISSEC) **13**(3) (2010)
30. Ciriani, V., De Capitani di Vimercati, S., Foresti, S., Samarati, P.: k-Anonymity. In: T. Yu, S. Jajodia (eds.) Secure Data Management in Decentralized Systems. Springer-Verlag (2007)
31. Crampton, J., Martin, K., Wild, P.: On key assignment for hierarchical access control. In: Proc. of the 19th IEEE Computer Security Foundations Workshop (CSFW 2006). Los Alamitos, CA (2006)
32. Damiani, E., De Capitani di Vimercati, S., Foresti, S., Jajodia, S., Paraboschi, S., Samarati, P.: Metadata management in outsourced encrypted databases. In: Proc. of the 2nd VLDB Workshop on Secure Data Management (SDM 2005). Trondheim, Norway (2005)
33. Damiani, E., De Capitani di Vimercati, S., Foresti, S., Jajodia, S., Paraboschi, S., Samarati, P.: Selective data encryption in outsourced dynamic environments. In: Proc. of the 2nd International Workshop on Views On Designing Complex Architectures (VODCA 2006). Bertinoro, Italy (2006)
34. Damiani, E., De Capitani di Vimercati, S., Foresti, S., Jajodia, S., Paraboschi, S., Samarati, P.: An experimental evaluation of multi-key strategies for data outsourcing. In: Proc. of the 22nd IFIP TC-11 International Information Security Conference (SEC 2007). Sandton, South Africa (2007)

35. Damiani, E., De Capitani di Vimercati, S., Jajodia, S., Paraboschi, S., Samarati, P.: Balancing confidentiality and efficiency in untrusted relational DBMSs. In: Proc. of the 10th ACM Conference on Computer and Communications Security (CCS 2003). Washington, DC (2003)
36. Damiani, E., di Vimercati, S.D.C., Finetti, M., Paraboschi, S., Samarati, P., Jajodia, S.: Implementation of a storage mechanism for untrusted DBMSs. In: Proc. of the 2nd International IEEE Security in Storage Workshop (SISW 2003). Washington, DC (2003)
37. Damiani, E., di Vimercati, S.D.C., Foresti, S., Samarati, P., Viviani, M.: Measuring inference exposure in outsourced encrypted databases. In: Proc. of the 1st Workshop on Quality of Protection (QoP 2005). Milan, Italy (2005)
38. Davida, G., Wells, D., Kam, J.: A database encryption system with subkeys. ACM Transactions on Database Systems $6(2)$, 312–328 (1981)
39. The DBLP computer science bibliography. http://dblp.uni-trier.de. Http://dblp.uni-trier.de
40. De Capitani di Vimercati, S., Foresti, S., Jajodia, S., Paraboschi, S., Pelosi, G., Samarati, P.: Preserving confidentiality of security policies in data outsourcing. In: Proc. of the Workshop on Privacy in the Electronic Society (WPES 2008). Alexandria, VA (2008)
41. De Capitani di Vimercati, S., Foresti, S., Jajodia, S., Paraboschi, S., Samarati, P.: Over-encryption: Management of access control evolution on outsourced data. In: Proc. of the 33rd International Conference on Very Large Data Bases (VLDB 2007). Vienna, Austria (2007)
42. De Capitani di Vimercati, S., Foresti, S., Jajodia, S., Paraboschi, S., Samarati, P.: Assessing query privileges via safe and efficient permission composition. In: Proc. of the 15th ACM Conference Conference on Computer and Communications Security (CCS 2008). Alexandria, VA (2008)
43. De Capitani di Vimercati, S., Foresti, S., Jajodia, S., Paraboschi, S., Samarati, P.: Controlled information sharing in collaborative distributed query processing. In: Proc. of the 28th International Conference on Distributed Computing Systems (ICDCS 2008). Beijing, China (2008)
44. De Capitani di Vimercati, S., Foresti, S., Jajodia, S., Paraboschi, S., Samarati, P.: Encryption policies for regulating access to outsourced data. ACM Transactions on Database Systems (TODS) $35(2)$ (2010)
45. De Capitani di Vimercati, S., Foresti, S., Paraboschi, S., Samarati, P.: Privacy of outsourced data. In: A. Acquisti, S. Gritzalis, C. Lambrinoudakis, S. De Capitani di Vimercati (eds.) Digital Privacy: Theory, Technologies and Practices. Auerbach Publications (Taylor and Francis Group) (2007)
46. Deutsch, A., Ludäscher, B., Nash, A.: Rewriting queries using views with access patterns under integrity constraints. In: Proc. of the 10th International Conference on Database Theory (ICDT 2005). Edinburgh, Scotland (2005)
47. Evdokimov, S., Fischmann, M., Gunther, O.: Provable security for outsourcing database operations. In: Proc. of the 22nd International Conference on Data Engineering (ICDE 2006). Atlanta, GA (2006)
48. Florescu, D., Levy, A., Manolescu, I., Suciu, D.: Query optimization in the presence of limited access patterns. In: Proc. of the SIGMOD International Conference on Management of Data (SIGMOD 1999). Philadelphia, PA (1999)
49. Garcia-Molina, H., Ullman, J., Widom, J.: Database Systems: The Complete Book. Prentice Hall (2001)
50. Garey, M., Johnson, D.: Computers and Intractability; a Guide to the Theory of NP-Completeness. W.H. Freeman (1979)
51. Goh, E.: Secure Indexes. http://eprint.iacr.org/2003/216/ (2003)
52. Gottlob, G., Nash, A.: Data exchange: Computing cores in polynomial time. In: Proc. of the 25th ACM SIGACT-SIGMOD-SIGART Symposium on Principles of Database Systems (PODS 2006). Chicago, IL (2006)
53. Graham, R., Knuth, D., Patashnik, O.: Concrete Mathematics: A Foundation for Computer Science, 2/E. Addison-Wesley Professional (1994)
54. Gudes, E.: The design of a cryptography based secure file system. IEEE Transactions on Software Engineering $6(5)$, 411–420 (1980)

55. Hacigümüs, H., Iyer, B., Mehrotra, S.: Providing database as a service. In: Proc. of 18th International Conference on Data Engineering (ICDE 2002). San Jose, CA (2002)
56. Hacigümüs, H., Iyer, B., Mehrotra, S.: Ensuring integrity of encrypted databases in database as a service model. In: Proc. of the IFIP TC-11 WG 11.3 Seventeenth Annual Working Conference on Data and Application Security (DBSsec 2003). Estes Park, CO (2003)
57. Hacigümüs, H., Iyer, B., Mehrotra, S.: Efficient execution of aggregation queries over encrypted relational databases. In: Proc. of the 9th International Conference on Database Systems for Advanced Applications (DASFAA 2004). Jeju Island, Korea (2004)
58. Hacigümüs, H., Iyer, B., Mehrotra, S., Li, C.: Executing SQL over encrypted data in the database-service-provider model. In: Proc. of the 21st SIGMOD Conference on Management of Data (SIGMOD 2002). Madison, WI (2002)
59. Harn, L., Lin, H.: A cryptographic key generation scheme for multilevel data security. Computers and Security 9(6), 539–546 (1990)
60. Hofmeister, T., Lefmann, H.: Approximating Maximum Independent Sets in Uniform Hypergraphs. In: Proc. of the 23rd International Symposium on Mathematical Foundations of Computer Science (MFCS 1998). Brno, Czech Republic (1998)
61. Hore, B., Mehrotra, S., Tsudik, G.: A privacy-preserving index for range queries. In: Proc. of the 30th International Conference on Very Large Data Bases (VLDB 2004). Toronto, Canada (2004)
62. Hwang, M., Yang, W.: Controlling access in large partially ordered hierarchies using cryptographic keys. The Journal of Systems and Software 67(2), 99–107 (2003)
63. Iyer, B., Mehrotra, S., Mykletun, E., Tsudik, G., Wu, Y.: A framework for efficient storage security in RDBMS. In: Proc. of International Conference on Extending Database Technology (EDBT 2004). Crete, Greece (2004)
64. Kossmann, D.: The state of the art in distributed query processing. ACM Computing Surveys 32(4), 422–469 (2000)
65. Krivelevich, M., Sudakov, B.: Approximate coloring of uniform hypergraphs. Journal of Algorithms 49(1), 2–12 (2003)
66. Li, C.: Computing complete answers to queries in the presence of limited access patterns. VLDB Journal 12(3), 211–227 (2003)
67. Liaw, H., Wang, S., Lei, C.: On the design of a single-key-lock mechanism based on Newton's interpolating polynomial. IEEE Transaction on Software Engineering 15(9), 1135–1137 (1989)
68. Lohman, G., Daniels, D., Haas, L., Kistler, R., Selinger, P.: Optimization of nested queries in a distributed relational database. In: Proc. of the 10th International Conference on Very Large Data Bases (VLDB 1984). Singapore (1984)
69. MacKinnon, S., Taylor, P., Meijer, H., S.Akl: An optimal algorithm for assigning cryptographic keys to control access in a hierarchy. IEEE Transactions on Computers 34(9), 797–802 (1985)
70. Miklau, G., Suciu, D.: Controlling access to published data using cryptography. In: Proc. of the 29th International Conference on Very Large Databases (VLDB 2003). Berlin, Germany (2003)
71. Motro, A.: An access authorization model for relational databases based on algebraic manipulation of view definitions. In: Proc. of the 5th International Conference on Data Engineering (ICDE 1989). Los Angeles, CA (1989)
72. Mykletun, E., Narasimha, M., Tsudik, G.: Signature bouquets: Immutability for aggregated/condensed signatures. In: Proc. of European Symposium On Research in Computer Security (ESORICS 2004). Sophia Antipolis, France (2004)
73. Mykletun, E., Narasimha, M., Tsudik, G.: Authentication and integrity in outsourced databases. ACM Transactions on Storage 2(2), 107–138 (2006)
74. Narasimha, M., Tsudik, G.: DSAC: integrity for outsourced databases with signature aggregation and chaining. In: Proc. of the 14th ACM International Conference on Information and Knowledge Management (CIKM 2005). Bremen, Germany (2005)
75. Nash, A., Deutsch, A.: Privacy in GLAV information integration. In: Proc. of the 10th International Conference on Database Theory (ICDT 2005). Barcelona, Spain (2007)

76. Özsu, M.T., Valduriez, P.: Principles of Distributed Database Systems, 2/E. Prentice-Hall, Inc. (1999)
77. Payment card industry (PCI) data security standard (2006). Https://www.pcisecuritystandards.org/pdfs/pci_dss_v1-1.pdf
78. Personal data protection code. Legislative Decree no. 196 (2003)
79. Ray, I., Ray, I., Narasimhamurthi, N.: A cryptographic solution to implement access control in a hierarchy and more. In: Proc. of the 11th ACM Symposium on Access control Models and Technologies (SACMAT'02). Monterey, CA, USA (2002)
80. Rizvi, S., Mendelzon, A., Sudarshan, S., Roy, P.: Extending query rewriting techniques for fine-grained access control. In: Proc. of the 23rd SIGMOD International Conference on Management of Data (SIGMOD 2004). Paris, France (2004)
81. Rosenthal, A., Sciore, E.: View security as the basis for data warehouse security. In: Proc. of the 2nd Intlernational Workshop on Design and Management of Data Warehouses (DMDW 2000). Stockholm, Sweden (2000)
82. Rosenthal, A., Sciore, E.: Administering permissions for distributed data: factoring and automated inference. In: Proc. of the IFIP TC-11 WG 11.3 Seventeenth Annual Working Conference on Data and Application Security (DBSec 2001). Niagara Canada (2001)
83. Samarati, P.: Protecting respondents' identities in microdata release. IEEE Transactions on Knowledge and Data Engineering 13(6), 1010–1027 (2001)
84. Samarati, P., De Capitani di Vimercati, S.: Access control: Policies, models, and mechanisms. In: R. Focardi, R. Gorrieri (eds.) Foundations of Security Analysis and Design, LNCS 2171. Springer-Verlag (2001)
85. Sandhu, R.: On some cryptographic solutions for access control in a tree hierarchy. In: Proc. of the 1987 Fall Joint Computer Conference on Exploring Technology: Today and Tomorrow (FJCC 1987). Dallas, TX (1987)
86. Sandhu, R.: Cryptographic implementation of a tree hierarchy for access control. Information Processing Letters 27(2), 95–98 (1988)
87. Santis, A.D., Ferrara, A., Masucci, B.: Cryptographic key assignment schemes for any access control policy. Information Processing Letters 92(4), 199–205 (2004)
88. Schneier, B.: Applied Cryptography, 2/E. John Wiley & Sons (1996)
89. Schneier, B., Kelsey, J., Whiting, D., Wagner, D., Hall, C., Ferguson, N.: On the twofish key schedule. In: Proc. of the 5th Annual Workshop on Selected Areas in Cryptography (SAC 1998). Atlanta, GA (1998)
90. Selinger, P., Astrahan, M., Chamberlin, D., Lorie, R., Price, T.: Access path selection in a relational database management system. In: Proc. of the SIGMOD International Conference on Management of Data (SIGMOD 1979) (1979)
91. Shen, V., Chen, T.: A novel key management scheme based on discrete logarithms and polynomial interpolations. Computer and Security 21(2), 164–171 (2002)
92. Sion, R.: Query execution assurance for outsourced databases. In: Proc. of the 31st International Conference on Very Large Data Bases (VLDB 2005). Trondheim, Norway (2005)
93. Song, D., Wagner, D., Perrig, A.: Practical techniques for searches on encrypted data. In: Proc. of the 21st IEEE Symposium on Research in Security and Privacy (S&P 2000). Berkeley, CA (2000)
94. Sun, Y., Liu, K.: Scalable hierarchical access control in secure group communications. In: Proc. of the 23rd Conference of the IEEE Communications Society (Infocom). Hong Kong, China (2004)
95. Tsai, H., Chang, C.: A cryptographic implementation for dynamic access control in a user hierarchy. Computer and Security 14(2), 159–166 (1995)
96. Wang, H., Lakshmanan, L.V.S.: Efficient secure query evaluation over encrypted XML databases. In: Proc. of the 32nd International Conference on Very Large Databases (VLDB 2006). Seoul, Korea (2006)
97. Wang, Z., Dai, J., Wang, W., Shi, B.: Fast query over encrypted character data in database. Communications in Information and Systems 4(4), 289–300 (2004)

98. Wang, Z., Wang, W., Shi, B.: Storage and query over encrypted character and numerical data in database. In: Proc. of the 5th International Conference on Computer and Information Technology (CIT 2005). Shanghai, China (2005)

99. Waters, B., Balfanz, D., Durfee, G., Smetters, D.: Building an encrypted and searchable audit log. In: Proc. of the 11th Annual Network and Distributed System Security Symposium (NDSS 2004). San Diego, CA (2004)

100. Wong, C., Gouda, M., Lam, S.: Secure group communications using key graphs. IEEE/ACM Transactions on Networking **8**(1), 16–30 (2000)

101. Yu, C., Chang, C.: Distributed query processing. ACM Computing Surveys **16**(4), 399–433 (1984)

102. Zych, A., Petkovic, M.: Key management method for cryptographically enforced access control. In: Proc. of the 1st Benelux Workshop on Information and System Security (WISSec 2006). Antwerpen, Belgium (2006)